THE
MOVIE MAKER'S
HANDBOOK

THE
MOVIE MAKER'S
HANDBOOK

Ziff Davis Books

New York

A QED BOOK

Published by Ziff-Davis Books,
One Park Avenue, New York, New York 10016

Library of Congress Catalog Card Number 79-65399
ISBN 0-87165-044-4
First printing

Filmset in Britain by Abettatype Ltd
Color origination by Scan Kolor Limited, Ilkley
Printed in Italy by New Interlitho SPA, Milan

Consulting Editor
Christopher Wordsworth

Contributing Editors
Stephen Fyles, Mike Kent, Keith Overend,
Michael Pearcy, Stuart Rumens, Peter West

This book was designed and produced by
QED Publishing Limited
32 Kingly Court, London W1

Editorial Director Jeremy Harwood
Art Director Alastair Campbell
Production Director Edward Kinsey

Designed by Nigel Osborne and James Marks
Illustrators Marion Appleton, Ray Brown, Paul Cooper,
John Crump, Paul Eustice, Nick Gibbard, Heather Jackson,
Elaine Keenan, Edwina Keene, Abdul Aziz Khan, Tony Lodge,
David Mallott, Simon Roulstone, Perry Taylor, Marnie Searchwell,
Alan Suttie, Ken Warren, John Woodcock, Martin Woodford
Editorial Cynthia Hill, Marion Casey, Francesca George,
Jim Roberts
Visual research Prue Grice, Anne Lyons
Photographers Jon Wyand, Roger Pring, Peter Cogram, Louis Jay

QED would like to thank the many individuals and organizations who have helped in the preparation of this book. Special thanks are due to Eumig (UK) Ltd., J. J. Silber Ltd., the Kodak Museum, Rank Taylor-Hobson, E. Leitz (Instruments) Ltd., Cresta Electronics Ltd., Cygnet Photographic Company, Hanimex (UK) Ltd., Bell and Howell, Polaroid (UK) Ltd., Ray Davis and Nigel Hodgeson of AV Distributors Ltd., Sony Ltd., Philips (UK) Ltd., Lee Enterprises Ltd., Photax Enterprises Ltd., CZ Scientific Instruments Ltd., KEM Electronic Mechanisms Ltd., Bush and Meissner Ltd., Top Line Equipment, Robert Rigby Ltd., Kafetz Cameras Ltd., Kodak Ltd., Bethnal Green Museum, Peter Gold, Adrian Mason and Alexandra Carr of Goldmason Productions, McCann Erickson, David Little and Dan Strodl of Little Strodl Advertising Limited, Di Biggs, Tony Rose of *Movie Maker* magazine, Sheila Graber Animated Films, Roy Mathews of Dixons Photographic Ltd., Mr. A. G. Green of Agfa-Gavaert Processing Ltd., Andrew Jones of Braun Electric (UK) Ltd., Mike Lane of Fujimex, Clive Insley of Introphoto, Mike Ryalls of Fotopia, Charlie Yianoullou of Rank Audio Visual Ltd., Corina Poore, Fletcher Films, Morris Hoyer of Balfour Photographic, Sarah Wyand, Louis Campbell, Sally Barrat.

Contents

Foreword

'The white eye of the screen need
only reflect the light that is properly its
own to blow up the universe'

Luis Bunuel 1953

Movies have been part of our way of life for nearly a century. Today, many take the miracle of motion pictures for granted, but this was not always so. From the early 1900s until the 1950s – and the birth of the television age – movie theatres all over the world played to packed houses; audiences of all races and creeds worshipped at the shrine of film.

Films were the product of a long quest in which many great thinkers, scientists and artists took part. They provided the answer to a question that had for long challenged, baffled and mystified man – how to make a moving record of events in the world around him in some kind of permanent form. Where, when and how they started is difficult to pinpoint exactly. The early pioneers – men such as Edison and Lumière – laid the technical foundations and established the basic technology. This was built on by directors as diversified as D. W. Griffith, Eisenstein and von Stroheim; these men – and many others – created a kind of film language that gave form to the basic stuff of the picture. However, it is impossible to date such events precisely; the speed with which movies developed from sideshow curiosities into a great and influential industry was

8

such that it is difficult to chart its progress in detail.

Certainly one fact about the early days of film is worth noting. Because the medium was so revolutionary, both professionals and amateurs started from the same position of advantage or disadvantage, depending on your point of view. Everything was new; everything was experimental; and the results were equally unpredictable. This amateur interest was quickly recognized by the manufacturers. The first film gauge to be introduced was 35mm, which remains the standard professional gauge. This, however, was soon followed by various weird and wonderful 'substandard' gauges – together with cameras and projectors – designed mainly for amateur use. Many of these were eventually discarded, but 16mm still survives – today joined by Super 8, the 'baby' of the 8mm family.

The amateur of today, of course, has far more advanced equipment at his or her disposal than the pioneers of yesteryear. But the basic goal – to produce the best possible movie with the means available – has always remained the same. This book has been prepared to help the movie maker – whether complete novice or skilled hobbyist – achieve this aim.

The motion picture – the idea of capturing the secret of movement in some kind of permanent form – has been a dream of man since earliest times. Primitive man's cave paintings of fleeing animals, for instance, must have seemed remarkably like what would be later a movie show, when seen by flickering firelight.

Over the thousands of years that followed, many attempts were made to reveal the secret in still pictures – but all of them failed. Even when Thomas Edison established the mechanical basis for the first motion picture camera, he still lacked the medium he needed to put his ideas into practice. This was flexible, ribbon-like film.

With the invention of film, however, development progressed in leaps and bounds, culminating in the vast range of movie equipment available today. Cameras, film types, lighting set-ups, tripods and light meters are all part of this array, designed to help the movie maker in the quest to produce the best possible movie.

Yet the sheer extent of this availability can sometimes seem bewildering, because of the variety of possible choice involved. The aim of the bulk of this section of the book is to establish the basic factors that should influence the choice. Starting with films and processing – the foundation stones of any movie – it progresses to discuss the facilities every good camera should possess, the difficulties of correct exposure and lighting and finally the accessories that are actually vital for the production of a satisfying film.

The Motion Picture Miracle

The human eye is an almost perfectly designed optical instrument. Perhaps the only significant advantage the camera has over it is its ability to record images. Each image received by the brain lasts only a fraction of a second before it fades and is replaced by another. Consequently , when the eye is presented with a series of images moving at a speed faster than about 14 per second, they appear to merge together to produce the impression of continuous movement. This effect, known as persistence of vision, is fundamental to all illusions of motion — from a child's 'flick' book to cinema and television.

The dream of movement

The idea of motion has always fascinated man. Since earliest times, he has attempted to capture the impression of movement in pictures. The primitive cave dwellers of southern France and Spain tried to capture the excitement of the hunt in art. Seen in the dark, lit only by flickering torchlight, the images they painted must have sprung into life and action.

Devices used to produce optical effects and illusions also have their place in the story. One of the earliest was the 'pinhole' camera or camera obscura — a very primitive ancestor of the modern cinema. Although the camera obscura was probably known to the ancient Greeks, the earliest description on record is by the Arab scholar Alhaza, written in about AD 1000. The device is based on a simple natural phenomenon; if light passes through a narrow hole into a darkened room, an inverted image of the scene outside is projected on to the opposite wall. During the Renaissance, the idea was developed further and it became possible to correct the

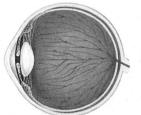
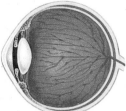

The pupil can be regarded as the variable aperture stop of the eye. Through a reflex action directed from the brain it contracts in a bright light and dilates in a dull one. It is in fact a ring of muscle situated in the colored part of the eye in front of the lens.

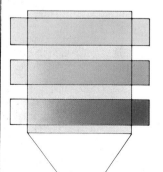

Below **Under optimum conditions the human eye can distinguish about 150 separate colors. It is almost certain that it does this through receptors sensitive to the three primary colors, blue, green and red, which overlap and thus make a greater range possible. By subdivision and recombination and by mixing with white these 150 colors can produce further hues and shades so that, in the end, the eye can probably distinguish about a million colors and shades.**

Retina
Lens
Pupil
Iris
Cornea

inversion. This was done by using mirrors and back-projected light to produce this image on a small, translucent screen.

Yet, although the principle underlying the appearance of movement is extremely simple, it was not until the late 19th century that the process of recording and playing back moving pictures was fully evolved. In part, of course, this was because the technology was lacking, but ultimate success was also in part due to the preoccupations of the time. In both Europe and

The range of brightness which the human eye can normally be expected to encounter is enormous. Strong sunlight and darkest night mark the effective|parameters.

America, the 19th century was the age of machinery — a time when it seemed possible to produce anything by mechanical means. Motion pictures were the natural offspring of an obsession with every aspect of movement — a dominant characteristic of the age.

From mechanical toys to moving pictures

Even before the invention of still photography, experiments were being carried out to produce realistic methods of showing motion. One such attempt was the Diorama, devised in 1822 by the French pioneer photographer Daguerre. This was a three dimensional panorama, featuring realistically painted translucent screens, magic lantern projection, dramatic lighting effects and a slow revolve. This was followed by optical toys, such as the Thaumatrope, Phenakistoscope and Zoetrope. These were the mechanical precursors of cinematography, since their intermittent movement relied on persistence of vision to create illusions of superimposition and motion.

However, the technology for cinema came from other roots — developments in still photography. An important figure in this was the British photographer Muybridge, who devised a system using a battery of still cameras operated by trip wires to record the sequential movement of horses, birds and human beings. The success of his method and the wide circulation of his results stimulated others to explore the possibility of combining a rapid sequence of photographs with the intermittent process developed through the optical toys. The result, they hoped, would be a moving picture system.

Development followed development. One of the most important of these took place in 1889, when a young inventor, George Eastman, introduced celluloid roll film. His Number 1 Kodak — 'You press the button, we do the rest' — had already brought still photography within the reach of the man in the street. The stage was now set for a similar development in movie making.

The movie pioneers

By now, the two halves of the formula for movie pictures — recording the images and their intermittent playback fast enough to make them fuse into continuous motion — were well known. All that was needed was a mechanically

Artists have long been aware that the camera obscura below **could be used to help reproduce perspective accurately. Chronophotography** right **is the recording of photographs at regular intervals. Muybridge pioneered this technique in his study of human and animal movement. Here a horse revealed the secrets of its movement.**

foolproof system to combine the principles.

First to establish a workable motion picture system was the American inventor Thomas Edison, who demonstrated the Kinetoscope in 1893. This was a kind of one-man peep show. It used film strips 35mm in width, with a revolving disc chopping the light source to produce an intermittent effect. The machine was extremely successful and coin-operated versions became very popular.

In turn, this development inspired other inventors. The French Lumière brothers swiftly brought out their own improved version, known as the Cinematographe, in 1895. This was a camera, projector and printer all in one; it also was the first device to use a claw to move the film strip. In addition, the equipment had the further advantage of being light, portable and easy to use.

In the euphoria that followed the extraordinarily successful debut of the Cinematographe, there seemed no reason why 'animated', or 'living', photographs, as they were called in contemporary advertizements, should not rival the popularity of still photography. Since the equipment was neither difficult to operate nor prohibitively expensive, it was possible for anyone with the time, mechanical aptitude and inclination to become a movie maker. Indeed, the line between amateur and professional was a thin one, since they both had everything to learn.

However, there were two main factors which prevented this. The first was the expense and cumbersome nature of 35mm, though this swiftly became the professional gauge. So-called 'sub-

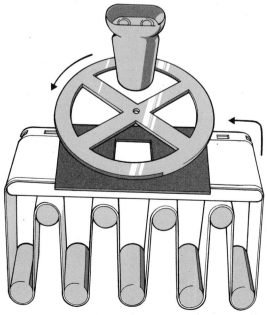

Marey improved on Muybridge's battery of cameras by devising a gun above **which could record twelve pictures on a circular plate in about one second. In 1887, when paper roll film became available,** he was able to devise a camera which could take 100 photographs a second. The first commercially successful motion pictures were viewed through Edison's Kinetoscope below.

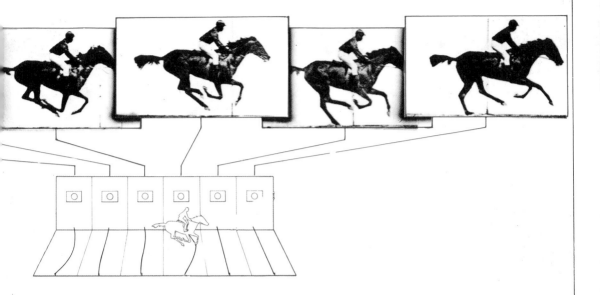

standard' gauge cameras were thus designed to take narrower film widths. Two of the first of these were the Birtac (1898) and the Biokam (1899). Both used 17.5mm film, obtained by splitting 35mm. Other gauges swiftly followed — 21mm, 15mm, 28mm, 11mm and even spiral film discs. But all these systems had one failing in common — the nature of the film stock.

For the modern movie maker, buying film and having it processed are both simple matters. This was not so in the pioneer days of film. It was often difficult to buy the right gauge, while professional processing was equally difficult to come by. Frequently, the only solution was for the amateur to process his own film, but even this presented problems. The early film types had to be developed to negative first and then printed to positive. This was a laborious and costly operation. Finally, most film gauges used a highly inflammable nitrate base for the emulsion.

Kodak and Pathé

Immediately after the First World War, however, the situation was transformed by two new systems which were to lay the foundations for true amateur movie making. In 1923, the great French movie mogul Charles Pathé unveiled his Baby projector, using 9.5mm film; a month later George Eastman launched the Ciné-Kodak 16mm system. Both systems were backed by giant corporations, which guaranteed their dependability; there were other similarities in common, too. Both films could be developed by reversal processing straight to positive, cutting

out the costly negative stage. They both also used a non-inflammable acetate 'safety' base, which Eastman and Pathé had pioneered independently in 1912.

There was a clear difference, however, in the philosophy behind each system. Pathé was probably the most prolific movie producer the world has ever known. His 9.5mm system was primarily intended, in this pre-television age, as a home viewing outlet for his vast library of commercial films. It was for this reason that the Baby projector, together with a library of 9.5mm 'featurettes', was launched first; the 9.5mm Baby camera only followed a year later.

Eastman's 16mm system, on the other hand, was designed and marketed from the start as a picture-taking system. The first advertizement for the Ciné-Kodak claimed that it offered 'a new simplicity, a new economy, a new compactness. It opens wide the door to personal motion pictures.'

Since those early days, the Eastman-Kodak company has been in the forefront of film developments. This strength on the retail market, this emphasis on quality and the keenness of this research have enabled the company to dominate small format movie making ever since the introduction of 16mm.

With the exception of Pathé, most manufacturers of equipment and film have been content to follow Kodak's lead.

From 16mm to Super 8

Though the 16mm format enjoyed a steady commercial success during the 1920s, it was still too expensive to spark off the anticipated breakthrough into the mass market. Eastman-Kodak's scientists therefore set to work; by 1928 they had so improved the quality of film emulsion that it was possible to devise an even smaller film format.

Several sizes were considered, but eventually a system using specially perforated 16mm was chosen. This could be processed using existing equipment. The film was run through the camera twice and then split into two 8mm strips for projection. Standard 8, as this new format was christened, was launched in 1932.

The next important landmark in the history of sub-standard movies was the introduction of Kodachrome in 1935. A primitive color film called Kodacolor had been produced for 16mm in 1928; the film was unsatisfactory, however, since the process required color filters on both camera and projector and a considerable amount of light was lost at both stages. Kodachrome, with its much brighter images and greater sensitivity rapidly found favor with amateur movie makers.

Meanwhile, important developments were also taking place in the 16mm field. Despite the much lower price of Standard 8, the survival of 16mm was assured because of its convenience as a projection medium for reduction prints from 35mm originals. Then came sound. In 1932, RCA took up Kodak's idea of replacing one row of the perforations on 16mm film with a soundtrack. The result was the first 16mm optical sound projector.

Paradoxically, this development affected the professional market much more than the amateur one. Optical sound was far too expensive for general amateur use — it was not until the introduction of magnetic stripe in the 1950s that sound became a practicable amateur proposition. However, the system had its attraction for professionals, particularly in the newsreel field. With the development of television after World War II, 16mm firmly established its professional status. It is now extensively used for news films and for documentaries.

The latest major link in the long chain of events since Edison introduced his primitive camera was forged in 1965, when Kodak introduced a revolutionary new cartridge loading system. This, the now universal Super 8, was designed to reduce the technical complexities of movie making to an absolute minimum.

Filming with Standard 8 necessitated running the first 50 feet of film through the camera, re-threading it and running it through again — a

Top when the card in the thaumatrope is rotated rapidly on its axis, the bird on one side and the cage on the other appear to be on the same side of the card. The zoetrope *middle* is a drum with viewing slits containing pictures which illustrate different stages of motion. The spinning drum only allows a brief viewing time through the slits, so motion seems to be continuous. The phenakistoscope *bottom* worked on similar principles.

laborious and time-consuming process that tended to put many potential movie makers off the subject of home movies. Moreover, the large sprocket holes inherited from 16mm wasted valuable film space, which could have been added to the picture area. Super 8, with its compact cartridge and smaller perforations, was intended to overcome both these problems. Kodak's hope was that the new system would rapidly replace Standard 8; all the two had in common was the 8mm film width.

Market response to the new format was immediate and other manufacturers quickly took up the new system. The Japanese manufacturer Fuji, however, decided to adopt only the film format itself, rejecting the cartridge in favor of their own Single 8 cassette. Equipment manufacturers followed suit, re-designing their cameras and projectors to take the new gauge. The old gauge did not go down without a struggle, however. For a time, certain companies

Below **Lumière's cinematographe,** *centre* **the all-in-one Biokam. Examples of Lumière and Biokam film are shown** *bottom left* **and**

right. Top **An advertisement for the Gaumont Chronophone, one of the first attempts at sound.**

Biokam camera

Biokam projector

Left **The Cine-Kodak Model A motion picture camera introduced in 1923. In contrast to the lightweight versatile cameras available today, this model weighed over seven pounds, was crank-driven and could only be used with a tripod.**

marketed 'dual gauge' projectors, which could be adapted for Super 8 or Standard 8. However, these are no longer being made; to all intents and purposes, the Standard 8 film gauge is now obsolete.

Kodak and its rivals continued to refine and improve the system in response to the increasing demands of the market for amateur film. In 1972 Kodak introduced low light capability for Super 8; in 1975 Super 8 sound cameras, with the cartridge of silent Super 8 re-designed and edged with magnetic stripe, were launched. On each occasion, other manufacturers swiftly designed new cameras and projectors to utilize the new concepts. Super 8 now offers a wide choice of cameras, projectors and accessories from most of the world's leading small-format equipment manufacturers. Film stockists and processing laboratories are established in most part of the world.

Super 8 thus represents the current state of the art as far as low budget movie making is concerned. But what of the future? Among the new developments, there is one that may well pose a threat to the present supremacy of Super 8 and, indeed, to the whole of amateur movie making as we understand it today. This is the challenge of video.

Video is, as yet, in its infancy, but the medium is the subject of major development programmes by every movie equipment manufacturer. The main problem at the time of writing is the lack of a suitable camera for the amateur market. If and when one is introduced, it will have to be seen whether such a development will make Super 8 as obsolete as the gauge it itself replaced.

Eastman's 16mm Cine-Kodak system *left* shared with Pathé the advantage of simpler and safer processing. It differed from the Pathé system in that it incorporated movie-making equipment from the outset. The system was more expensive than its rival, but managed to take the lead partly because a 'total system' seems to have been what was called for, and partly because of the interests of the big US film manufacturers.

Films and
Processing

Film is the lifeblood of the movie industry. Without it, cameras, projectors and the rest of the movie enthusiast's equipment would be totally useless. The early pioneers were well aware of this fact; from the first days of film, scientists and inventors all over the world were experimenting to find the perfect film format. The goal was to find one that ensured maximum efficiency and flexibility at a price that all could afford.

This last consideration ruled 35mm — the standard professional format since the late 19th century — out of court. Over the years, there have therefore been many attempts to introduce an internationally acceptable sub-standard gauge. Many such gauges were short-lived; even today, two of the four basic sub-standard film formats are falling into disuse.

16mm — the first substandard gauge

The first sub-standard gauge to be commercially successful was 16mm, which the US - based Eastman Kodak company introduced in 1922 for amateur use. Unlike early formats, which used highly inflammable materials, it was produced on a safety base, which added to its appeal.

The film has a projectable picture area of 9.65 by 7.21mm — the camera exposes a fractionally larger area — and there are 40 frames per foot. Initially, the film had a set of perforations running down each edge; as far as amateur use was concerned, this persisted into the 1950s. At the professional level, though, one set of perforations was replaced by an optical soundtrack as early as the 1930s. The expense of this system put it out of the running for amateurs.

16mm

9.5mm

Standard 8

Super 8

Above The four basic film formats currently in use. Their fortunes have diverged considerably. 16mm film used as a medium for optical sound as early as 1932, has survived because of its convenience as a projection medium for reduction prints. 9.5mm, on the other hand, now lives on nostalgia alone. It was appreciated for a long time that there was a large number of potential buyers deterred by the technical complexity of threading every 50ft run of Standard 8 film twice. The Super 8 cartridge silenced all complaints on this score and is now the norm for small-format film equipment the world over.

With the introduction of the much cheaper magnetic stripe in the 1950s, however, single-perf. 16mm was soon recognized as the best format for the new medium. It became a simple matter, even for the non-professional user, to record sound; the magnetic stripe, with a width of 2.5mm and a linear speed of 7.2mm at 24 feet per second, was found to produce results of the highest quality.

Interestingly enough, magnetic stripe also boosted the use of 16mm professionally, as well as in the amateur market. There had always been some professional interest in the medium — during World War II, for instance, both sides made extensive use of 16mm because of its compactness and relatively low running costs — but it was the introduction of magnetic sound that made it commercially respectable. Television, in particular, makes extensive use of 16mm film; largely because of this, there are a wide range of film stocks and services available today.

9. 5mm — the format that failed
At about the time that Eastman Kodak were launching 16mm in the USA, Pathé were introducing this gauge in France, in conjunction with a specially designed camera. One special feature of the format was its design; to make the most economical use of the film area, a single set of perforations were placed centrally between the frames. This produced a picture 8.3mm by 6.5mm — 70 per cent of the surface area thus being used, as opposed to only 57 per cent on 16mm.

9.5mm had one great failing, however. The original format could not be used with an optical soundtrack and so, when sound was introduced, it had to be re-designed. The only solution was to reduce the picture width, producing an almost square image. Commercially, too, 9.5mm's success was confined to Europe; it never managed to compete with Eastman Kodak's 16mm in North America and, today, it has virtually ceased to exist outside France and Germany. There, it is mainly used by specialized amateurs.

Regular 8mm
Regular, or Standard, 8mm film was another product of the Eastman Kodak laboratories. It was introduced in 1932 as the result of a series of experiments to find a derivative of 16mm to suit the growing amateur market. The Kodak scientists found that, by halving the width and height of the 16mm frame, it became possible to record two sets of pictures side-by-side on a length of 16mm film. Thus Standard 8 — the child of 16mm — was born.

The principle on which Standard 8 works is simple. The camera is loaded with a 15 foot length of 16mm film, with twice the normal number of perforations. When one side of the film has been exposed, it is turned over and run through the camera again to produce a second set of pictures down the other. After processing the film is split down the centre and the two ends joined together to give a 50 foot length of Standard 8 film.

Regular 8mm film has a printable picture

Right **Early attempts to achieve reasonably convincing color reproduction resulted in two color technicolor.**

area of 4.37mm by 3.28mm; a 25 foot double run length gives a running time of three minutes 40 seconds at 18 fps. The system achieved considerable success, but this lasted only until a less cumbersome rival was produced. This came with the introduction of Super 8 and now no new equipment is being produced for the older format.

Super 8 and Single 8

Super 8 film was launched on the market by Eastman Kodak in the mid-1960s. Its success was immediate and, today, it is regarded as the principal non-professional gauge. Virtually all the vast range of amateur equipment is produced in this format.

Super 8's chief rival is Single 8, which was introduced by the Japanese company Fuji at about the same time. As far as the film is concerned, the two gauges are identical; the difference lies in the design of the camera cartridge.

Both Super and Single 8 film have a projectable picture area of 5.31mm by 4.01mm. This is effectively 30 per cent greater than that of Regular 8mm and is largely achieved by reducing the size of the perforations to make better use of the available film area. The picture definition is also improved. However, the greatest advantage of the format is the cartridges in which the film is supplied. These are less cumbersome than the traditional reels and are extremely quick and

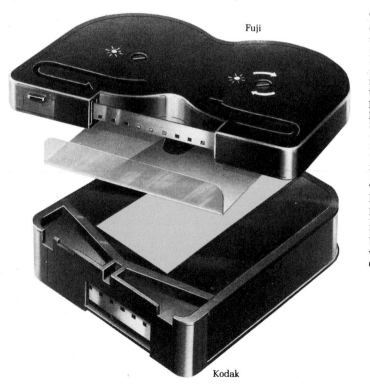

Fuji

Kodak

There are two major differences between the silent Fuji and Kodak cartridges illustrated here. The layout of the supply and take-up reels, is dissimilar. In addition to this, the pressure plates, whose job it is to position each successive frame properly, have different locations. The metal Fuji plate is part of the camera and has a fixed relationship to the aperture and shutter. The plastic, spring-loaded Kodak plate is part of the cartridge and pushes against the film to a degree determined by three protrusions which are part of the camera's aperture plate.

Both cartridges key in automatic film speed settings through notches which engage feeler thrusts; the longer the notch, B the deeper the feelers and the greater the film speed. Most cameras have a built-in 85, or Type A, filter which allows film **balanced for indoor exposure to be used outdoors when it is moved into the optical path of the lens. The bottom notch controls this movement. The two middle notches assist location and sorting at processors.**

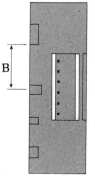

Whereas the Kodak cartridge is squat, the Fuji single 8 *below* is thin and flat. This is because the feed core is directly above the take-up core, supplying the film from top to bottom. Because this design allows any amount of backwinding, double exposures and dissolves are facilitated. The Kodak cartridge *bottom* is sometimes called a coaxial cartridge because feed and take-up core are side by side and centre on the same axis. The path of the film to its exposure at the optical interface is curved.

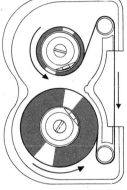

Fuji

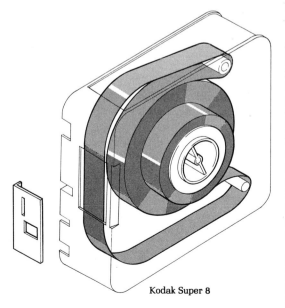

Kodak Super 8

easy to load into the camera.

Super 8 cartridges contain 50 feet of film, usually on an acetate base. The compactness is achieved by arranging the feed and take-up film chambers co-axially. The other unique feature is the built-in pressure plate. By contrast, the Single 8 cartridge has a co-planar layout; here, size is kept to a minimum by using an ultra-thin, but nevertheless extremely strong, film.

Both systems were originally designed for silent filming, but now both have modified cartridges on the market, containing pre-striped film for use in sound cameras. The original 50 foot length has also been surpassed; Super 8 film can now be obtained in 200 foot cartridges, which, provided that the camera is designed to accept them, give an uninterrupted run of 13 minutes 20 seconds at 18 fps.

Fundamentals of color

In common with still photography, movie film started off life in black and white. Today, however, the vast majority of movie enthusiasts film almost exclusively in color.

A modern color movie film is a remarkable and extremely complex product. Not only is it able to record faithfully even the most subtle colors in a scene, but its ability to reproduce the finest details is little short of miraculous. It is easy to use, tolerant and dependable — yet, for all its sophistication, it depends on properties first discovered centuries ago.

In 1666 the British physicist Sir Isaac Newton discovered that white light was made up of seven basic colors — red, orange, yellow, green, blue, indigo and violet. This is termed the spectrum. He found that he could split sunlight into these colors using a prism and that by using another one he could recombine them into white light again. But he also discovered that, if he blocked out part of the spectrum, light of a completely different color was produced on recombination. If the green part of the spectrum were blocked, for instance, the recombined light would be magenta in color. Blocking off other parts produces cyan and yellow respectively. These new colors, formed by a mixture of the incomplete spectrum, are known as 'complementaries'.

The next giant step forward came just under 200 years later. On 17 May 1861 James Clerk-Maxwell, another British physicist, demonstrated that, by using light of the three primary colors — red, blue and green — all other colors could be created. He used three lanterns fitted with filters to combine the three colors to produce white light.

Clerk-Maxwell's next step was to apply his discoveries to color photography. He took three pictures of a tartan riband through primary filters. When positives of these photographs were projected in register, using lanterns also fitted with filters, a color picture of the riband was produced.

Unfortunately, because of the poor response of the photographic plates to red and green, the image produced was predominantly blue. Nevertheless, Clerk-Maxwell had shown the feasibility of color photography based on the addition of light of the three primary colors. The next advance, which made color photography viable, was the development of film with a wide spectral response in the early 1900s.

Sir Isaac Newton devised the first experiments to show that white light is a mixture of the spectral colors. Each frequency in the spectrum, on travelling through a prism, is deviated through a slightly different angle. The beams which emerge are thus fanned out into an array of the spectral colors. If the spectrum is then made to pass through a second prism held the opposite way up, it will be reconstituted into white light. Newton's experiment was not entirely objective; he had a semi-religious commitment to the number seven which led him to identify seven colors. In fact, indigo is not really identifiable as a separate color. What was not known at the time was that each color represented light waves of different frequencies.

Thomas Young, an Englishman of very wide-ranging abilities, working in the early nineteenth century, was acknowledged by Clerk Maxwell as the first to look for the explanation of the fact that there are three primary colors in the human perceptual system rather than in light itself. Young's experiment is illustrated *below*. If green, blue and red light are added together they form white light. A mixture of any two primary colors produces the complementary of the third. An ordinary Kodachrome film consists only of Young's three lights. Mixing these colors to produce any of the others forms the basis of additive color systems. *Bottom* if white light is viewed through overlapping filters of the complementary colors then the primary colors and black are formed. Each filter subtracts the other two complementaries. This is the basis of modern subtractive color films.

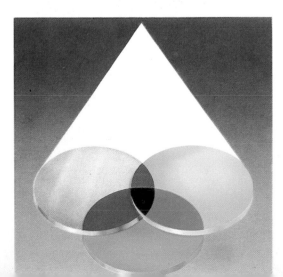

Nature of film

Almost without exception, film depends on the light-sensitive properties of silver halides to make the formation of an image possible. These light-sensitive salts are suspended in a binding agent, such as gelatine; it is this binding agent which is coated in the form of an emulsion on to the transparent base of the film.

When the film is exposed to light as it runs through the camera, the silver halide crystals react. If the light falling on a given part of the film is intense, all, or most, of the crystals will be affected. If the light is weak, only a few will be changed and, if no light falls on the film at all, they will remain completely unaffected. The crystals affected by the light can be developed to produce black metallic silver.

Normally, white areas of the object reproduce black, while black areas are rendered as unaffected white emulsion. In other words, the image produced is a negative of the object. To convert this to a positive, the film must undergo 'reversal'. There are two ways in which this can be done. In the first, special reversal processing is used to obtain a positive image on the camera film; in the second, a print is made on a separate film material to produce an image suitable for projection. All 8mm films are of the reversal type, but negative films are often used in 16mm for professional work when a number of copies are required.

Additive color

This system is the basis of all black and white movies and the processes described above also have their applications to color. Most of the early color film systems were based on the 'additive' principle, discovered by Clerk-Maxwell. Of these, probably the most successful was Dufaycolor. This consisted of a fine mesh of red, green and blue transparent lines, ruled on the base of a conventional panchromatic black and white film. Exposure took place through this fine colored mosaic; reversal processing produced a positive image in full color ready for projection.

Dufaycolor was available in cine formats from the early 1930s until the 1950s, when it was replaced by more efficient systems. The one major disadvantage of additive color films is that they never use more than a third of the light available from the projector lamp and therefore are extremely inefficient. Nevertheless, the Polaroid Corporation's Polavision process is an additive one, while, today, the most common use of additive color is in the color TV tube. A close inspection of the screen will reveal that it is made up of thousands of tiny phosphor dots, emitting red, green and blue light.

Subtractive color

All modern color films, with the exception of Polavision, are based on the subtractive system. Here, unwanted colors can be subtracted from a particular part of the image by using filters of the complementary color in the white light of the projection beam. These are superimposed over each other, so white areas of the image will have no filtration. This means that almost 100 per cent of the available projection light reaches the screen in the highlights.

If, for instance, any area of the scene is required to be green, the other two primary colors — red and blue — have to be removed from the white light. This is done by using a cyan and a yellow filter in combination; a cyan filter, being the complementary of red, will pass all colors except red and similarly a yellow one will pass everything except blue. Most colors are, in fact, a subtle blend of two or more primary colors. These are reproduced in the subtractive color system by an equally subtle use of complementary filters.

Film consists of an image forming layer called the emulsion and a transparent support material called the base. In the conventional black and white negative film, silver halide particles in the emulsion are activated in proportion to the amount of light striking them.

Reversal color films

Subtractive color film consists of an emulsion made up of three light-sensitive layers. Usually the top layer is sensitive to blue light, the second to green and the third to red. A yellow filter layer is used to subtract blue from the light reaching the lower green and red layers, as these are also sensitive to blue. Some types of film have additional layers of filter — most probably an opaque layer on the film base to prevent halation or 'fogging'.

The colored dyes in the emulsion are formed during processing. The dye-forming chemicals are usually introduced into the film during

Developer would in time reduce all the halide to metallic silver, but it acts first on those particles made more susceptible to it by the action of light.

In the unexposed area A few if any of the particles become black metallic silver. Moderate exposure area B produces a 'grey' number of grains. In the heavily exposed area C most of the grains are developed to black.

A strip of 22mm film, produced in 1912 for Edison's Home Kinetoscope. One of the problems with many early films was the sheer difficulty of getting them processed. Another was the inflammable nature of their base emulsion.

manufacture; these react with a color coupling agent in the color developing bath. A different dye-former is required for each layer and it is important that there is no layer-to-layer migration. In Agfachrome film, for instance, this is prevented by anchoring the dye-formers in place with long-chain molecules; in Ektachrome 'oily' globules are used.

Kodachrome, however, is now unique in being the only film stock which contains no dye-formers in the emulsion. Instead, they are introduced during processing. Because of the absence of the relatively large dye-forming molecules, Kodachrome tends to give sharper, finer-grained images than emulsions incorporating dye-formers.

Negative color films

Color negative films are available only in 16mm and larger formats. They are basically similar to reversal films, but there is one important difference. After processing, not only are the tone values the opposite of those of the original scene, but the colors are also negative. Green objects,

for instance, appear magenta, red ones cyan and blue ones yellow. Usually an orange mask is formed during processing. This helps to reduce contrast and improve color quality in the finished print.

Processing

With the exception of Kodachrome, all color reversal films are processed in much the same way, though the detailed chemistry of the various processes may differ. Initially, the film is developed in a developer very similar to that used for ordinary black and white negative film. This converts the silver halide crystals affected by light during exposure into black metallic silver, the exposed areas of all three layers reacting in exactly the same way. An exposure of a red, green and blue flag, for instance, would result in appropriate areas of metallic silver on the respective light-sensitive layers. Black objects in the original scene would not affect any of the layers; white objects would affect all of them.

So far the developing process is identical to that used for black and white film and, in fact, the color film looks much the same as a black and white one at this stage. The next step, however, is very different. This is reversal, in which the areas of the three emulsions not affected by exposure must be fogged. This is either done by exposing the whole film to white light or by immersion in a special chemical.

Color development

The film is now re-developed in another developer. This contains chemicals that react with the dye-formers in the film emulsion to produce colored dyes. These form only in the areas fogged during the reversal process.

No dye, for instance, will form in the areas of red-sensitive emulsion affected by light during the original exposure and subsequently converted to metallic silver during the first stage of development. On the other hand, magenta and yellow dyes will form in the blue and green-sensitive emulsions immediately above the red one, because no original exposure took place there.

Finally, the metallic silver is bleached away and any developed silver halide removed through a process known as bleach-fix. The end result is a full color film, consisting solely of pure dyes.

Home processing

The previous section gave a simplified outline of the various stages in the commercial processing of a color reversal film. Depending on the particular type of film being used, there may well be other steps involved. Washing the film between each process is usually essential, while, with some films, stabilization and immersion in a hardening bath are necessary. Nevertheless, it is possible to process many types of color film at home, provided that it is accepted that laboratory standards cannot be fully achieved.

The reasons for this are simple. Without exception, movie films are designed to be processed by sophisticated machines operating under carefully controlled conditions of time and temperature. In addition, there are no color processing kits specifically designed for use with movie film at present on the market, although some still reversal kits are adequate substitutes.

In the Dufaycolor system, the maximum amount of light was passed by preventing the stripes and squares from overlapping. The red filters were horizontal stripes, interlaced with vertical green filters but not crossing them. Blue was allocated the square rectangles in between.

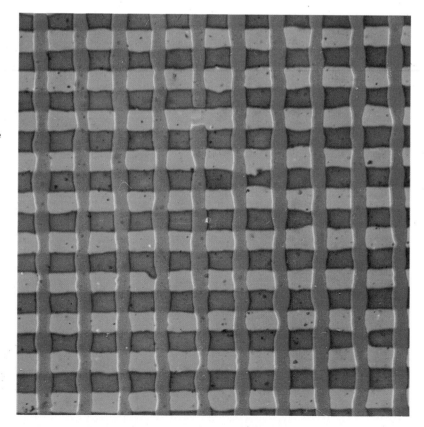

And unexpected problems can occur. The carbon-based anti-halation backing on Ektachrome Super 8 film is particularly difficult to remove outside the laboratory.

Equipment required

The first piece of equipment required by any home processor is some means of holding the film while it is immersed in the processing solution. Various types of processing drums, aprons and spirals are on the market; the choice, obviously, will depend on the film gauge being used and the length of film to be processed. Film spirals and drums normally come complete with a lightproof tank. This means that the processing solutions can be poured in and out in normal daylight — a useful facility if a fully equipped darkroom is not available.

The quantity of processing solution to be used is also an important consideration. It is obviously wasteful to buy an over-large tank, but it must have a large enough capacity to do the job properly.

Though it is not necessary to use the tank in a darkroom, it is vital to load it with film in total darkness. An improvised darkroom can be created by blacking out a bathroom or cupboard; alternatively, a large photographic changing bag can often be used. The various solutions being used will also need to be stored in dark bottles. Some of these — particularly developers — oxidize quickly, so as little air as possible should be left trapped in the bottles with the fluid. If prolonged storage is necessary, it is best to use collapsible plastic bottles which allow all the air to be expelled. Another important item of equipment is an accurate thermometer. This is essential if consistent results are to be achieved.

Choice of kit

The processing kit should suit the film being used. With the exception of Kodachrome and Agfachrome, most movie films are of the Ektachrome type. The best type of kit to use with these is an E4 still type, but, as these are hard to obtain, a universal kit can be substituted. If in any doubt, take the advice of your movie equipment store.

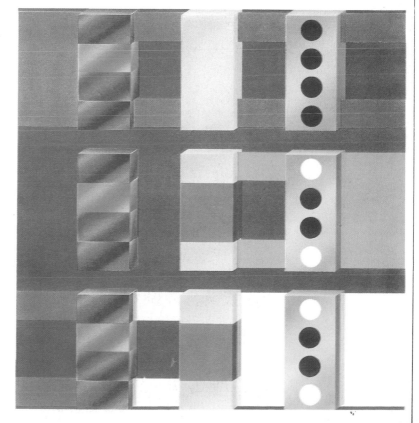

How Polavision works.
When the film is exposed to red, the stripes function as color filters. The exposed grains behind the red will form a negative image. The unexposed grains behind green and blue will form a positive.

Processing.
Seconds after the reagent is applied, the exposed grains start to develop to form a low covering power negative image. The unexposed grains begin to dissolve and move to the positive image receiving layer.

Projection.
The unexposed grains have dissolved and migrated to the thin layer to form the positive image. The exposed grains have meanwhile developed into a negative. The wide differences in covering power allow positive and negative to coexist.

Before mixing up any of the processing solutions, the manufacturer's instructions should be carefully read, as they must be followed precisely. This not only ensures safety — it also produces the best results. Absolute cleanliness is essential, particularly since many of the chemicals are toxic and some of the developing and bleaching agents are very harmful to the skin and eyes. All chemicals must therefore be handled with extreme care, while cross-contamination must also be avoided. If this happens, the film will be ruined.

Processing the film
During processing, it is essential to adhere to the times and temperatures of the various stages specified by the kit manufacturer. Even seemingly small deviations can ruin the final result. This is particularly important when the developer is being used.

Similarly, the washes must be carried out according to the instructions. Time spent on this is never wasted; insufficient washing can cause unpleasant color casts. Again, the temperature should be checked carefully. Too high a temperature can damage the film emulsion.

Because of the difficulty in obtaining an exactly matched film and processing kit, however, deviations from the instructions may sometimes be necessary. For instance, if Ektachrome 160 film is developed using the E4 kit, it will lose about one stop in speed. The answer to

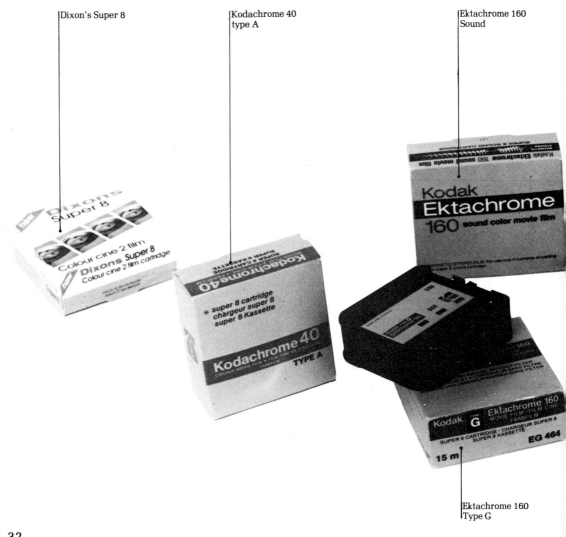

Dixon's Super 8

Kodachrome 40 type A

Ektachrome 160 Sound

Ektachrome 160 Type G

this is to increase the time allowed for the first developing stage by about 30 per cent to compensate for the loss. However, as far as the novice is concerned, it is always best to seek expert advice before embarking on such experiments.

Special effects

Home processing has many advantages. The film can be screened much more quickly and it is also far cheaper than professional processing. For a creative movie maker, it also opens the door to the creation of his or her own special effects.

An interesting result can be achieved, for instance, by extending the time the film spends in the first developer. This will increase the effective speed of the film; generally, 25 per cent longer in the developer should produce about a one stop increase in speed. However, it should be noted that there are some unfortunate side-effects — notably an increase in grain size with a shift in color balance — so the film maker must judge whether technical perfection or the effect are more important. This obviously depends on the subject of the film.

Spectacular 'science fiction' effects can be achieved simply by subjecting ordinary reversal film to negative film processing — in other words, omitting all processing stages before color development. In the finished product, all the colors will be the complementary of the originals; green grass, for instance, will be magenta and a

Kodachrome 40
Sound type A

Some of the many brands of film available in cassette form. Always choose the right type of film for the job in hand, checking the information on the packet or box carefully.

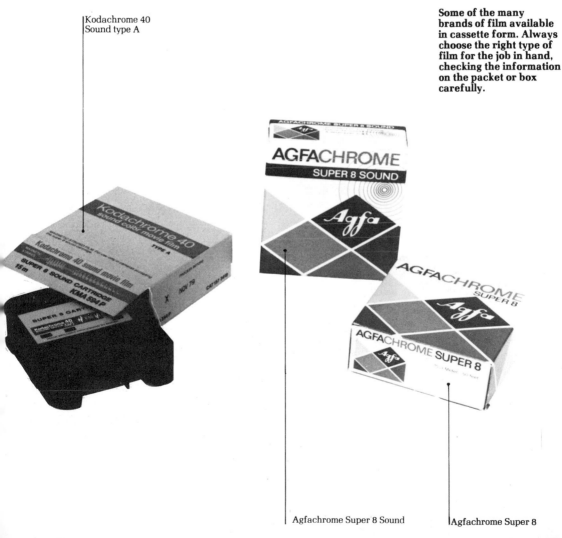

Agfachrome Super 8 Sound

Agfachrome Super 8

blue sky will be yellow.

Black and white film can be toned to give an old-time movie effect. Sepia is the most commonly used shade. Other colors can also be used; blue, for example, was often used in the silent cinema to create the effect of night.

Duplication

Both professional and amateur movie makers often want copies of their films. In the professional's case, the reason for this is obvious; in the amateur's the copies may well be intended for distribution among friends and relations or for entry into competitions. Whatever the reason, correct copying is important; a damaged original is difficult, if not impossible, to restore.

Producing a good copy of a film is not as easy as it may seem. The major problem is the control of

film contrast. This is important since it enables dark objects to be distinguished from lighter ones.

Each type of film, when correctly processed, has a definite relationship between exposure and optical density. In a reversal film, for instance, no exposure at all will reproduce as dense black, while a great deal of exposure will reproduce as clear white. Between these two extremes, the rate of change of density is known as contrast.

In practice, however, even a perfect film would not reproduce the inherent contrast in a scene exactly. The tone range is always compressed, especially in the darker and lighter parts of the scene. This has the effect of extending the exposure latitude and retaining 'highlight' and 'shadow' detail. All such factors are taken into account by manufacturers when designing emulsions intended for projection. Then, contrast

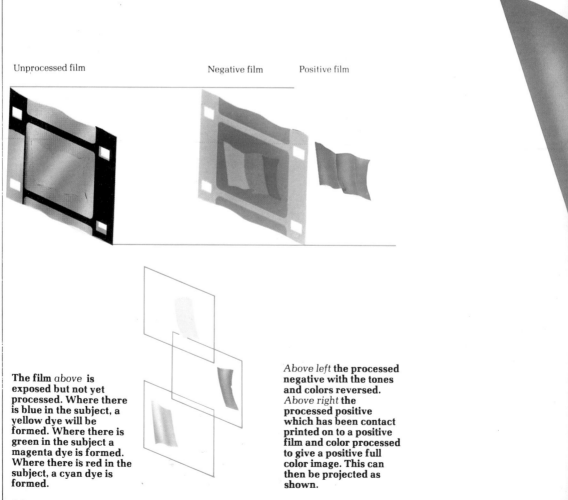

Unprocessed film   Negative film   Positive film

The film *above* **is exposed but not yet processed. Where there is blue in the subject, a yellow dye will be formed. Where there is green in the subject a magenta dye is formed. Where there is red in the subject, a cyan dye is formed.**

Above left **the processed negative with the tones and colors reversed.** *Above right* **the processed positive which has been contact printed on to a positive film and color processed to give a positive full color image. This can then be projected as shown.**

Subtractive color works on the principle of taking out a portion of the spectrum from received light and using what is allowed to pass through. All colors can be made from the three primaries — red, blue and green. A red sensitive filter will take out red and allow blue and green to pass through, thus forming cyan. Similarly, if green is taken out, the remaining red and blue will form magenta; if blue is taken out, the remaining red and green will form yellow. These 'secondary' colors can be used to stop their opposite primaries: yellow will pass red and green and stop blue, for example, cyan will stop red and magenta will stop green.

is chosen to make the result on the screen satisfactory to the audience.

When a film is copied on to another one, however, there is always the risk of a loss of contrast. This is particularly the case if the characteristics of the two emulsions are not complementary, when the results may well be unacceptable. The best copies are obtained from films shot on special low contrast emulsions specifically designed for the purpose. These can be either reversal or negative. Unfortunately, they are only available in 16mm, while, in both cases, the camera original is not suitable for projection.

All Super 8 films are reversal and designed for projection, so here the problem is particularly acute. In some cases, a certain amount of pre-fogging can improve the final result, while the right choice of printing stock is essential.

Though contrast is the main problem with copying, it is not the only one. There can be color shifts and there is an inevitable loss of resolution. At best, if the original and the copy emulsions both have the same potential resolving power, the copy will only have half the resolution of the original. However, with modern high resolution emulsions, this loss is by no means disastrous.

Printing options

Prints can be produced in several ways. The simplest method is to place the film in contact with a suitable print stock and to run them both past a light. This normally produces good results and it is used extremely frequently. However, it has one drawback. Contact copies are frequently not as sharp as the originals because of the finite thickness of the two emulsions.

The way to overcome this problem is to have

Projected image

The negative film *left* shows the secondary colors, the positive film *right* the primary.

A comparison of the results produced by filming on Super 8 *left* and 16mm *right*. **The image area of Super 8 is** naturally smaller than that of 16mm and the quality and sharpness of the image itself is inferior. 16mm equipment, however, is far more costly than Super 8 equipment.

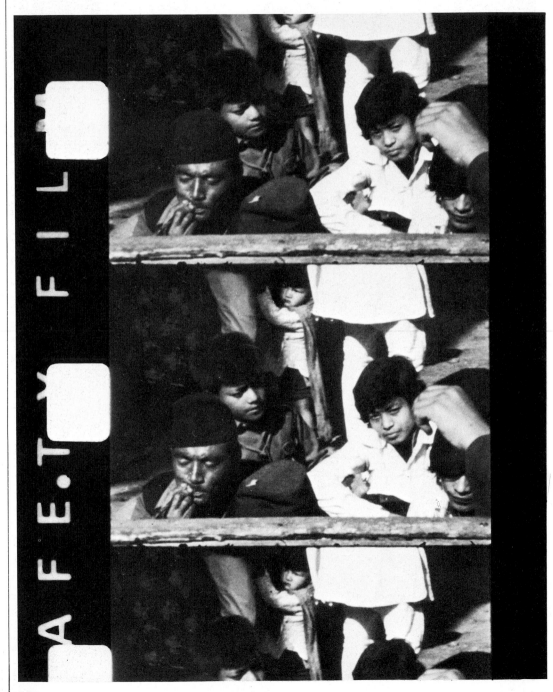

the image optically projected from the original on to the printing stock via a high quality lens system. Though both emulsions still have their finite thickness, the effects of the depth of field and focus make the resultant print much sharper.

The optical qualities of a print can be improved still further by running the original through what is known as a liquid gate during printing. The film is immersed in a liquid with optical qualities similar to those of the film base. By this means, the effect of any scratches can be minimized or even eliminated.

It is also possible to change the size of a print during optical printing by increasing or reducing its size to that of another gauge. This is now a common commercial practice; 35mm feature films, for instance, are widely available in 16mm versions. Reduction prints from 16mm to Super 8 are also fairly common, while blow-ups from Super 8 to 16mm are similarly satisfactory. Even films shot at silent speed can be stretch-printed to sound speed by printing every third frame twice.

Most prints are now graded. This involves a close inspection of the original to assess the intensity of the printing needed to create a print that is evenly exposed. If the original's color balance is inconsistent, this can be compensated for at the printing stage through the use of filters. In general, modern developments in printing mean that considerable correction is possible, with a commensurate improvement in visual consistency.

Home copying

One factor influencing the decision whether or not to have a print of a film made is the question of the cost. Even having a few feet of film copied professionally can be very expensive, since most laboratories make a minimum change for making a print. The alternative is, once again, for the movie maker to undertake the task at home.

In many cases — just as with home processing — amateur copying can be very successful, provided the movie maker is prepared to accept the inevitable drop in quality. The process is basically very simple. The sequence to be copied is projected on to a flat, matt white screen and re-filmed with an ordinary movie camera. A carefully focused bright screen image is essential; the best results are given by one about

After exposure, the reversal process involves developing to black and white, then, after a fogging exposure, formation of the complementary colors by a color developer. The silver is **bleached out, and, after fixing, the full color image is produced. The color forming agents in this process are large molecules which have a tendency to produce less sharp, slightly grainy definition.**

Components

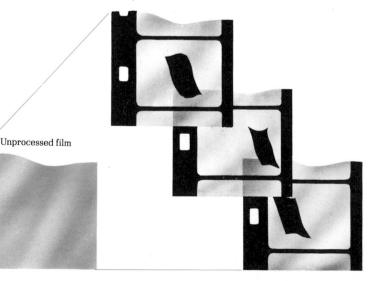

Unprocessed film

two foot wide. The camera should be lined-up as close as possible to the axis of the projection lens to minimize the effect known as 'keystoning'.

To find the correct exposure, it is usually best to shoot an experimental length of the copy first. Often, it will be found that the exposure should be one stop greater than that indicated by an exposure meter. The best type of film to use is Type A film — that is, film balanced for use with tungsten lights. This may create a slight blue cast, but this can be compensated for through the use of a 10 or 20 'yellow' color correction filter.

To avoid a strobing effect, the camera and projector must be precisely synchronized. Really accurate sync can only be achieved through the use of an electronic synchronizer, accurate to within a fraction of a frame.

Care of film

All photographic materials change over a period of time and it is obviously important to check them carefully before use. Film cartons, for instance, are usually stamped with an expiry date. This indicates that, given average conditions, the film will begin to noticeably deteriorate after this date. The rule is therefore never to use over-age film, unless you are prepared to risk the disappointment of inadequate results.

As far as film is concerned, color is less stable than black and white. This is because the color dyes tend to fade, unless the film is kept under proper conditions. The two greatest enemies of film emulsion — particularly color — are humidity and heat. If film stock is stored at a low temperature, its shelf life will increase

Components after second stage of development   Final print

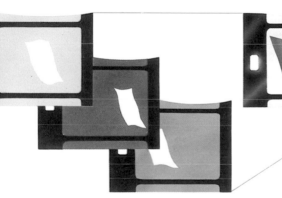

In the process each primary has been formed from two complementaries.

Kodachrome attempts to overcome this problem by having the color forming dyes in the developer. Exposure to red, following the black and white negative stage, fogs the bottom layer of silver halides.

The developer in the next stage contains a cyan dye former. Exposure to blue from the top then fogs the blue sensitive silver halide in the top layer, and the next developer contains a yellow dye former. Exposure to white light fogs the undeveloped middle layer and the next developer contains a magenta dye former. The silver which is also developed at each stage is bleached out and a pure dye image in the natural colors remains.

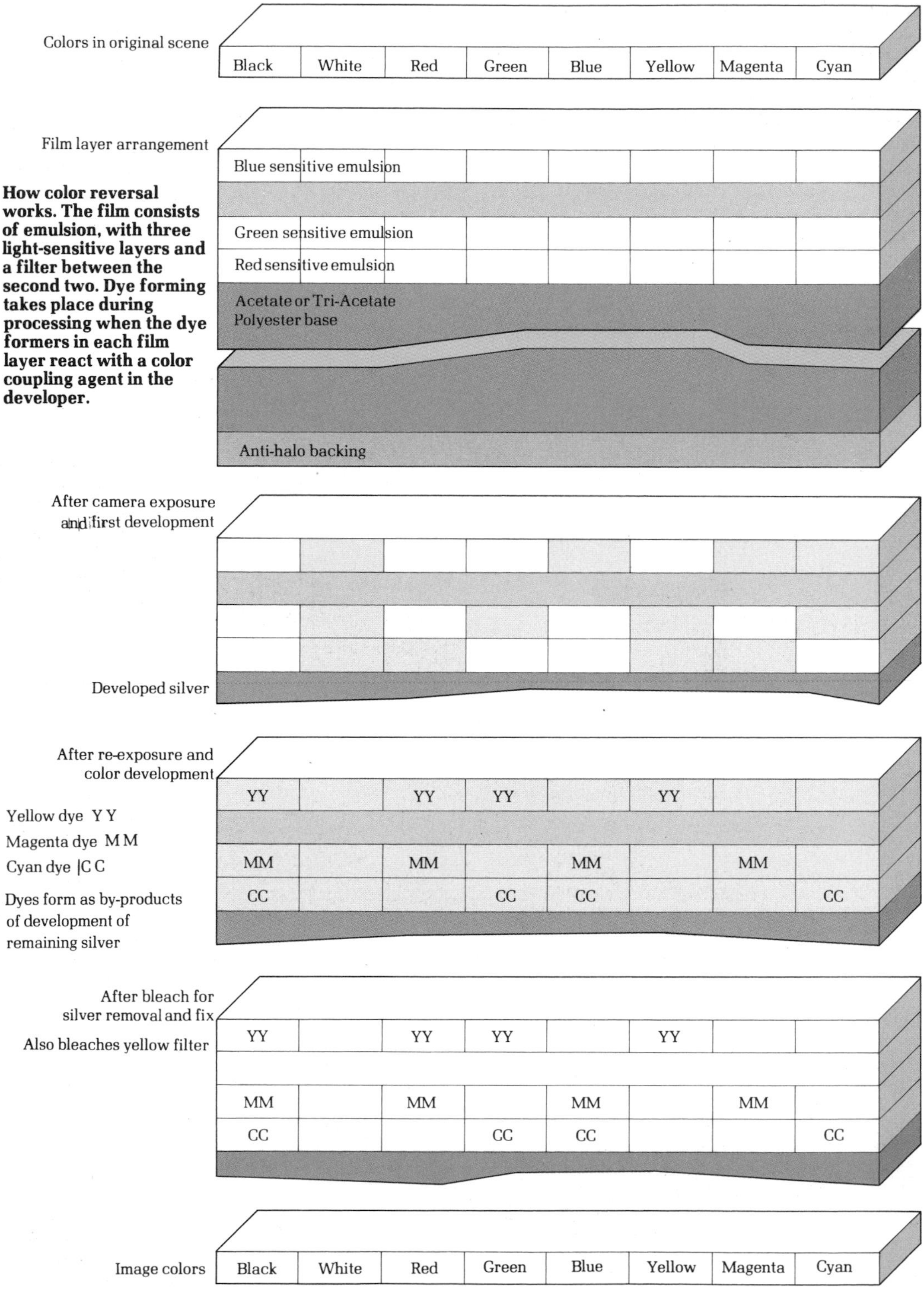

Colors in original scene

Black	White	Red	Green	Blue	Yellow	Magenta	Cyan

Film layer arrangement

How color reversal works. The film consists of emulsion, with three light-sensitive layers and a filter between the second two. Dye forming takes place during processing when the dye formers in each film layer react with a color coupling agent in the developer.

Blue sensitive emulsion

Green sensitive emulsion

Red sensitive emulsion

Acetate or Tri-Acetate Polyester base

Anti-halo backing

After camera exposure and first development

Developed silver

After re-exposure and color development

Yellow dye Y Y
Magenta dye M M
Cyan dye |C C

Dyes form as by-products of development of remaining silver

Black	White	Red	Green	Blue	Yellow	Magenta	Cyan
YY		YY	YY		YY		
MM		MM		MM	MM		
CC			CC	CC			CC

After bleach for silver removal and fix

Also bleaches yellow filter

Black	White	Red	Green	Blue	Yellow	Magenta	Cyan
YY		YY	YY		YY		
MM		MM		MM	MM		
CC			CC	CC			CC

Image colors

Black	White	Red	Green	Blue	Yellow	Magenta	Cyan

dramatically; if, for instance, unexposed film is wrapped in a plastic bag and frozen until it is required for use, its working life will be increased by at least a year. Ideally, however, film stock should be as fresh as possible. Even under the best storage conditions, it will deteriorate with time. Usually, the older the film, the more insensitive it becomes to light. There is often an increase in graininess, while, with color films, the color reproduction shifts.

The same rule applies to processing. This should always be done as soon as possible after the completion of shooting. Any long delay, particularly in hot and humid climates, can lead to a considerable deterioration in the latent image.

Buying film
Always purchase film from a reliable professional store. Cut-price film 'bargains' may look tempting, but there is always the considerable possibility that the film has been wrongly stored. Most film footage is irreplaceable; it is not worth taking the risk to save on the cost of proper raw film stock. Though the price of raw film is often the largest item in any movie maker's budget — once the capital cost of the equipment has been allowed for — it still represents less than one third of the raw-stock-development-printing expense.

The Kodak Supermatic processor was designed for the mass processing of Super 8 film.

The typical processing sequence at a modern film laboratory. *Far left, top* Up to 40 cartridges are fixed together for processing, so each cartridge must be carefully identified. *Far left, middle* The cartridge is placed in a box for eventual linking to an automatic splicer which will feed the heat seal machine, illustrated *far left, bottom.* One operator normally controls about five of these machines, loading and unloading them and watching the display panel. This indicates any faults in machine, cartridge and film and gives instructions on how to deal with them. Up to 40 cartridges are wound on to a main reel, sealed, taken out, and transported to the dark room, *top left.* The cassette is opened in the dark and joined on to the end of the preceding reel on its way through the continuous

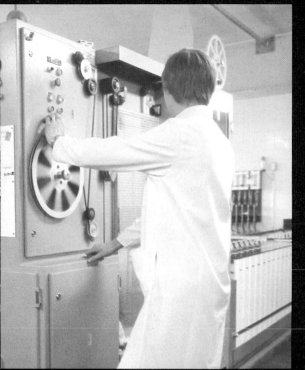

processing machine. Alternatively, it may be added on to a test strip, *bottom left.* This will pinpoint any scratching, density fluctuations, color or chemical changes, and so on. The continuous processing machine *above* takes the film through two developers, bleach baths, fixers, stabilizers and several washes in the course of about one hour. *Above right* The take-up spool at the finished end of the processing machine must be changed at intervals, but it is obviously not possible to stop the process inside the machine when this is necessary. The hopper carefully collects surplus film during this change-over and the new spool works at a faster speed for a time to empty it. In fact the hopper will collect several minutes of film if this proves necessary. *Right* The rolls are taken

away and separated out. Numbers are checked, leaders are attached and individual cassettes are placed in their correct bags. These are heat sealed and dropped in the post bag.

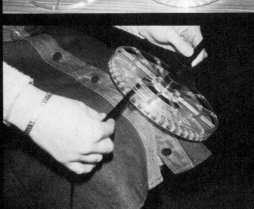

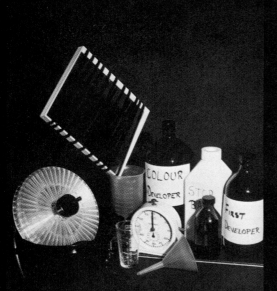

Various stages in home processing. After the film has been wound on to the tank spirals *top right* and *below*, it is placed in the developing tank and developer added *near right*. In this, timing is vital. The film must be agitated constantly for 30 seconds and then for 5 seconds every 30 seconds for 12½ minutes. The film is then quickly rinsed and the first stop bath given (10 seconds agitation per minute. After 4 minutes, the film is washed for the same amount of time. It is then exposed to white light *bottom* for 3 minutes on both sides. The temperature is stabilized with water, a second stop bath is given (4 minutes), and then a 5 minute wash is followed by a 6 minute bleach and a five minute final fix. One last 10 minute wash, a minute in stabilizer and the film is ready to dry.

Know your Camera

In the pioneer days of movie making, the functions of recording and replaying images were quite frequently combined in one machine. Today, however, they are always performed by separate ones — camera and projector. The former's basic function is to record a series of images in quick succession on photographic film. These can later be used to recreate an illusion of movement.

How the camera works

Mechanically, the camera works in a very simple way. When you press the start button, a number of things happen almost simultaneously many times a second. The starting of the motor activates a claw. This engages with the perforations along the edge of the film to transport it through the camera. When a frame of film reaches the camera gate, the claw retracts to halt the film and a shutter then opens to expose it. The shutter closes and the claw goes back into action to transport the film on to the next frame. During transport, the shutter must remain closed; otherwise vertical streaks will appear to come from the lighter part of the picture.

A take-up mechanism, powered by the camera motor, winds up the exposed footage. When you finish filming, the mechanism usually stops with the shutter in the closed position to prevent 'fogging' of the frame of film left in the camera gate.

The camera gate itself consists of two sections — a fixed front plate, which has a cut out

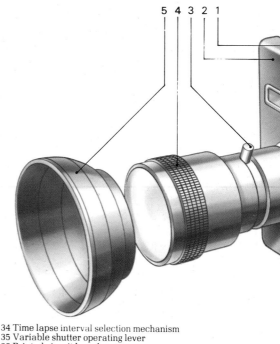

1 Lens mounting plate
2 Front housing
3 Manual zoom lever
4 Zooming and focusing parts of lens
5 Flexible lens hood
6 Rackbar with film sensitivity setting feeler
7 Viewfinder tube and optics
8 Exposure setting galvanometer movement
9 Aperture scale
10 45° mirror
11 Reflex finder objectives lens
12 Aperture setting blades
13 Photo-conductive element
14 Can of film sensitivity setting mechanism
15 Sensitivity setting plate
16 Parabolic mirror
17 Swing-in conversion filter
18 Zooming motor
19 Lock-on run lever
20 Impulse generator printed circuit board
21 Run-stop micro switch
22 Cable release socket
23 See-saw run/single frame select mechanism
24 Release button
25 Drive battery container
26 Pistol grip lock
27/28 Power zoom operating buttons
29 Power zoom switches
30 Camera body housing
31 Locating notch for half-closed shutter
32 Auto/manual exposure selection/setting
33 Battery test button

34 Time lapse interval selection mechanism
35 Variable shutter operating lever
36 Printed circuit board
37 Running speed selector
38 Conversion filter setting machine
39 Drive battery test and isolating switch
40 Batteries powering exposure meter
41 Pistol grip
42 Left hand cover plate
43 Right hand cover plate
44 Two-speed zoom contact set
45 Variable section shutter
46 Drive motor
47 Eye-cup
48 Eyepiece focus adjustment
49 Loading door
50 Take-up drive dog
51 Footage counter
52 Rack and pinion drive
53 Motor starting solenoid
54 Claw
55 Counter mechanism
56 Counter window

An exploded view of the movie camera *left,* **showing all the working parts, is seen** *below.*

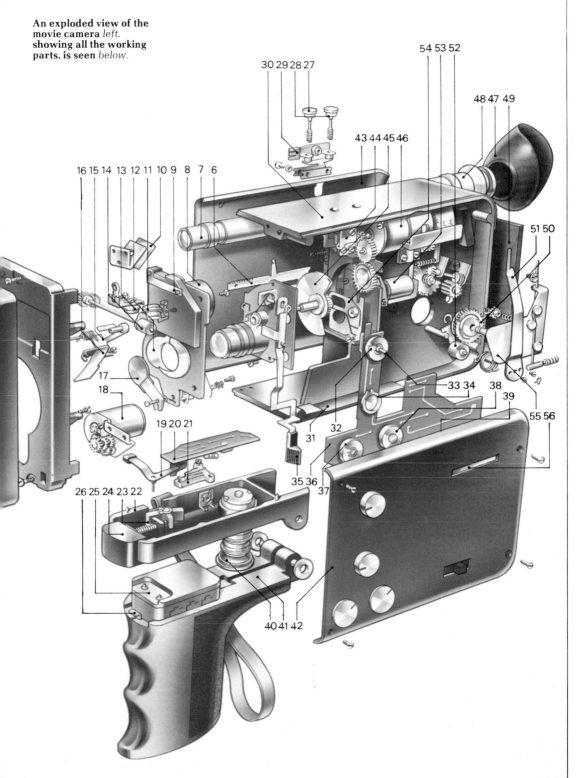

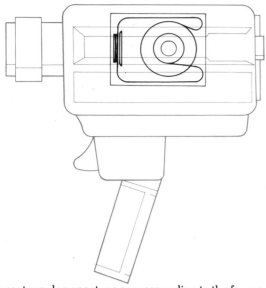

Left *Left* **The movie-camera's transport system in schematic form.** *Below* **Starting the film drive motor makes the take-up core rotate and wind on the film. At the same time the shutter and claw come into action. The claw is inserted into a perforation and pushes the film down one frame. It holds the film for the exposure, and is then withdrawn as the shutter moves across. Movement of shutter and claw are synchronized so that the shutter prevents exposure while the film is moving. In most Super 8 cameras the claw advances the frame for half the cycle, and the frame is exposed for the other half. This is made possible by the use of a semicircular shutter.**

rectangular aperture corresponding to the frame area of the film, and a rear sprung pressure plate. In Super 8 cameras, the pressure plate is omitted, since it is built into the film cartridge. Its function is to ensure that the film is held at a constant distance from the lens and remains perfectly flat during exposure. The gate is relieved so that it does not touch the film in the picture area and so cause scratching.

Movie camera shutters usually take the form of a disc rotating once per frame, with a cut-out sector to enable light to pass through it. The larger the angle of the opening, the greater the amount of light reaching the film and the longer the effective exposure time. The majority of cameras have a fixed shutter with an open sector of around 160°; this corresponds to an exposure time of 1/40th of a frame per second at an 18 fps running speed. Cameras designed for shooting under low light conditions have an increased shutter opening of 220°; this corresponds to an exposure time of 1/30th of a second at 18 fps.

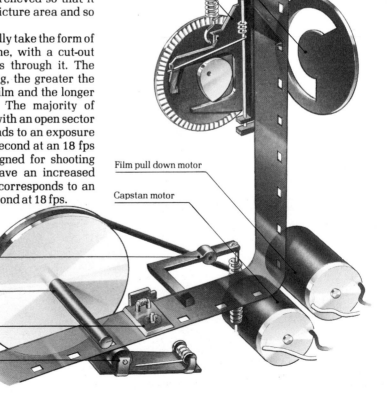

Shutter

Pull down claw

Film pull down motor

Capstan motor

Loop sensing switch

Capstan

Pressure roller

Recording head

Some cameras are fitted with variable shutters. These allow the size of the opening to be reduced, so that a fade can be produced.

Motors and running speeds

Nearly all modern cameras have electric motor drives, powered by batteries. These have several advantages over the older spring-driven types; chief of these is their very constant running speed — a very important consideration when shooting sound — and the ability to shoot for extended periods. With the recently introduced Kodak 200ft Super 8 cartridge, shooting can be done continuously for 13¼ minutes at 18 fps, the standard speed for both sound and silent Super 8 cameras. Several models also operate at 24 fps; this gives slightly improved sound quality from striped film and smoother, flicker-free images, but at increased cost. All 16mm sound films are shot at 24 fps (or 25 fps for television, except for America and Japan), since these are the standard professional filming speeds.

In addition to the normal filming speeds, some cameras have slower speeds, such as 9 fps, for producing accelerated motion on the screen and also faster speeds, such as 36 fps or 54 fps, for producing slow motion when projected at the normal running speed. Since the exposure required at 9 fps is half that required at 18 fps, the slower speed is useful for filming in poor light, providing there is very little movement in the shot.

Another extra is the ability to shoot frames one at a time, a technique used for animation and time lapse photography. Time lapse can compress several hours of real time into a few seconds. Some cameras are equipped with interval timers, which enable single frames to be taken automatically at pre-determined intervals. They also have attachments for electronic flash.

The sole disadvantage of electric drive is the risk of power failure if the batteries are allowed to run down. Most cameras are fitted with a meter to check this, but it is always advisable to fit new batteries if a prolonged shooting session is planned.

Release mechanisms

All cameras have start buttons, but many offer additional methods of stopping and starting the motor. One involves the use of a flexible cable

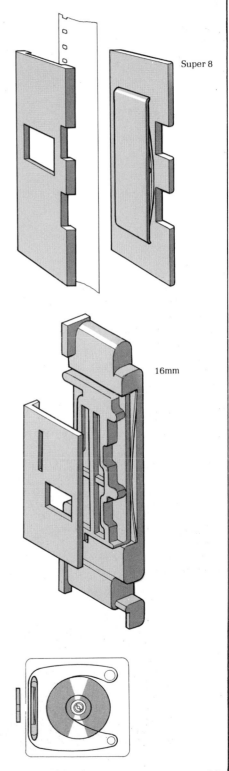

Super 8

16mm

Three projections on the camera's aperture pad determine how much the plastic spring-loaded pressure pad in the film cartridge pushes against the film. This cuts out side weave. The claw takes care of most of the vertical alignment.

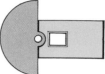

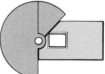

A film's exposure is determined by the amount of light passing through the lens (the f stop) and by the amount allowed through the shutter. The shutter is a metal disc between the lens and the aperture which whirls in time with the claw or shuttle so that light is admitted when the film is stationary and in position and kept out when it is in motion.

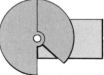

release, which is screwed into a small internally-threaded socket on the camera. An alternative is electronic remote control. This serves the same purpose as the cable release, with the additional advantage that the operator can be several feet away from the camera.

Reverse running

A further useful facility to look for in any camera is the ability to run it in reverse. This enables the film to be wound back to make superimpositions and produce lap-dissolves — a fade-in superimposed over a fade-out.

On several 16mm and Single 8 models, the drive can be disengaged and the film wound back manually; as far as Super 8 is concerned, however, the facility is far more limited. Only a few cameras have the necessary mechanism to be run in reverse, while the amount of film that can be wound back is limited by the design of the Super 8 cartridge. With some cameras, though, lap-dissolves can be achieved automatically at the push of a single button.

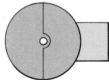

In most cameras the shutter's opening is fixed at between 160° and 180°. The range of exposure times is limited by the fact that it takes time to bring each frame into position. If the shutter is half a disc, then the film spends about the same amount of time moving as it does in exposure.

The variable shutters built in to some cameras allow the size of the opening to be reduced. Reduction of the opening from 180° to 90° means that exposure is halved. A variable shutter can control depth of field. Closing down the shutter, and opening the diaphragm to compensate, results in a decrease in depth.

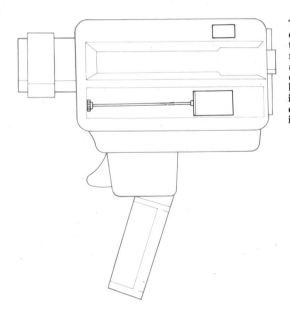

The great advantage of electric motors is that they make constant running speeds easy to achieve. This advantage can be lost if the batteries run down, and it is a good idea to buy a camera which incorporates a battery checking system. Filming speeds range from those for time-lapse photography, measured in frames per minute or hour, to very high speeds which allow for slow motion effects on projection.

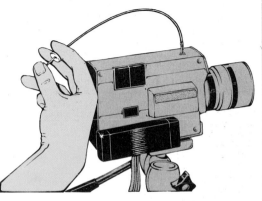

Cable release is always used in conjunction with a tripod. Steady filming is allowed then, as well as distancing of the operator. Depression of the cable release drives a wire into the cable release socket which starts the camera. Some cable releases lock to allow continuous filming.

The camera lens

Apart from the actual film itself, the most important factor determining the quality of the picture is the design of the lens. The camera lens consists of several spherically curved pieces of glass, which focus the rays of light passing through it on to the film plane. The image formed on the film is, in fact, inverted, but this is of little consequence since it is turned the right way up by the projector lens to appear correctly.

The two most important characteristics of a lens are its maximum aperture and its focal length. The maximum aperture of a lens indicates its greatest light-gathering capacity; this is measured in terms of f/numbers. The larger the lens aperture, the smaller the value of the f/number. A lens aperture of f/1.2, for instance, will pass more light than an aperture of f/1.8; cameras designed for use under low light conditions usually have a maximum aperture of f/1.2 or larger. The focal length of a lens is quoted in millimetres. This measurement determines the size of the image formed on the film and hence the angle of view of the lens.

Lenses are divided into three main groups, according to their focal length. By convention, normal focal length lenses cover a horizontal viewing angle of about 22°-23°. This corresponds to a focal length of 15mm for Super and Single 8 film, 12.5mm for Standard 8 and 25mm for 16mm. The focal length varies between film gauges because the apparent taking angle is related to the size of the image formed on the film — and hence the available frame area.

A wide-angle lens, as its name suggests, covers a wider field of view than a normal focus lens. It is thus particularly useful for filming in confined spaces. The shortest Super 8 lenses in common use — these have a focal length of around 6mm-7mm — include more than twice as much in the frame area as a normal lens at the same distance from the subject.

A long-focus lens, on the other hand, covers a narrower angle of view than a normal focus lens. Such lenses are commonly referred to as telephoto lenses. Strictly speaking, however, this description is inaccurate; it applies only to certain types of long-focus lens which are

Stages in the manufacture of a camera at the Sankyo and Nikon factories. *Above* Pitching lens elements prior to grinding to attach them to the grinding jug *below. Right* The semi-finished lens blanks.

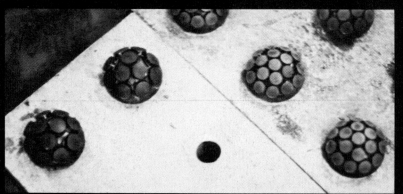

Far left Mounting the lens cell for polishing and *left* the automatic lens grinding machine. *Above* Assembling the lenses in a clean-air cabinet, followed by a thorough check and examination on the work bench.

Above **Checking the camera speed prior to assembly, shown** *right*. *Below* **After completion the camera is tested in a climatic chamber to ensure it can withstand extremes of heat and cold.**

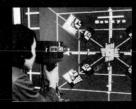

Above left **Checking the picture steadiness of the camera.** *Above right* **Testing the lens resolution.** *Right* **Testing the camera with a beam of light in a specially designed chamber.**

optically constructed to physically shorten the length of the lens.

The effect produced is the telescoping of the subject, bringing it apparently closer in the frame. Today's Super 8 cameras have focal lenses of up to 90mm; these will cover as little as one-sixth of the subject width as taken by a normal focal length lens. These extra-long lenses are tricky to operate and therefore a tripod should always be used if they exceed 40 mm in focal length.

Zoom lenses

A zoom lens has an infinitely variable focal length between a maximum and minimum limit. Its

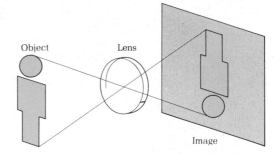

The size of an image produced by a lens is determined by its focal length. For a simple positive lens this is the distance from its centre to the point at which a sharp image is formed of a distant object. The longer the focal length the larger the image.

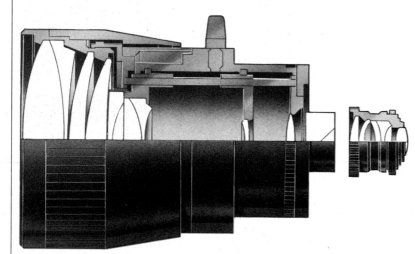

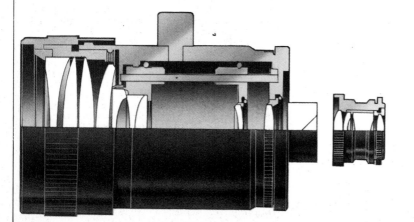

An XL (existing light) lens has, basically, a larger aperture than a slower lens, and is normally coupled with two light saving features. The shutter is designed to have a longer opening time, and light losses to the viewfinder and light meter systems are reduced. In addition, it is normally used in conjunction with a faster film. The larger aperture means that accuracy in focusing is critical and that if a focusing aid such as a rangefinder is used, then its operation is easier because the move in and out of focus is more positive.

The basic factor governing picture quality is the quality of the camera lens. A bad lens *above* will only produce a soft, badly defined image; a good lens will normally produce a sharp, clear image *right* unless the basic rules of movie making are ignored.

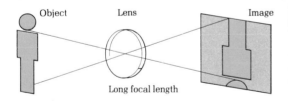

Long focal length

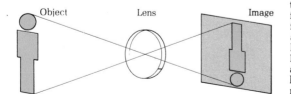

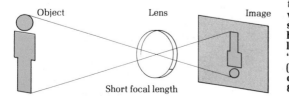

Short focal length

Focal length determines the size of the object filmed. The longer the focal length, the less the area covered and the larger the subject. Lenses are grouped according to focal length, and the three main groups are illustrated left. The long lens in schematic form *top left* (called telephoto when it is mounted in a short, compact barrel) has the longest focal length. The fixed 'normal' focal length (centre) is no longer in common use with Super 8 because zoom lenses are more or less standard. Most Super 8 zoom focal lengths start at 7mm to 9mm and extend to 40mm to 70mm. It is important to remember, however, that in terms of angle of coverage, you add many more degrees by reducing focal length from 7mm to 6mm than by raising it from 40mm to 70mm. The wide angle lens *bottom* is not so common. The conventional zoom range is easier to design than one which could reach down to, say, a 5mm focal length.

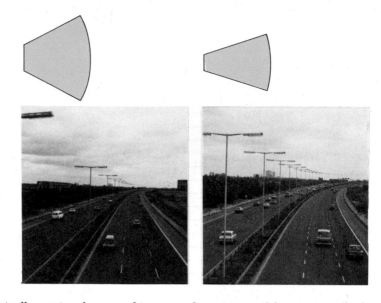

Right **The shorter the focal length the smaller a subject will appear at a given distance, but the greater will be the depth of field and the greater the proportion of the scene which will be included in the shot. The most important use of varying focal length is controlling the size of the main subject in the overall image.**

effect is rather similar to physically moving the camera closer to, or further from, the subject, but there is one important difference. Moving the camera — a tracking or a dolly shot — produces a change in perspective. This does not occur with zooming, when both subject and background are magnified or diminished equally.

All but the most basic cameras are now supplied with zoom lenses. The cheapest usually have a zoom range of around 2-1 or 3-1 — a zoom range is the ratio between the focal lengths at the extreme telephoto and extreme wide-angle settings. Thus, a lens with focal lengths varying between 9mm and 27mm will have a zoom range of 3-1; a more expensive lens, with focal lengths variable between 6.5mm and 65mm, will have a zoom range of 10-1.

Many cameras are equipped with motorized (or power) zooming, while some models have a choice of two zooming speeds. A few of the most expensive have infinitely variable zooming speeds. The advantage of power zooming is that it enables the focal length to be changed much more smoothly than with manual execution.

Focusing

The simplest cameras are fitted with a correspondingly simple form of lens — the fixed focus lens. This has been pre-focused by the manufacturer to produce an acceptably sharp image, irrespective of how far or near the lens is to or from the subject. This, however, is only a compromise solution to a problem that faces every movie maker — depth of field.

Depth of field sounds a complex term to understand, but, in reality, it is relatively simple. What happens is that the aberrations present in all lenses and the thickness of the film emulsion

combine to produce a range of distances at which an object will appear reasonably sharp and it is this range which is known as depth of field. It value depends on three contributing factors — focal length, aperture and the distance being focused upon. When the focal length is short, the working aperture small and the distance focused upon is far, the depth of field is great. The depth of fi...d is shallow when the focal length is long, the working aperture large and the distance focused

If only focal length is varied then perspective is unaltered. However, if the distance between camera and subject is changed in order to control the size of the subject, then the relationship between foreground and background will also be altered. With the wide-angle lens, the distance of the background is maintained, but, as the angle is narrowed and

upon is near. Under the latter conditions, it is essential that the lens is focused accurately; for this reason, many cameras with focusing lenses are also equipped with some form of focusing aid.

Autofocusing

To overcome the problem of focusing, many modern cameras are fitted with an automatic system to do the job. This employs two small mirrors, which are positioned on either side of a prism. The prism deflects light rays to two identical photo-cells, which are connected to a complex electronic comparator circuit.

The scene before the camera is viewed by both mirrors, one of which is fixed at a preset angle to the prism, while the other vibrates about its pivot to scan the scene. When the images presented to the prism coincide, a tiny microprocessor measures the angle of the scanning mirror to calculate the camera-to-subject distance. A small

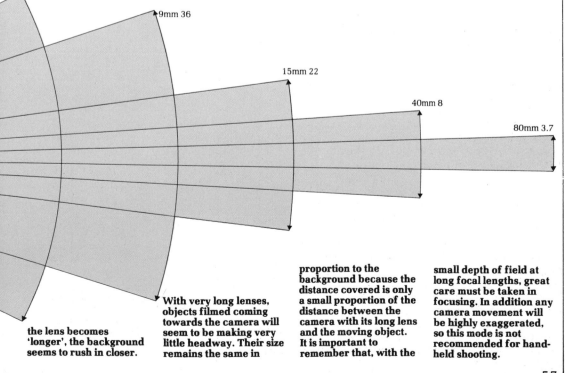

6mm 55
9mm 36
15mm 22
40mm 8
80mm 3.7

the lens becomes 'longer', the background seems to rush in closer.

With very long lenses, objects filmed coming towards the camera will seem to be making very little headway. Their size remains the same in

proportion to the background because the distance covered is only a small proportion of the distance between the camera with its long lens and the moving object. It is important to remember that, with the

small depth of field at long focal lengths, great care must be taken in focusing. In addition any camera movement will be highly exaggerated, so this mode is not recommended for hand-held shooting.

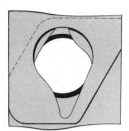

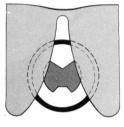

sensor mounted on the lens focusing ring tells the micro-processor how the lens is set; if this setting is incorrect, the microprocessor then sends a signal to a focusing motor, which adjusts the lens setting motor accordingly.

Autofocus systems, however, are not foolproof. They will always focus upon the nearest dominant object to the camera, but this may not always be the subject which the operator wishes to focus upon. For this reason, autofocus cameras have a manual override to deal with such situations.

Macrofocusing

Macrofocusing makes extreme close-up photography possible — in some cases right up to the front element of the lens — without the need for supplementary lenses. This is achieved by moving an internal lens element, thus causing the whole lens to focus to very short distances. A frame of film can be filled with subjects an inch wide and this usually more than compensates for the loss of ability to zoom.

Interchangeable lenses and lens attachments

Though the majority of Super 8 cameras have fixed lenses, there are a few types available —

Depth of field is the range of acceptably sharp focus in front of and behind a subject which is being focused on. Three factors affect it: f/stop setting (stop down to increase depth); distance of subject (rapid decrease in depth as lens is focused close); focal length (less depth for long focal length, more for short focal length).

Above **three kinds of diaphragm.** *Centre* **is the traditional multi-leaf, which almost manages to achieve consistently circular opening. The twin moving vane method** *top* **comes reasonably close to this, but with the system of one moving vane and one fixed vane, the fixed vane persistently decreases the lens speed.**

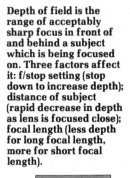

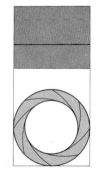

The importance of focusing correctly when working at the numerically lower end of the f scale is illustrated *above.* **Left at f/1.4 the aperture is almost fully open. The depth of field,**

about one third in front of the object and two thirds behind, is very narrow. At f/8 the smaller aperture allows less light and correspondingly greater depth until at f/32 *right*

much of the field in front of the subject and all of the background is in focus. To make a smaller stop possible, and thus increase the depth of field, you can: use a faster film, decrease the

frames per second rate and use more light. You can also zoom down to a low focal length or put more distance between camera and subject.

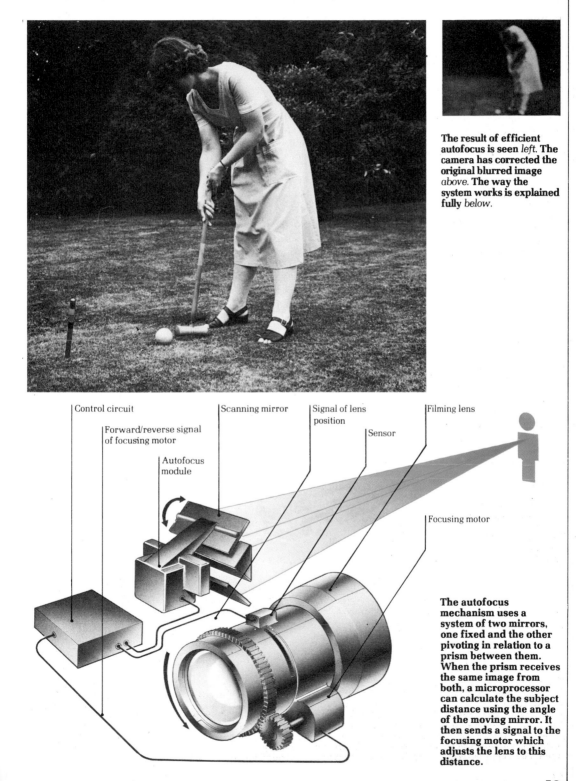

The result of efficient autofocus is seen *left*. The camera has corrected the original blurred image *above*. The way the system works is explained fully *below*.

Control circuit

Forward/reverse signal of focusing motor

Autofocus module

Scanning mirror

Signal of lens position

Sensor

Filming lens

Focusing motor

The autofocus mechanism uses a system of two mirrors, one fixed and the other pivoting in relation to a prism between them. When the prism receives the same image from both, a microprocessor can calculate the subject distance using the angle of the moving mirror. It then sends a signal to the focusing motor which adjusts the lens to this distance.

and many 16mm models — with interchangeable lenses. Some cameras employ bayonet-type lens mounts, while many 16mm cameras have turret mounts, which are capable of accepting three (in a few cases four) different lenses. The turret rotates so that the selected lens can be quickly swung into position.

Most cameras, however, use threaded 'C' mounts. The 'C' refers to a standard thread and mount size used almost exclusively by lower-priced interchangeable lens movie cameras.

The front of the lens barrel is usually threaded to accept screw-in attachments, such as supplementary lenses, lens hoods and filters. Supplementary lenses are used when the camera is required to focus on objects closer than the normal focusing range of its own lens will allow. They are used for close-up work, such as titling, with cameras without macrofocusing ability, or in cases when the ability to zoom needs to be retained, as in animation.

The power of a supplementary lens is measured in dioptres; its value is inversely proportional to the focal length (in metres) of the supplementary lens. Normally, supplementary lenses are used with the camera lens focused on infinity, in which case a one dioptre lens will focus on a subject one metre (39ins) from the lens. Similarly a two dioptre lens will focus on a subject half a metre (19½ins) from the lens and a three dioptre one on a subject one-third of a metre (13ins) away. When using more than one supplementary lens at a time, their combined power is calculated by adding their individual dioptre values together.

To vary the focusing distance, the focus of the camera's own lens must be adjusted. To work this out the equation $D = \dfrac{C \times F}{C + F}$ is used. D is the working distance from the supplementary lens to the subject, C is the camera scale setting and F is the focal length of the supplementary lens. It is usually easier to work this out in metres and to multiply by 39 to convert the result to inches.

Filters
Extensive coverage of filters is given in the chapter on Exposure and Lighting. However, since they are an essential camera fitting, a brief account of some of the more common types is also given here. All are intended for use with color film.

By absorbing ultra-violet (UV) light, skylight filters help to reduce the blue/green cast

The f stop is the ratio between the focal length and the diameter of a lens. Changing the f stop involves changing the diameter of the lens by means of a diaphragm. As the diaphragm is

closed down the diameter becomes smaller and the ratio of diameter to focal length is thus increased. This explains why the f stop numbers go in the opposite direction to the

one which many people expect them to. Most light is admitted through the lens when the diaphragm is open and the diameter is widest (fast). But it is here that the ratio of diameter to

f/2.8

f/5.6

f/8

sometimes evident in the shadowy areas of an image or on film shot on rainy days. They absorb very little light and therefore no exposure increase is required.

Polarizing filters, on the other hand, do require the exposure to be increased — usually by two f/stops. They are extremely useful for eliminating unwanted reflections from non-metallic surfaces, such as water and glass, while on bright, sunny days they can make the sky appear a more intense blue. The filters are usually available in rotatable mounts, so that the plane of polarization can be varied as desired.

Color conversion filters enable film balanced for one type of light — tungsten, for instance — to be used with another, such as daylight. The exposure increase required for this is two-thirds of an f/stop. All commonly available Super 8 films are balanced for tungsten light, so all Super 8 cameras have a built-in filter to achieve this. The filter can be retracted from the light path for use under artificial light conditions.

Conversely, other color filters are available to enable daylight balanced film to be used with artificial light. The exposure increase required in this case is somewhat lower. Other color filters produce more subtle changes in color

temperature and are frequently used when a particular effect is required.

Neutral density (ND) filters are designed to reduce the intensity of the light entering the lens without altering the color temperature. They are used when the working aperture of the lens has to be increased — to reduce the depth of field, for instance — or to give a satisfactory aperture fade under very bright conditions. A x 2 ND filter will require an exposure increase of one f/stop : an x4 ND filter requires an increase of two stops; and an x8 requires an extra three stops exposure.

Exposure control

All cameras have some form of exposure control, so that the intensity of light passing through the lens to reach the film can be adjusted. This is done by incorporating a diaphragm in the lens system; the aperture of this diaphragm can be varied to pass more or less light, depending on the amount required to achieve the right exposure.

The size of the diaphragm opening is related to the effective lens aperture and is expressed in terms of f/stops. A typical exposure system is calibrated as follows — f/1.4, f/2, f/2.8, f/4, f/5.6, f/8, f/11, f/16, f/22, f/32 and so on. Each successive number in the sequence enables twice as much

focal length is lowest. In moving from low values of f to higher ones, the light allowed through decreases. Conventional f values are as follows: 1, 1.4, 2, 2.8, 4, 5.6, 8, 11, 16, 22, 32. Numbers at

either end of the scale are often omitted. Each step indicates a halving of the exposure and each consecutive number is obtained by multiplying by the square root of 2. The

pictures *below* show the effect of closing down the f stop, with the ones on the left admitting too much light and the ones on the right too little.

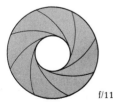

f/11

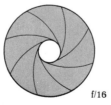

f/16

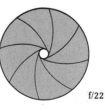

f/22

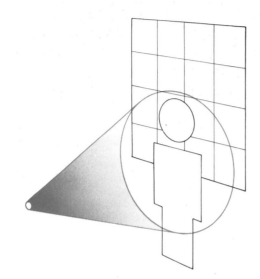

light to pass as its predecessor; thus, f/2.8 passes twice as much light as f/2 and f/4 passes twice as much again — that is, four times as much as f/2.

The aperture setting required to correctly expose a film depends on the following factors: the intensity of the available light; the sensitivity of the film in use; the effective speed of the camera shutter, related to the filming speed in fps; and the amount of light absorbed by the camera's optical system. With modern cameras, this last factor can be extremely significant. Light can be absorbed by the lens itself, particularly with long zoom, multi-element lenses, while it can also be lost to a reflex view-finding system and built-in light meter.

Professional cameras are calibrated in units known as T (or transmission) stops, which take these factors into account. Amateur cameras with built-in automatic light meters automatically compensate for it; if an external metering system is used, however, the correction factor must be determined and allowed for by experiment.

Exposure determination

There are two main ways of determining what

The usefulness of a backlight control when working with a camera with automatic light metering is illustrated *above* and *right*. If a subject is viewed against a light background such as a window the meter tends to under-expose the subject. This results in a silhouette such as the one|*below*|. This situation can be dealt with either by employing a manual control which overrides the automatic one, or by having an in-built backlight button or notch which will automatically increase the exposure by one stop. *right.*

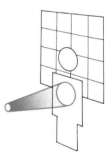

The automatic exposure control works by receiving light in a cell made of a substance such as cadmium sulphide. This has an electrical resistance which varies according to the amount of light. This cell can then power the motors which drive the diaphragm blades in accordance with the amount of light impinging on it.

Aperture control motor

Photo-electric cell

Diaphragm

Exposure control beamsplitter

Viewfinder beamsplitter

exposure should be used. The first is to use printed exposure tables. These give a list of the recommended apertures for use under various lighting conditions at a specified running speed. This is usually 18 fps in the case of Super 8 film. Correction factors of filming at other speeds are also normally quoted.

Far more consistent results, however, can be obtained by using an exposure meter to measure the amount of light falling on a subject. An exposure meter consists of a photo-electric cell, which passes an electrical current according to the amount of light falling on it, and a galvanometer, to measure the strength of the current. Some meters use cells, such as the Selenium type, which are photo-generative — that is, they produce a small electric current proportional to the light received. Others employ photo-conductive cells, such as Cadmium Sulphide (CdS), whose electrical resistance varies according to the level of illumination.

The latter type need a battery to work, but they are far more accurate at low lighting levels than the photo-generative types; these only produce a weak current under such conditions. The values registered on the galvanometer scale are converted to exposure terms via a calculator, which is calibrated in both shutter speeds and f/numbers.

Exposure indexing
Before an exposure meter can be used, its exposure index must be set according to the sensitivity of the film in the camera. Film sensitivity, or 'speed' as it is also known, is expressed in ASA (American Standards Association) units or in DIN (Deutsche Industrie Norm). ASA is an arithmetic rating; a doubling of its value denotes a doubling of sensitivity. DIN is a logarithmic rating; here, a doubling of film sensitivity is denoted by a numerical increase of three. The two scales are related — ASA25 is the same as 15DIN. Hence, ASA50 equals 18DIN, ASA100 equals 21DIN and so on.

Manual setting of the exposure is unnecessary in virtually all Super 8 cameras fitted with built-in exposure meters. In these, the film sensitivity is set automatically by a small notch in the cartridge.

Built-in metering
The majority of cameras available today are equipped with built-in exposure meters. Of these, many make their measurements through the lens — an ability known as TTL metering. This is achieved by a tiny beam-splitting prism, or

mirror, inside the lens, which diverts a small amount of the light to the built-in meter. Many Super 8 cameras and some 16mm models have their metering systems coupled to the lens diaphragm to provide fully automatic adjustment, though other 16mm cameras are only semi-automatic.

On many cameras, too, the aperture can also be set manually, while some allow the automatic control to be partially overriden by various exposure compensation devices. One such system is the so-called backlight control, featured on several Super 8 cameras. This automatically increases the exposure by one stop more than normal, enabling the lens to cope with subjects posed against predominantly bright backgrounds. Without this increase, the result would be a silhouette.

How exposure is measured
Exposure can be determined either by measuring the light reflected by the subject or by measuring the light falling on to the subject. The latter is known as the incident light method. Of the two this gives the more consistent results, since reflected light readings can be influenced by the nature of the subject. Dark objects, for instance, reflect less light than light ones.

Incident light readings can only be made using a separate meter, fitted with a white opaque

There are basically two types of light meter — the reflected light meter and the incident light meter. The former measures the light reflected by the subject. The latter is positioned at the subject and aimed at the camera. They can be powered by selenium cells, which work indefinitely, or by a CdS cell, which needs batteries. Some meters combine both functions.

baffle — known as an incident light attachment — covering the cell window. To make an incident reading, the meter is placed in the subject's position and pointed in the direction of the camera.

Built-in light meters always use the reflected light principle, with the reading being averaged over the whole frame area. However, spot metering is possible if the camera has a zoom lens and an automatic meter with manual override. The operator zooms-in to the subject, notes the aperture indicated by the automatic meter and sets it manually. The zoom is then adjusted to produce the desired framing.

Aperture fades

The easiest way to produce a fade-out is by closing the aperture smoothly during filming. A fade-in is produced by reversing the procedure. Many cameras have a fading button, which automatically opens and closes the lens to produce these results.

The best diaphragm fades are produced with a large working aperture; they tend to become less satisfactory as the aperture decreases. If the sun is very bright, a neutral density filter should be used to reduce the intensity of the light entering the lens, so increasing the working aperture.

Viewfinders

The cheapest cameras on the market are usually

Right **Fade-outs and fade-ins can be produced simply by closing or opening the lens aperture during filming. In bright conditions, a neutral density filter should be used when undertaking the effect.**

Spotmeters are special versions of reflected light meters. They are used to make a reading for a very small field of view and are particularly useful when shooting small areas from a long way off. You could not use an ordinary meter if you were shooting a night camp-fire scene from a distance, or a lighted house surrounded by darkness, unless you went right up to the subject. A spotmeter solves the problem.

fitted with the simplest kind of viewfinder. This is a direct optical device, which consists of an arrangement of lenses whose field of view closely approximates that of the actual picture-taking lens. Error increases, however, the nearer the camera is to the subject. This is because the viewfinder lens is slightly offset from the picture lens, producing a discrepancy in framing known as parallax error.

More expensive cameras are normally fitted with reflex viewfinders. These overcome the problem of parallax by enabling the operator to look through the actual picture-taking lens. This is achieved in one of two ways — the most common being the use of a beam-splitting prism.

The prism is situated in the lens system, where it diverts some of the light to the viewfinder (and metering) system while the remainder is allowed to pass through to the film. The prism itself is located in front of the lens diaphragm, so that the brightness of the image in the viewfinder is not affected by the working aperture.

The other system uses a small mirror which is located on the shutter itself. When the shutter is closed, the mirror diverts any light entering the lens to the viewfinder. When the shutter opens, the mirror is removed from the light path and all of the light is allowed to pass through to the film. This system makes the most efficient use of the light, but it suffers from one disadvantage. This is

On most cameras, the lens system will take away between 25 and 50 per cent of the light reaching the front of the lens, the viewfinder will take another 20 per cent, and the light meter another 10. The rest exposes the film. The diagram *below* shows how the viewfinder beamsplitter takes away some of the light which has passed through the front lens, so that the image seen through the viewfinder will be the same as the one reaching the film.

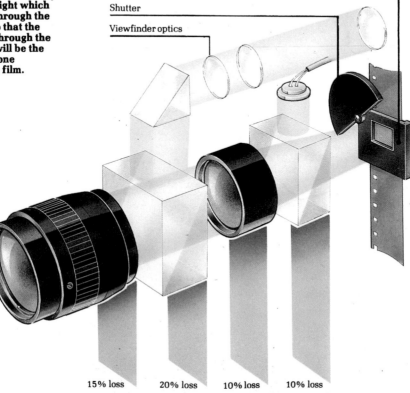

Aperture plate

Shutter

Viewfinder optics

15% loss   20% loss   10% loss   10% loss

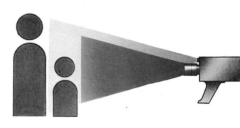

When a camera has a viewfinder separate from the lens, the image in the finder *left* will be slightly different from the one seen by the lens which eventually appears on the film *below*. **This difference is called parallax and is greatest for close-ups or long focal lengths.**

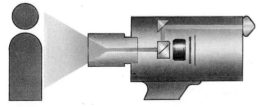

Reflex systems allow the camera user to see the image which reaches the film. The beamsplitter method/is less expensive than the moving mirror method, but it does not allow so much light to the film.

split image

microprism

that the image in the viewfinder darkens as the aperture diaphragm is closed. Another characteristic is the slight flickering which can be seen in the viewfinder during filming.

Focusing aids

One problem with a reflex viewfinder is that though the image may appear to be perfectly focused in it, the camera lens may be out of focus in reality. This is because the image is what is known as an aerial image — that is, it is projected on a plane in space. To help overcome this, several cameras have some form of focusing aid actually in the viewfinder. The commonest of these are the split-image rangefinder and the microprism.

The split-image rangefinder appears in the centre of the viewfinder as a small circle, bisected by a horizontal or diagonal line. If the lens is not correctly focused, the two halves of the image on either side of the circle will appear to be misaligned. When correctly focused, they will be in perfect alignment. The only problem comes when a subject does not have clearly defined vertical lines on which to focus.

The microprism is also located in the centre of the viewfinder. It consists of a circular matrix containing several tiny prisms, which appear to 'break up' an incorrectly focused image. When focused correctly, the image appears 'whole', while the microprism pattern itself is less noticeable.

When the two halves of the circle in the split image rangefinder are aligned then the image is focused correctly. The system works well for a scene with plenty of horizontals and verticals./The microprism is a central grid of tiny lenses which break up the image when it is out of focus. This system is more useful for action shots, but not so effective for fuzzy surfaces. Ground

glass makes any out-of-focus image look indistinct. However, it produces a dark image, which the ground glass spot attempts to remedy. The coincident image rangefinder produces two images until the correct focus is found. It is useful for extreme close-ups. The information given through a typical modern viewfinder is indicated *below.*

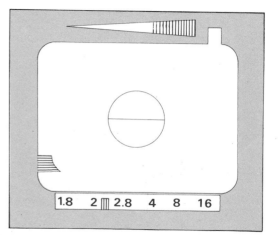

1.8   2 ▥ 2.8   4   8   16

ground glass

co-incident image

Other, less commonly used, focusing systems include the ground glass screen and the co-incident image rangefinder. The former provides a textured surface upon which an image can be formed. Focusing is then determined visually. The disadvantage of this system is that the image appears relatively dark on the screen.

The co-incident image rangefinder produces a double image when the lens is wrongly focused. As this is corrected, the two images come together and eventually are exactly superimposed.

The accuracy of any built-in focusing aid depends on the accuracy of adjustment of the viewfinder eyepiece to suit the user's eyesight. This is carried out by sighting the camera on a distant object and adjusting the zoom to its maximum focal length. The lens is focused on infinity. The eyepiece is then adjusted until the object appears sharp in the viewfinder and the correct focus is indicated.

Once the eyepiece has been adjusted, it need not be altered again, unless there is an appreciable change in the user's eyesight, or another operator takes over the camera.

Critical focusing
To make the focusing of the camera lens as precise as possible, set the zoom to its extreme telephoto setting, since this will produce a limited depth of field. Once the lens has been focused, the zoom can be adjusted to give the desired framing.

Low-light cameras
Cameras specifically designed for filming in low light conditions are known as XL (existing light) models. Their special design features are planned to increase their light-gathering efficiency. These include a very fast — that is, highly sensitive — lens of f/1.3 or greater; a shutter with an open sector of around 220° to increase exposure time; while the film used is fast 160ASA film. Some models also have a running speed of 9 fps for filming in extremely poor light.

The most efficiently designed XL cameras have simple non-zoom lenses, non-reflex viewfinders and separate non-TTL metering systems.

Sound cameras
Sound cameras are described in detail in the sections on sound. Several silent models have sync contacts enabling the camera to be used in conjunction with a tape recorder. Single-system sound cameras have built-in circuitry and magnetic heads for recording sound directly on to special magnetically striped film. These are the most commonly used types.

All of the sound cameras currently available have automatic recording level control, while some also allow the level to be set manually. Nearly all of them enable the sound to be monitored via headphones and give some form of indication of the input signal level — usually by flashing LEDs — light emitting diodes. This is an extremely useful feature.

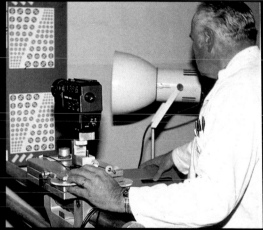

Precision is the key word in the manufacture of modern movie cameras. Here, various stages in the production process are seen, culminating in an array of finished cameras ready for final inspection before dispatch. Every stage involves close attention to detail and rigorous testing of individual parts and actions, such as the focus. Even the tiniest fittings are in individual bowls *top right* for ease of handling and cleanliness.

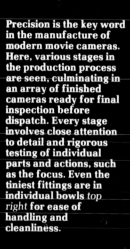

Above **Four views of a completed Beaulieu 6008S. Cameras such as this are now extremely sophisticated, as the industry responds to the demands of the market. The features they offer make it possible for the amateur to produce** **films of near professional standard on an extremely limited budget. Sound is just one of these capabilities; built-in filters, automatic light-reading systems and zoom lenses are among the others now taken as standard.**

Exposure and Lighting

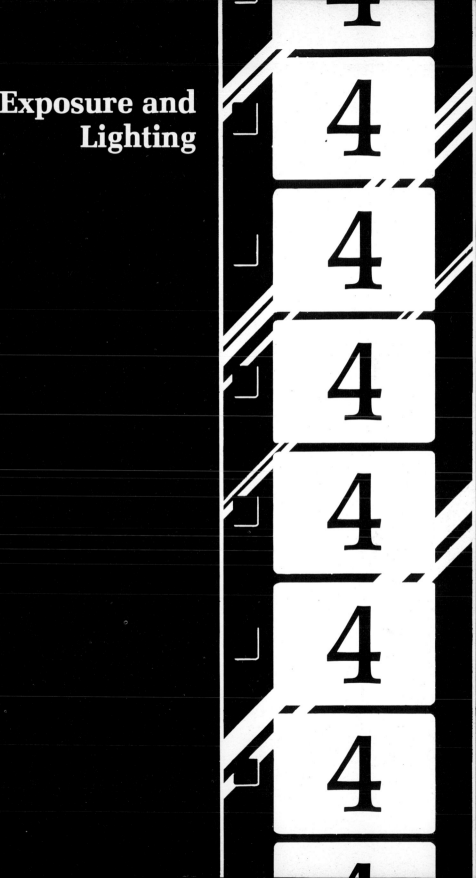

An awareness of the properties of light is essential for good movie making. Too many films are shot totally in bright sunlight or over-lit interiors, sacrificing visual mood for the sake of full exposure. For, though movies can never recreate the full sensation of natural light, they can isolate many of the nuances that go unnoticed in everyday living.

Light, wavelength and color

Light is part of the range of energy that makes up the electromagnetic spectrum. The forms this energy can take range from radio to gamma waves. These are categorized by wavelength — that is, the distance between each crest in the wave pattern — and range from the short wavelengths employed in TV and radio broadcasts to the long wavelengths of gamma rays. Visible light forms only a tiny part of the whole electromagnetic spectrum.

Visible light can be further divided by wavelength into its various component colors — short wavelengths for violets and blues to longer wavelengths for orange and red. Infra-red, ultra-violet and X-rays fall at different ends of the spectrum, just outside the visible range. These rays also have applications in photography.

The color of light is related to its wavelength, each specific wavelength having its own particular energy value. Thus, a flood of white light will contain a mixture of all the wavelengths of visible light, each with its specific energy rating. When this light hits an object, it is either absorbed or reflected in a particular way, according to the nature of the substance.

When the electromagnetic spectrum is divided into wavelengths, it can be seen that visible light only takes up a small proportion of it. Beyond red (that is, with longer wavelengths) are infra-red, radar, TV and radio waves. Beyond violet (with shorter wavelengths) are ultra violet, X rays and gamma rays.

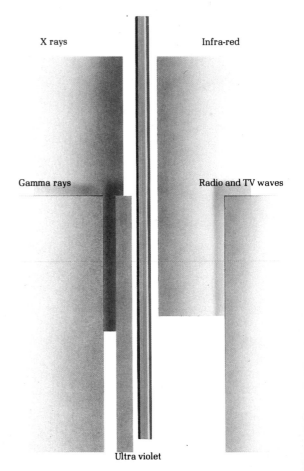

X rays

Infra-red

Gamma rays

Radio and TV waves

Ultra violet

In color photography the spectrum of visible light is broken down into the photo-primary colors.

Visible spectrum

Photographic primaries

Red

Blue

Light absorption

The way in which a substance absorbs light accounts directly for its color. For example, when you look at a blue shirt, the appearance of color is created by the action of the dye. This absorbs all the red and green parts of the visible spectrum that strike it, leaving only the blue to be reflected. If the shirt was lit by light which contained no blue wavelengths, there would be nothing for the shirt to reflect and it would therefore appear black. This is what happens if a normally blue object is viewed under the very yellow light of a sodium street lamp.

Photographic filters operate on this principal. They contain substances which absorb exact amounts of certain wavelengths and therefore allow the filter to control the overall color of the light.

Color temperatures

If a substance is to remain stable, the amount of energy it contains must be strictly limited. Therefore, when a substance absorbs light and

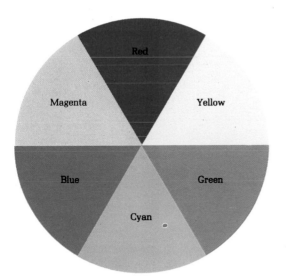

The varying effect of light at different times of day are seen in these stills. Whenever and whatever you are filming, it is vital to ensure that such changes are accounted for. Exposure setting and color correction are the main things to check.

its associated energy, it must eventually find a way of disposing of it. The chief way it does this is by dispelling the energy as heat. Light shone on to an object produces heat; conversely, the application of heat will produce light. This forms the basis of the color temperature scale, which was created so that light sources could be standardized to match the color balance of film.

To determine color temperature, a substance known as a black body radiator is used. This absorbs all the light that falls on it and therefore reflects none. The radiator is heated until it gives off light; depending on the temperature, this ranges from dull red to a brighter red, orange, yellow, white and bluish white. At certain temperatures, the color of the black body matches that of a light source and, by measuring the temperature at the match, the color temperature of the light can be defined. This is measured in degrees Kelvin (K); zero on the Kelvin scale is 273° below Centigrade.

Daylight — actually noon sunlight in Washington DC — is balanced by a black body at 5,600K; photographic film intended for daylight use is balanced around this color temperature. Because light filaments have a much lower melting point, film for artificial light use has much lower color temperatures — 3,400K for photofloods (Type A film) and 3,200K for tungsten-halogen lamps (Type B film).

How light behaves

Light travels in straight lines from its source, so it follows that it will spread as it travels. Consequently, the output from a photographic lamp covers a wider and wider area the further it is from its source; as it does so, it becomes progressively weaker. It is possible, however, to calculate the alteration in camera exposure needed to compensate for this loss of strength.

Suppose, for example, you are shooting a 3m square painting, the first shot being a close-up of an area approximately 1.5m square. You might find with the lamp 2mm away, you can shoot at an aperture of f/5.6. Next, a general view is required and, to ensure even illumination, the light must be moved back to a distance of 4mm from the subject. The exposure now changes to f/2.8 — two stops larger than the first setting.

The reason for this is that the quantity of light used to illuminate the first shot (1.5m square) is being spread to cover an area four times as large (3m square). Since the light is spread more thinly, the aperture setting needs to be larger so that the film is fully exposed. The area to be lit has increased by four, so each part of the painting

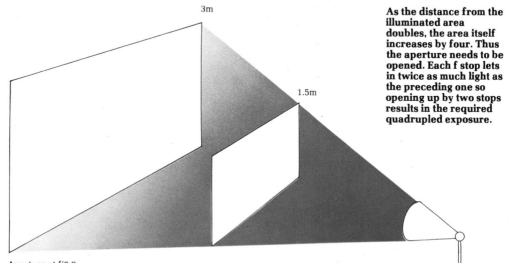

3m

1.5m

As the distance from the illuminated area doubles, the area itself increases by four. Thus the aperture needs to be opened. Each f stop lets in twice as much light as the preceding one so opening up by two stops results in the required quadrupled exposure.

Aperture at f/2.8

Camera aperture at f/5.6

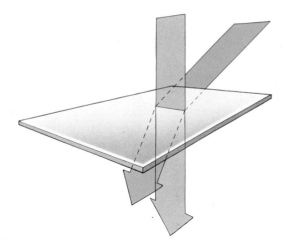

receives only one quarter of the light used for the close-up shot. Four times less light requires an increase of four times in the exposure. Because each f/stop lets through twice as much light as the preceding one, the lens aperture must be opened by two f/stops to maintain the correct level of exposure.

Another important factor is the movement of the lamps away from the subject. For the general view, the distance between the light source and the painting is doubled. This ratio is constant — when the lighting distance is doubled, four times the light is required. This rule is known as the inverse square law; this states that light deteriorates as the square of the distance from the source.

Refraction and reflection

Light is affected by the density of the medium in which it is travelling and particularly by sudden changes of density. If light passes from air into water, say, its direction changes slightly at the point where the two mediums meet. This effect is known as refraction; it accounts for the apparent displacement or bending of objects that are partially submerged in water. It also explains why the glass in a camera lens must have a carefully controlled density.

The way light behaves when it passes from one medium to another is consistent; it is the angle at which the light enters the new medium that is critical in deciding in which direction and to what extent the light path will be altered. As camera lenses must therefore be uniform at every point of their curved surface, lengthy calculations are necessary to ensure that the final lens will be capable of producing a high-quality image.

When light falls on an object and is neither fully absorbed or transmitted, it is reflected. The angle of reflection is the same, but opposite to, the angle at which the light arrives. This angle is measured from a theoretical line drawn at right angles to the surface at the point of impact. A very smooth surface — polished metal, for instance — will reflect all the incident light in one direction, provided that it arrived from the same one. It is very like bouncing a ball off a wall, even

Refraction occurs when light travels from one medium to another of different density. As it enters the denser medium, it will be bent towards a line perpendicular to the surface at the point at which it enters.

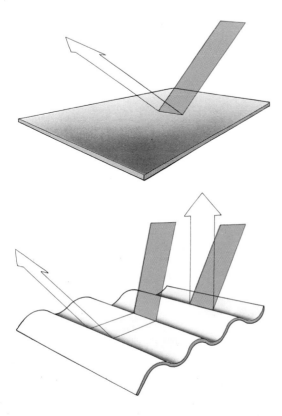

When light strikes an even surface then the angle made with the surface when it travels away is the same as that made when it strikes (the angle of incidence is equal to the angle of reflection). This law still applies when the surface is uneven, even though the light is scattered in all directions.

if the surface changes from smooth to rough. If this happens, it is just as difficult to predict how light will behave as to anticipate how the ball will bounce.

The point at which each single ray of light strikes the surface of an object acts as a tiny smooth surface which reflects the light ray at the same angle as it arrived. Therefore a smooth surface will provide a uniform reflection. The effect of a rough surface is to scatter the light; on a rough surface each point of impact offers a slightly different surface angle which sends the ray off in a different direction.

This factor must always be taken into account when filming. The way a nearby surface reflects light into the shot will almost certainly affect the appearance of the film and, at worst, may control it completely.

Light and dark surfaces

The intensity of a reflection is controlled by the tone of the surface on which light falls. A true black absorbs all the light that arrives on it. When we 'see' an object as black, what we are really aware of is the absence of light rather than its presence. Since black objects do not reflect any light, they cannot expose photographic film and shooting them is extremely difficult as a result. A

The color of an object depends on the color of the light which falls on it and the colors which it absorbs. When a blue object is struck by a combination of blue, green and red light, then it absorbs green and red and reflects blue. The same principle operates for other colors. However, if the original light was passed through a yellow filter, the blue would be absorbed before it reached the 'blue' surface and that surface would appear black.

A green surface will absorb green and reflect magenta — a combination of red and blue. The blue surface will reflect yellow, made up of red and green, and the red surface will reflect a mixture of blue and green.

The color temperature produced by different types of light is illustrated here. Candlelight is the lowest, followed by artificial tungsten light, ordinary daylight and the same scene clouded over.

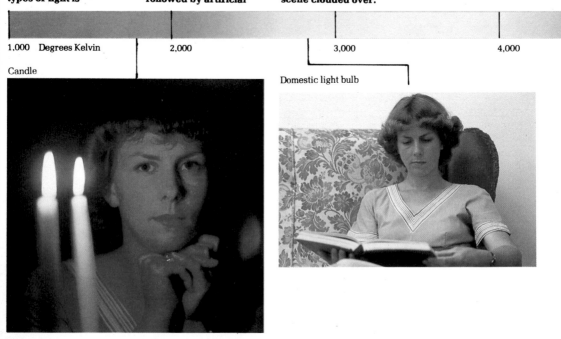

| 1,000 Degrees Kelvin | 2,000 | 3,000 | 4,000 |

Candle

Domestic light bulb

white object, however, acts in the opposite manner, reflecting a very high proportion of the light that falls on it.

This difference is particularly apparent to the cameraman if the walls of a film location are either very dark or very light. In a room with white walls, the subject will be lit by direct light from the source in a room with white walls and by the light reflected from the walls. This has the effect of filling-in the shadows cast by the main light and increasing the overall amount of light available to expose the film.

In a black room, very little of the light is reflected from the walls, so the subject will be lit simply from the source. The shadows receive no reflected light, so they remain relatively dark and the whole scene will have a slightly lower level of illumination. The slight difference in exposure levels can be easily dealt with; however, the appearance of shots employing the same lighting, but made in dark and light rooms, will differ considerably.

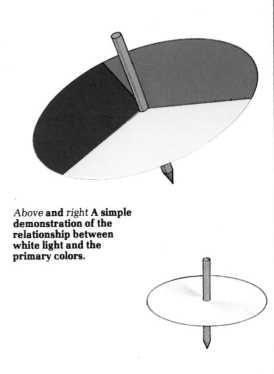

Above **and** *right* **A simple demonstration of the relationship between white light and the primary colors.**

Types of light
The two main considerations for the cameraman are, firstly, the quantity of light, and, secondly, the quality of light available for filming. Quantity is the most critical factor because correct

| 5,000 | 6,000 | 7,000 | 8,000 |

Early and late sunlight

Overcast sky

exposure depends on it — under or over-exposure can ruin even the most perfect set-up.

Having ensured this, the cameraman can then turn to its quality. The prime concern here is to avoid mixed color sources, as these can create obtrusive and disturbing effects on screen. Although the lighting mix should be apparent during filming, the natural tendency of the brain is to compensate for differences in color; so, without concentrated attention, the problem can easily be ignored until it is too late.

When the difference in color is extreme — say, between noon daylight and late evening light — the eye can easily identify it and make a qualitative assessment. However, in film, more accurate methods are needed to calculate the amount of color correction that will be required. The instrument used for this is known as a color temperature meter. As well as measuring the color of light, it indicates which color filters can be used to correct the light, either as it leaves the source or as it passes through the lens.

Certain types of light, notably fluorescent light, cannot be measured with the normal single reading color temperature meter. In these cases, a special two color meter is required. This measures the red, green and blue parts of the spectrum in turn, instead of the overall, mixed effect.

A comparison of a figure lit from a single source in a room with white walls *below* and dark walls *bottom*.

Light walls have the effect of filling-in shadows cast by the light source; dark colors, however, do not reflect the light so the whole scene has a slightly lower level of illumination.

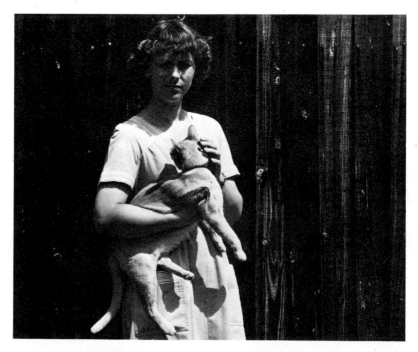

Standard corrections

The main aim in all lighting is to achieve a color to suit the film stock being used. Whether the light being used is natural or artificial, the color of the source must be carefully matched to the response of the film.

This is usually achieved by a simple system of standardization. For color matching, daylight is taken as standard; by comparison artificial light is yellow (in other words, daylight is more blue than artificial light). As stated previously, the daylight temperature is 5,600K but, in fact, the scale does go beyond this. The higher the temperature, the bluer the light; correspondingly, the lower the temperature, the more yellow the light becomes. Photographic lamps are either 3,200K or 3,400K and, in practice, are both called 'Tungsten'.

Daylight film is balanced to sunlight, which stands at 5,600K. However, average daylight, allowing for the effect of blue skylight, has a color temperature of around 6,000°K. The color quality of daylight also varies greatly; dawn or dusk light can fall to temperatures around 2,000K (much more yellow than artificial light) and summer shade areas lit only by light from a blue sky — can reach 8,000K.

Tungsten halogen lamps do not alter in color during their lives, but non-halogen sources — photofloods and incandescent lamps — drop by several hundred degrees Kelvin at the end of their life-span. This means that they produce a noticeably yellower light. In practice, this drop can usually be discounted, unless two lights are being used to illuminate a single object. Here, an old photoflood on one side would give a very yellow light compared, say, with a tungsten halogen lamp on the other.

Film balance

Movie film is balanced to produce the correct

Reflectors are used to fill-in shadows when the light source is too harsh and the contrasts too **high. One of the best reflector surfaces easily available is the dull side of cooking foil, but any** **white material or paper can be used to do the job. The picture *left* was taken using a single light** **source; the one *right* used a reflector as well.**

colors in either daylight or artificial light. Assuming that all the sources are matched to produce uniform illumination, filters can be applied to the camera lens according to the film stock in use. To convert daylight to match Type A film a yellow/brown filter, such as the Kodak Wratten 85, is needed. This is a built-in attachment on Super 8 cameras. Professional (Type B) films need a slightly more orange filter (Wratten 85B). If tungsten light is matched with daylight film, the color correction can be achieved by using a blue filter, such as the Wratten 80A.

Matching sources

Matching the lighting to the film stock is a simple matter provided the lighting is all the same color. If there is more than one source, however, the situation can become more complex. For example, if filming is being done in a room with large windows and photographic lamps are also being used, the intrusive daylight can pose problems. In such a case the color of one of the sources must be altered to maintain consistency.

One solution is to change the daylight to match the artificial light. This can be achieved by fixing large sheets of yellow/brown filter material over the window. This is an expensive and time consuming approach, but it has two main advantages. Firstly, the lamps can be used as normal; secondly, the scene outside the window will be slightly reduced in brightness. This means that the levels of inside and outside exposure will be closer.

Even with the window filter in place, the view through the window may well be overexposed compared to the interior scene. If they are

Light sources must always be matched. The shot of the sodium street light *above* clearly shows the effect of filming a mixed source without a filter. *Left* and *right* — one without a filter and one with — demonstrate the correct and incorrect approach.

Filter	Use	Comments
85A	Over lens when exposing tungsten film in daylight	Amber color. Exposure increase ⅔ stop. Fitted to most Super 8 cameras.
80A	Over lens when exposing daylight film in artificial light	Blue color. Requires 2 stops exposure increase. Only necessary for Single 8 and 16mm
Ultra-violet (UV)	Over lens to suppress the effect of ultra-violet light on subject color	No exposure increase required. Some UV filters have a pink color tinge which slightly warms the color of the subject. Usually left permanently on the lens.
Neutral density	Controls the density of light passing through the lens. Useful when fast film is being used in bright light	Various densities of grey which do not affect the color of the subject, its contrast or the definition. Filters are coded by density: ND 0.3 transmits half the light and needs an exposure increase of 1 f/stop; ND 0.6 requires 2 stops; ND 0.9 needs 3 stops. The filters can be used in combination — ND 0.3 (+ 1 stop) + ND 0.6 (+ 2 stops) = ND 0.9 (+ 3 stops). Some cameras have a built-in ND filter
Polarizing	On lens mainly to control reflections from non-metallic surfaces. Will darken blue sky when sun is at right angles to it.	If source of illumination is also polarized, reflections from metallic surfaces can be controlled. The exposure increase required is 1⅓ stops. Some Super 8 cameras have a polarizing element in the optical system. This would result in cross-polarization of the light, which means that none reaches the film. Check the camera for this. Polarizing filters do not affect color and reduce haze on landscapes.
Daylight Blue	Large plastic sheets to convert tungsten light to daylight used in front of artificial lamps.	Blue color, available as full blue, half and quarter blue, depending on the degree of correction required. Necessary on photo lamps mixed with daylight but not suitable for use on lenses
Soft focus	On lens to reduce overall definition	Available in varying degrees. Best on close shots as they tend to obscure detail in long ones. Difficult to inter-cut soft focus and straight shots in one scene. Do not affect color
Fog	On lens to simulate fog	Available in varying degrees and in either grey or slight color (blueish or greenish). Do not give feeling of depth since effect is at same level in close and long shots. Flat lit scenes requires less fog filter than brightly lit contrasty scenes. Work best when combined with the use of smoke in shot.
Starburst	On lens to produce star effects or bright points of light	Different patterns give either 4, 6 or 8 point stars. Difficult to control
Graduated color	On lens to alter color of part of the scene	Partly colored and partly clear filters in a range of colors. If the clear part is correctly exposed, the colored area will be dark on the film unless it has a neutral density to match the color portion of the filter.
Graduated neutral density	On lens to darken part of the scene without altering color	Useful to darken skies in day for night shots. Also helps to correctly expose bright skies in normal shooting.

When using filters, it is essential to know whether the light reading includes the effect of the filter. If it does not, then an allowance must be made according to the density of the filter as shown in the chart.

required to match, the only answer is to put more filters over the window. Here, neutral density filters should be used. These are grey filters which do not alter the color of the light but reduce its intensity. The degree of intensity depends on the density (darkness) of the filter. An ND 0.3 filter sheet, for example, transmits 50% of the light and produces an exposure loss of one f/stop.

The alternative to altering the daylight color is to change the color of the photographic lamps. Again, large sheets of filter, called gels, are used, attached to the lamps. The filters — known as daylight blues — are blue in color. They come in a range of strengths from quarter and half blue to a full blue, the last being identical with the 80A filter used on the camera lens. The full blue will match 3,200K lamps to 5,600K daylight, but since normal room lighting is in reality often of a warmer tone than natural daylight, the cameraman can use one of the weaker filters and leave the lamps slightly more yellow than daylight.

In situations where the balance between light sources is critical, a color temperature meter can be used to determine the exact color of the daylight. This enables the cameraman to decide on the correct filter to apply to the window or lamps to produce the required effect.

If, for example, the interior and exterior of a location are to be recorded in one shot, it is obviously important that the exposure levels of the two areas should match. The only way to control the brightness of the outside scene is to place neutral density filters over the windows. The alternative would be to wait for the light level outside to drop naturally at dawn or dusk, but this would give very little time for shooting and also lead to color problems as the sun rose or set.

When shooting mixed lighting interiors, the filter on the camera lens must be carefully selected. The main factors to consider are the color of the light after it has passed through the filters and the film stock being used. For example, with artificial light film in the camera, unfiltered daylight at the window, and blue filters on the lamps, the lens should carry a yellow/brown 85B filter. This is because the general level of illumination is of a daylight color quality. If the same film is being used with the daylight filtered to match artificial light but without filters on the lamps, the lighting will match the film balance and no filter is required. If a daylight-balanced film is used, then a blue (80A) filter is needed.

With black and white film, photographic lamps can be used naked with daylight because this film is only slightly affected by the mixture. If photo-graphic lamps are used outdoors and mixed with daylight on a color film shoot, the only solution to the mixed color problem is to attach full blue filters to the lights.

Exposure and filters

Photographic filters control the color of light by absorbing the wavelengths associated with certain colors and allowing others to pass unaffected. Consequently, as the filter acts to

When filming a landscape with a large expanse of sky, it is very easy to under expose the whole scene and end up with a dark shot. The solution is to take the light meter reading with the camera pointing below the horizon. This will ensure that the details of the landscape, as well as the sky, appear.

Matching the color of the light source to the response of the film is a vital preliminary, especially when both day and artificial light are present. *Above* **One solution is to filter the daylight so that it matches the lamp light. One way of doing this is to fix large sheets of yellow/brown filter over the window. The results of this are seen** *below.*

change the color it also reduced the total amount of light available to expose the film.

If the filter is placed over the light source, the intensity of the illumination is altered before it reaches the exposure meter and so exposure can be calculated in the normal way. If the filter is positioned on the camera lens, however, normal calculations would result in under exposure, because some of the light is absorbed by the filter after it has been measured.

All manufacturers supply details of the exposure allowances required by particular filters. These are usually expressed as factors to be applied to the chosen exposure. A 2x filter factor requires an increase of one f/stop; 4x requires two f/stops, and so on. In practice it is not always convenient to alter the exposure for each filter, according to the meter. It is simpler to adjust the ASA setting on the meter so that the filter factor is programmed in to each reading. Each time the ASA number is doubled or halved, the exposure is altered by one f/stop. For example, f/5.6 at ASA50 equals f/8 at ASA160 or f/11 at ASA200. If a filter with a factor of 2x is being used, one extra f/stop is needed to allow for the light absorbed by the filter. Thus if the meter indicates an exposure of f/11, the lens should be set to f/8 (one f/stop larger) to allow for the filter. If the film in use is a normal ASA40, altering the meter setting to ASA20 will provide readings

Fixing the sheets of filter material in position is time-consuming business, while the material itself is fairly expensive. However, its use helps to reduce the difference between inside/outside exposure levels and also means that the lamps can be used normally.

There are two broad categories of filters for camera lenses. The first group consists of light balancing and color conversion filters, the second of non-specific color filters to give total color control. The filters illustrated *left* are green, yellow, orange, polarizing, haze and color burst.

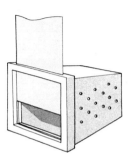

Another method of matching light sources is to change the color of the lamps themselves with blue filters known as Daylight Blues.

using an extra f/stop to allow for the 2x filter being used.

These rules apply only to separate hand meters or camera meters which do not read through the lens. Through-the-lens (TTL) metering systems allow for lens filters without requiring any adjustment.

Though the information given above may seem somewhat abstract, a basic grounding in color temperatures and filters will enable you to obtain good results, even under adverse lighting conditions. If, for example, you are shooting under an overcast sky, the Kelvin scale will indicate a color temperature of around 6,000K. This is 400K higher than the standard value for daylight film and without color correction, the resulting film would be noticeably blue. To remedy this, a CC10Y filter can be positioned over the camera lens. This will replace the missing warmth and require only a slight exposure correction of about 1/3 f/stop.

Filter types

There are two broad groups of filters for camera lenses. The first contains two types: color conversion and light-balancing. These are intended for major and minor corrections in color

temperature respectively, so that light sources can be adapted to match particular film types. These filters have codes such as 85 and 80A for conversion types and 81 and 82 for the balancing models. Full instructions are normally supplied with each filter; otherwise information can be obtained from the manufacturer.

The second group consists of non-specific color filters designed to give total color control in any direction and to any extent. These come in six colors and range in density from very weak to very strong. They are available in three primary and three secondary colors in various strengths. The key is based on initials — R (red), B (blue), G (green), Y (yellow), M (Magenta) and C (cyan).

The more commonly used color conversion and light-balancing filters are generally available in glass; this makes them tough and long lasting. Color compensating filters, however, are usually available only in square plastic sheets of two or three sizes. These are then cut to fit the lens. Plastic filters must be absolutely flat in front of the lens and placed as close to the front element as possible. If a glass mounted filter, such as a 1A skylight filter, is being used, the plastic filter can be dropped behind it. Some cameras have a filter slot, which allows a tiny piece of filter to be inserted behind the lens.

It is vital that filters are absolutely clean, because any blemish in the image forming path behind the lens may destroy picture definition. Except in an emergency, filters designed for lamps should not be used on lenses.

Light readings

All photographic film has a particular speed, which varies according to the type of film and its intended use. This tells the cameraman how much light the film requires to form a correct image and the camera controls must be adjusted accordingly. The 'amount' or exposure is a product of two factors — the intensity of the light reaching the film multiplied by the time it takes to do so. In movie making, the time is usually fixed, so the main way of adjusting exposure is to vary the f/stop of the lens.

The first thing to do is to take an exposure reading to measure the amount of light shining into the lens. The aperture and sometimes the shutter controls are then adjusted to ensure that the correct intensity of light reaches the film.

Each particular film requires a specific quantity of light to record an image. This can be measured in various ways. Reflected light readings are taken by pointing the meter at the subject and measuring the light that is reflected. In general, this system is perfectly adequate, as film speeds are standardized to reproduce subjects which reflect an average of 18% of the light falling on them. Sometimes, however, objects may reflect substantially more or less light than this norm and, as light meters cannot allow for unusually bright or dark elements, problems can be caused. The meter may give more than one reading or it may fail to give a correct measurement.

Take, for example, a film of a business conference. The first scene consists of rows of men in grey suits. The lights are set up, readings taken, exposure levels set and the first shots filmed. When the cameras return to the audience later, however, the situation has changed. Under the warm lights the businessmen have removed their dark grey jackets, revealing a sea of bright white shirts. Obviously the amount of reflected light will have increased dramatically, so the reflected light reading will be much higher. Nevertheless, many of the objects — the faces, furniture and trousers — remain constant. In these circumstances the exposure should not be altered from the average reflection reading, so another solution must be found to compensate for the extreme brightness of the shirts.

Grey card readings

In such a situation, where conventional reflected light readings fail to produce an objectively correct exposure value, one solution is to take what is known as a grey card reading. The measurement is taken from an object which can be relied upon to represent the average in terms of reflected light. A piece of grey card which reflects exactly 18% of the light which falls upon it is used for this purpose; most major film manufacturers will be able to supply 18% reflectance grey card. However, this system can

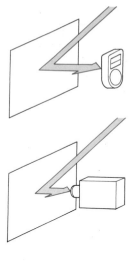

A grey card reading using a hand meter. Note the meter must be held close to the card so that nothing else can intervene to affect the reading.

A grey card reading using a camera with a built-in light meter. For an accurate reading the card should fill the viewfinder.

To take an incident light reading, the meter is placed near the subject and pointed at the camera so that it measures the light falling on the subject and not reflected light.

When filming in front of a light background — whether inside or outdoors — it is important to take a light reading from the subject of the shot. Otherwise the film will be underexposed.

Flare is the term used when extra, unwanted light reaches the film and mars the image. One method of preventing this is to use a shade, such as the french flag *above,* to stop the extra light reaching the lens.

Right An example of the ruinous effects of flare on film. To test for the risk of flare, a hand should be held six inches in front of the lens, if it casts a shadow there is a possibility of flare and precautions must be taken.

only be used if the camera will allow manual override of the exposure settings.

If separate hand meters are used, they must be held close to the card so that no extraneous subjects intrude. With through-the-lens meters the card should fill the viewfinder. Although the grey card is the technically perfect answer, in an emergency almost any suitably toned object can be substituted — such as a grey sweater, or a neutral area of the scene.

Incident light readings
Incident light readings offer another solution to the problems of reflected light. The exposure meter is held at the subject and pointed at the camera, so that it measures the amount of light actually falling on the subject as seen by the camera, rather than the reflected light. A special baffle is fitted over the meter's light-sensitive cell. This is designed to present an integrated overall impression of the light falling on the scene. It also allows for the fact that average subjects do not reflect all the light falling upon them. Unlike reflected light readings, incident light measurements are not affected by changes in the subject; hence the conference example described above could be filmed without difficulty.

An incident light reading meter is vital for setting different light levels. A single location may require several separate lamps, either matching or set at different levels. By using an incident meter to measure each part of the set, the lamps can be adjusted to the appropriate intensities.

Exposure cheats
The primary function of the exposure meter is to measure the light and indicate the necessary adjustments. However, this setting need not necessarily be the one finally used — the choice is always up to the film maker, particularly as exposure can be used to create spectacular special effects.

Taking the example of a film shot in a cellar, the obvious need is for the end product to be suitably dark and atmospheric. Under artificial lights, the correct exposure for a clear, bright picture would be f/4. But by slightly underexposing the film at a setting of f/5.6, the film maker can obtain a much more appropriate gloomy effect. In another case it may be necessary for part of a scene to appear lighter or darker than the main action area. This can be achieved by adjusting the lighting levels until the meter gives an exposure sufficiently different from the main one to produce the right effect.

Flare

Flare is extra light that reaches the film but is not required to make the image. Its presence therefore results in over-exposure and it is vital to eliminate it, or the whole effect may be ruined. Even the slightest flare will reduce contrast, while the worst will completely desaturate the colors in the film. Reversal movie film gets lighter as it receives more exposure; the effect of surplus flare is to reduce the density of the darkest part of the image and leave weak, flat colors.

If a crew is working in a small room with two or three floodlights, light can frequently penetrate the lens accidentally. Precautions should therefore be taken to avoid the problem. When all the lights are set in position, no light should be falling directly on the lens. A shadow test will ascertain this — if a hand is held about six inches in front of the lens and moved about, it should not cast a shadow on the lens. If it does, there is direct light falling on the lens and therefore the possibility of flare.

To prevent flare, the source of the direct light must be moved. Alternatively, some form of shade can be set up to stop the light reaching the lens — making sure that it does not enter the shot. The best shade is a french flag. This is a small rectangle of black metal; it is attached to an arm which has several ball and socket joints to enable the tiny flag to be placed in any position to shade the lens.

Single light units

Often, as in much documentary work, for instance, there will be only time or the facilities for one lighting unit to be used. But even this can achieve very effective results in difficult circumstances.

The worst place to put a single lighting unit is close to the camera. This causes flat lighting, with ugly shadows thrown behind the subject. The

When using one light, the shadows on the subject become more noticeable as the angle between camera view and light direction grows. Normally shadows are avoided, but they can be used to great effect.

When the main, or key, light is placed at 45° to the camera view, and the second, or 'fill', light is placed close to the camera with a direction close to its viewpoint, extremes of light and darkness are avoided. Detail in the darker areas can thus be recorded.

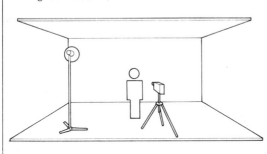

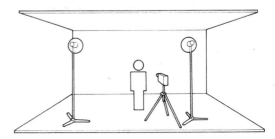

ideal position is 60-70cm above the camera and 30-40cm to one side. This will give the subject an appearance of depth and the shadows cast will be less obtrusive. If the subject is at some distance from the background, reflected light meter readings will be unreliable and incident or grey card readings should be used.

Normally, when shooting with one light, the objective is to obtain shadow-free lighting on the subject. However, shadows can be used very effectively in film to create special effects. In a dramatic scene in a fiction film, say, the shadows cast by the light can add to the atmosphere. As the angle between the direction of light and the view of the camera grows, the shadows cast on the performers' faces become more noticeable. Eventually, if the light source is at right angles to the camera's view, half the actor's face will be in shadow. The result can be very dramatic, but flare may be a problem. Another dramatic use of one light is to place it as a very high or very low angle relative to the subject. This causes distorted and unnatural views which can be quite disturbing.

Reflectors

The possibilities of one unit lighting can be further extended by using additional equipment and techniques. A reflector can considerably increase the available light. It can lighten the shadows cast by the light and also allow the film to record highlight and shadow detail more accurately. If the reflector is positioned on the shadow side of the subject, it collects the light that would otherwise miss the subject completely. This is then re-directed back into the shadows, so that the single source is used most efficiently.

The larger the reflector the more effective it will be. A 1m square reflector is a convenient size for close and medium shots. The dull side of cooking foil makes an excellent reflector surface, but any white object can serve — card, newspaper, a white shirt or sheet, for instance. If the location has white or light walls these will

The addition of a third light means that the background can be illuminated. Any shadows left on the walls can be eliminated **and the background given the best exposure level. Care must be taken to ensure that other parts of the scene are not affected.** **The fourth light is normally a backlight, which can add a halo glow to the subject and depth and dimension to a scene. There is a risk of** **flare, even when, as is usually the case, the light is highly placed.**

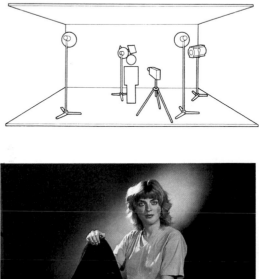

One of the most effective ways of using a single light is to 'bounce' its light from a white wall or ceiling on to the subject. Here the lamp stand has been extended to bring the lamp to within 30cm of the ceiling. It is positioned at 45° to direct light on to the subject.

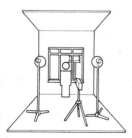

The use of shadow can give a scene atmosphere. Here this is being created by the use of two lights. Black cards fixed to the reflectors act as barn doors, or focusing lenses, and control the width of the beam.

make very good reflectors and the positioning of subject, light and the camera should be arranged with this in mind.

Bounced lighting

Bounced lighting is another method of increasing light from a single source. This is a term used to describe a method of lighting in which the subject is illuminated indirectly. It is usually achieved by pointing the lights up at the ceiling. Where only one light is available, this method produces an extremely natural effect; the light is diffused and, since it reaches the subject from many different directions, it is able to fill in the shadows. The intensity of bounced light is lower than that of direct light, but its use helps avoid the heavy shadows and dark backgrounds caused by the latter.

Colored surfaces should not be used for bounced lighting, as this will affect the color of the image. Ceilings are regularly employed, while white walls can give a very attractive soft side light. In this case, a reflector would be needed opposite the bouncing wall to fill in the shadows. For soft side lighting, a cine screen makes a very useful portable bouncing surface.

A 1000 watt movie light is powerful enough for filming medium or close shots in an average sized room with a white ceiling. The light should be positioned about 0.5m from the bouncing surface, at an angle to throw as much light as possible on to the subject. Extra lamps can easily be added, since each casts only a slight shadow. Take particular care, however, if surfaces are

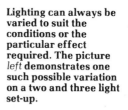

Lighting can always be varied to suit the conditions or the particular effect required. The picture *left* demonstrates one such possible variation on a two and three light set-up.

yellowed or discolored by tobacco smoke — they can make the whole picture look 'warm'.

Two lights

When two lights are used, the cameraman has more creative control over shadow effects. The first lamp can be placed to cast the most flattering or expressive shadows. The second is then used to lighten these shadows so that the detail in the darker areas of the scene can be recorded. The exposure is normally set according to the light falling on those areas of the subject that are lit directly and not the areas in shadow. The shadows must be carefully controlled so that they do not create extremes of light or darkness outside the film's range of response. For normal reproduction, shadows should be lit to a level between half and one stop less than the main part of the picture.

As a guide to the setting of two lights, the main, or key light, is often placed at an angle of about 45 degrees to the camera's sightline, and about 0.50m higher than the subject. The second unit is placed as close as possible to the camera's sightline, level with the camera. In this position the second lamp will cast its shadow directly behind the subject so that it is effectively hidden. The second light is called a fill light, because it fills in the shadows; its intensity can be controlled by altering its distance from the subject. The relative exposures of the two lights can be easily checked with a light meter by switching off the key light, measuring the other and comparing the

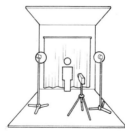

The use of a third light adds further flexibility to a lighting set-up. The 1000 watt third light shines through the net curtains to give the effect of daylight.

result with both lights on.

As an alternative, one of the lamps could be placed near the camera position, and the other one set up to bounce light from the ceiling. This would give a directional light, and also provide fill-in for the shadows. This also cuts down the problem posed by a dark background, which exists even with a two-light system.

Three lights

By adding a third light unit the cameraman can

light the main subject fully and use the additional lamp to illuminate the background. Normally the background lamp is placed in front of the camera and to one side of the shot. It should be arranged so that the shadows of objects or people in the background fall in roughly the same direction as those cast by the main lighting.

If, however, the background light spills over on to the subject it will spoil the effect of the key light. This risk can be avoided by using a flag — a large sheet of black card or metal, fixed to a stand and placed next to the lamp, to prevent the light from affecting other areas of the scene.

Four lights

As the number of lighting units used in any set-up increases, the problems of control and positioning become more complex. The classic position for a fourth light is high up at the back of the set, so that it shines on the back of the subject's head — in the case of an actor. However, this means that the fourth lamp, or rim light, is pointing towards the camera, which creates the risk of flare.

A rim light requires careful control. Ideally, the type used should be a spotlight, whilst the other three units will probably be standard floodlights. If a spotlight is not available, a snoot can be fitted to a floodlight. This is an open-ended cone fitted over the rim of a floodlight.

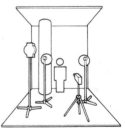

Here the lamps perform the same basic functions as in the previous four light arrangement, but have different positions in relation to the subject.

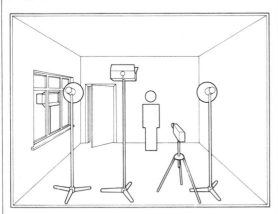

Above **Area lighting.** Lamps positioned like this allow actors to move around on the set and still remain effectively lit.

Area lighting

These lighting set-ups are designed for situations where the subject is likely to move within a very small area. When people start to move on a longer scale — to walk round a room, say, general area lighting will be required and the cameraman's problems consequently increase.

The first step is to work out with the director and the actors all the moves to be made. After this, the lighting can be physically plotted. For some films, such as those dealing with factual subjects or using amateur actors, it is often best to illuminate the entire working area to avoid inhibiting the performance. Ideally, the location should be divided into lighting areas, related to the positions and movements of the characters. This means that each area can be lit in turn, progressing throughout the location. Even if no general views of the location are required, it is

You will probably use photofloods or halogen lamps for supplementary illumination. Photofloods have built-in reflectors and power ratings of 100 watts to 1000 watts.

Color temperatures range from 2,900K to 3,400K, but this can alter with changes in mains voltage: the greater the voltage, the colder the light. Intensity will also decrease with age.

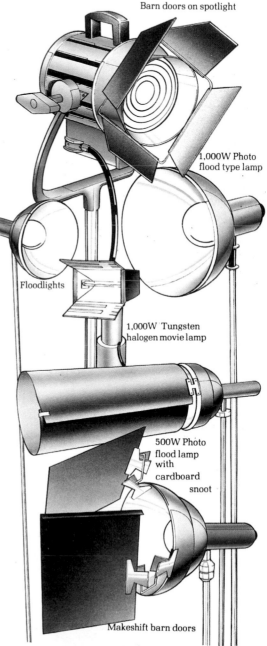

Barn doors on spotlight

1,000W Photo flood type lamp

Floodlights

1,000W Tungsten halogen movie lamp

500W Photo flood lamp with cardboard snoot

Makeshift barn doors

Adjustable Quartzcolor lamp: Full flood

Adjustable Quartzcolor lamp; Full spot with barn door

1,000W Tungsten halogen lamp

Whereas the filament in photofloods is surrounded by a glass envelope, that in halogen lamps is encased in a material such as quartz. The atmosphere is a halogen, such as vaporized iodine or chlorine. Halogen lamps have a long life and constant color temperature, most commonly 3,200K. Because they are so bright, you can use filters and still have good enough illumination to use film balanced for daylight.

wise to light the set to an overall plan so that there is a general continuity throughout.

In arranging the lighting set-up, remember to allow for natural sources of light, such as windows. If any doors are to be opened during the action, the rooms they open into must also be lit. Similarly, if the script indicates a particular time of day, this will affect the lighting of the scene. Another important factor is the mood or atmosphere required by the director, which can be created or intensified by the appropriate lighting.

Unless a special effect — such as night — is required, the lighting of the location should be fairly uniform. In some areas the light of two lamps may overlap, but, provided that the exposure varies by no more than half a stop to a full stop, this can be safely ignored. The general level of light can be checked by taking an incident reading light meter around the location and watching how the needle moves as the light changes.

When area lighting is being used, moving the lamps may not be the best way of controlling the various intensities. The set-up is likely to become so complex that curing one problem by moving the unit simply causes another one elsewhere. The most convenient solution to the problem is to use scrims. These are pieces of wire mesh placed over the light source to reduce its intensity. They can be fitted over all or part of a lamp in order to even out the effect.

Hand-held lights give extra flexibility if you want to make minor adjustments to an arranged setting and do not need the resulting arrangement maintained for a long period.

Mini-halogen quartz 1,000W lamp

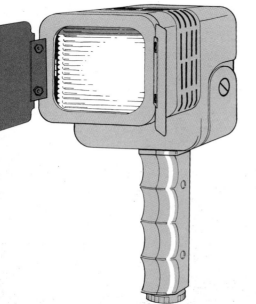

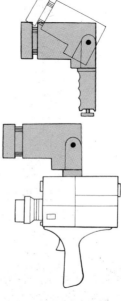

Vital Accessories

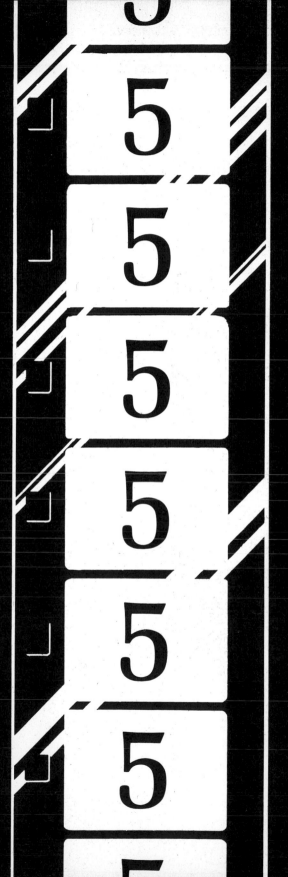

The camera is the heart of the film-making system and its most important accessory is its operator. Sophisticated accessories are useful only in so far as they permit an extension of your own imagination and invention. No accessory can make your film for you.

Nevertheless, some accessories are extremely useful in the quest for the best possible pictures. The question every movie maker has to ask is what exactly is required; too much hardware can be as restricting as too little. There is also the factor of expense to be taken into consideration. Some accessories can cost more than the camera itself, so it is best to plan carefully around what you really need and can afford.

Travelling light

The key to successful camera work is accessibility. This means placing your camera in exactly the best place and at the right angle in relation to the subject being filmed. This is not always easy to achieve, but however difficult it may be — whether you are trying to look into a swallow's nest, through a hole in a fence or up an exhaust pipe — it is always easier with a lightweight camera and a minimum of ancillary gear. Indeed, one of the chief advantages that an amateur has over the professional is flexibility, especially in terms of camera angle and movement.

However, some professional hardware undoubtedly helps to improve the final result. The most essential accessory is a camera support. In the first place, this provides something for the camera to rest safely on between takes. More importantly, it produces picture steadiness; the need for this is paramount whoever you are and whatever your camera.

Tripods and monopods

The commonest type of support is a tripod. The

Tripod

There are literally thousands of movie accessories on the market today, presenting the amateur with a bewildering array of choice. Some, such as a camera support, are essential, whatever the level and ability of the movie maker.

Super 8 editor

Splicer

Movie light

Camera case

Stop watch

Leader tape

Filters

Headphones

A camera support is an essential accessory for all movie makers. Its use is the only way to ensure picture steadiness; it also provides a safe place for the camera to stand between shots. The commonest form of support is a tripod made out of wood or metal and fitted with collapsible legs to make it easily portable. However, it is a mistake to make portability the prime consideration; too light a tripod may not provide a steady support for the camera, while tripods with many-jointed legs tend to be insufficiently stable. The most practical alternative to the tripod is the monopod, which, as its name suggests, only has one leg. Although a monopod is less stable then its rival, good static shots and even pans and tilts can be achieved with practice.

Heavy duty

Three section

Four section

Minipod

Monopod

Left **A selection of tripods. All of them are fitted with an adjustable head, known as a pan-and-tilt head, which can pan, tilt or swing the camera from side to side; in expensive tripods the fitting is usually more sophisticated and is bought separately. In movie-making it is especially important to have good control over the pan head; a simple ball joint head is rarely secure enough.**

In certain conditions a conventional tripod, or even a monopod, can be too cumbersome a support. In such cases aids such as a shoulder stop, a carpod or a cramp tripod should be used instead. For tracking shots, a special tripod with a dolly attachment can be bought to enable the camera to be wheeled smoothly across the floor or on tracks.

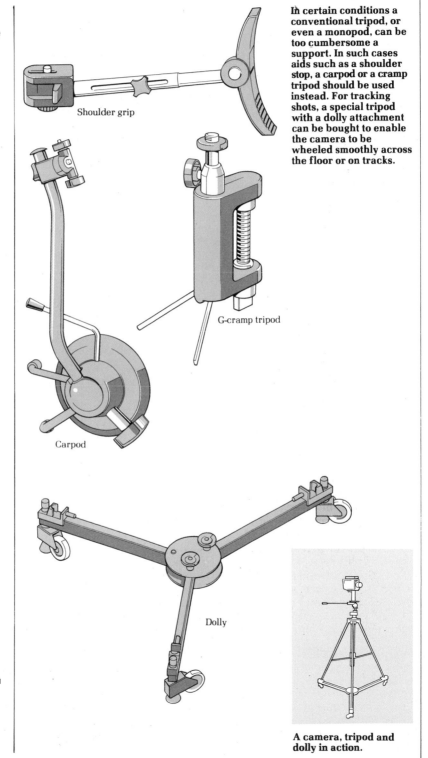

Shoulder grip

G-cramp tripod

Carpod

Lightweight

Dolly

Table-top

A camera, tripod and dolly in action.

problem is to find one that is sufficiently rigid yet portable enough for ease of use. It is a mistake to choose anything extremely lightweight, as extremely light tripods are not sturdy enough to steady the camera. To test for rigidity, place the camera in position on the tripod head, move it around and press it down. An unsuitable tripod's legs will whip and even collapse. It is also worth noting that the more joints there are in the legs, the less stable the tripod will usually be. All joints should be locked during filming.

A pan and tilt head is an essential tripod fitting. Do not buy a tripod with a ball and socket head, as it will not be suitable for film work. The pan and tilt head fits on top of the tripod, so a further test for stability should be carried out with both it and the camera in position. Most heads are fitted with locking devices; these are extremely useful, as it means that the tilt can be locked when you want to pan and vice versa. When using the head, it is important to check that it is absolutely level. This can be done by lining the camera up on a vertical object, panning, and checking through the viewfinder.

However, there are situations when a tripod can be very awkward and even dangerous. A crowded street is a good example; here there is quite a high risk of somebody tripping over a tripod leg. The worst outcome would be that you might find yourself defendant in a lawsuit; the least is that the camera might be dashed to the ground. Remember, too, that in many places it is illegal to use a tripod in a public place without permission from the local authorities.

The monopod is probably the most practical alternative to the tripod. Unlike the latter, it has only one leg, but it is nonetheless extremely useful. The instability produced by hand-holding a camera mostly occurs in the vertical plane and a monopod arrests all vertical movement. This enables you to achieve almost perfect static shots and very even pans and tilts. The monopod, too, is a somewhat more flexible tool than the tripod and there are occasions when it offers a definite advantage. Fast moving subjects, such as airplanes and racing cars, are much more easily panned on a single leg.

Improvising a support
Monopods are cheap to buy and their telescopic construction enables you to operate at any height from about five feet down. But there is always the possibility of improvisation. If you do not have either a monopod or tripod with you, keep your eyes open and you will see many useful implements lying around. In the countryside, a

A pan and tilt head is an essential tripod fitting. Practice will produce a smooth pan even with cheap equipment though comparatively little skill is required to use the more expensive heads, such as the fluid type illustrated right. The needle head type is shown *below*. These heads are designed to offer a resistance to the intended motion of direction and to smooth out motion by forcing a fluid from one chamber to another.

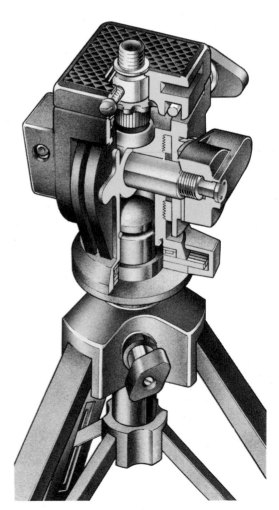

wooden stave is easily come by and this makes an excellent improvised support. Naturally, it will be impossible to actually attach the camera to it; nor will it be telescopic, so if you want to shoot at a low angle, you will have to break a bit off or find a shorter length. But a little improvisation is well worth the trouble if picture steadiness is to be the reward. Remember that improvised camera supports are devised to stabilize the hand that holds the camera, rather than the camera itself.

If there is not a suitable monopod substitute lying around, there will be almost certainly something standing up that can be used. The world bristles with upright features — trees, lamp-posts, fences, walls and so on. All these provide adequate support, though different features require different techniques. When using a lowish wall, say, it is usually best to rest both elbows on the wall. This way, the two forearms form two legs of a tripod and the body and head the third. If the wall is too high for this method to work conveniently, rest the camera in the hand directly on, or against, the wall, using your free hand as a cushion against abrasion. When using a post, grip it with your left hand, thus making a bridge of your left forearm. Then rest the camera, or the wrist of your camera hand, on that bridge.

Even a car's radio aerial can be used to stabilize a hand-held camera. Remember, it is only the vertical motion that needs to be arrested, since it is quite easy to avoid making erratic sideways motions.

Increasing stability
In fact, the lighter the camera the greater the disadvantage for some people. Many find it easier to hold a heavy load stable than a lighter one. The way to overcome this is to artificially increase the load.

There are several ways of doing this. By hanging your accessory bag — containing an exposure meter, say — on your camera wrist, you can bear up against an additional weight. Alternatively, you can achieve increased loading with a piece of string. Tie a loop at one end and

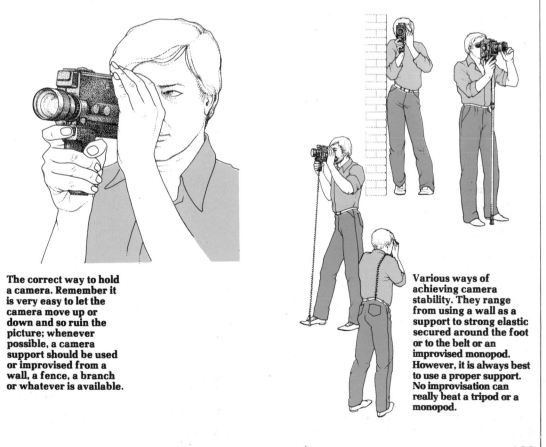

The correct way to hold a camera. Remember it is very easy to let the camera move up or down and so ruin the picture; whenever possible, a camera support should be used or improvised from a wall, a fence, a branch or whatever is available.

Various ways of achieving camera stability. They range from using a wall as a support to strong elastic secured around the foot or to the belt or an improvised monopod. However, it is always best to use a proper support. No improvisation can really beat a tripod or a monopod.

put your foot through it. Fix the other end to the camera, or simply wrap it around your wrist, and then bear up against the tautened string.

Elastic is even better than string, especially if you intend to pan, tilt, or make some other intentional camera movement. The heavy duty pannier elastics used to secure loads on motor cycles and cars are very useful. A short length passed through your waistband belt and up to the camera grip has a very steadying, yet flexible, effect. If you prefer to bear down, you can thread the elastic through the back of your belt and pass it over your shoulder to the camera.

Steadiness and movement

Elastics are particularly useful when you are attempting to steady the camera against greater forces, such as those in a moving vehicle or your own bodily locomotion in a walking shot. In a moving car, for instance, camera steadiness poses a considerable problem. If you brace yourself against the car door, your body will transmit a stream of vibrations to the camera. If you fail to brace yourself, you will simply bounce up and down on the seat.

In such cases, elastics can achieve a considerable damping effect, provided that you can arrange fixings for them. The ideal is to support the camera on shock-absorbing elastics from as many different positions as possible. This is because the forces at play in a moving vehicle occur in many different directions.

Passenger handgrips, seat belt mountings, sun visors and rear view mirrors all provide potential anchorage points. The greater the elastic cushioning you provide, the less the camera needs to be in contact with you, but even if you support the camera from just one place — say, from a sun visor mounting — a very real damping is achieved. The results will well justify the effort involved.

Camera placement

Never be niggardly in your efforts to improvise camera placement devices. They can mean the difference between success and failure in the final film. Remember that anyone can press the start button; it is what is done in preparation that counts. If, say, you are interested in birds and you decide to make a film about them, one of the obvious preliminary steps is to build some kind of hide. If you want candid shots of people in the street, you may decide to conceal the camera, perhaps in a parcel under the arm.

It is not necessary to improvise devices for every conceivable situation, but only for those

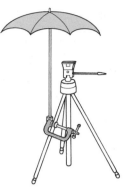

Shooting in the rain is sometimes essential but causes problems if you are not prepared. An umbrella fixed over the tripod is often the best solution, unless a helper is on the spot.

A cheap boom can easily be improvised with the aid of a broom handle. A boom and boom operator are invaluable when shooting sound to ensure that the microphone is at exactly the right distance and angle from the subject without letting it appear in the shot.

necessary for the production in hand. When apportioning your efforts, you should be guided by the relative importance of one shot to another. If you want one single outdoor shot during a rain shower, for instance, a plastic bag to protect the camera will be sufficient. If three or four shots are required, you might take an umbrella along. For twenty or thirty shots, you should devise some means of securing the umbrella over the camera support.

Tracking made easy

Tracking shots are rarely seen in amateur movies because there is a general belief that it is difficult to set them up. In fact, this is not so; in studio conditions — that is to say, on a smooth floor — anything on wheels will do. Professional movie makers use a purpose-built camera dolly, but you can use anything from a wheel chair to a supermarket trolley.

Rough ground presents a greater problem. Here, professionals set up a railed track on which the camera bogey rides. You may find it impossible to go to this extreme, but, again, improvisation provides a solution. You could move your wheel chair on a couple of scaffold boards. You could build a bogey and track using

nylon curtain rails fixed to the supports of a ladder. Everything depends on just how desirable tracking shots are in terms of the film and how much trouble you are prepared to take.

Equipment and crewing

The more equipment you use — whether it is improvised or purchased — the more people you will need to operate it. However lightweight they may be, there is a limit to the number of items that you can manage alone. Extra hands enable the film maker to use techniques which he could not achieve on his own and, to this extent, a film produced by a camera crew is likely to be more technically accomplished than the one-man production. Tracking shots are a good example; however simple the dolly, there has to be somebody to push it.

There are many more instances of the advantages that crewing can bring. A boom operator, for instance, is invaluable when you are shooting sound. Single handed, it is often impossible to get the microphone close enough to the subject, particularly if it is moving around. By attaching the microphone to a boom — either purpose-built or improvised — the problem usually can be solved. But there must be a pair of hands available to operate the boom — the hands of someone who can concentrate all his efforts to hold the microphone at exactly the right distance and angle without letting it appear in the shot.

The same principle applies to lighting. You can use highly efficient, but expensive, halogen lighting units, or you can improvise with homemade units, using photoflood bulbs. The real efficiency, however, comes from having someone on the crew who devotes his attention and enthusiasm exclusively to lighting the subject. Even the operation of the camera itself can be eased by having an assistant available. No single operator can reliably pan, zoom and change focus in the same shot.

Vital accessories

It is up to the individual to decide whether to remain a lone operator or become the director of a crew. The decision might well be to crew one

Tracking shots need not cause problems if you have a wheeled chair or trolly, a smooth floor and an assistant to push at the required speed. Both the shot which the camera takes from the vehicle and the vehicle itself are called a dolly.

production and operate another entirely alone, depending on the complexities of the film. But, whatever the decision, equipment — manufactured or improvised — will play an increasingly important role as you become more experienced and imaginative in your techniques.

It is important to remember, however, that an accessory is of no use if it is never used. So you must consider carefully what kind of films you want to make and what accessories will be needed for such films. There is little point, for instance, in buying a close-up lens if you want to film motor sports or in buying an interval timer unless you are particularly interested in time lapse techniques (see Chapter 6). When buying any accessory, you should ask yourself how often you will use it and whether there are other items of which you could make greater use. In the following section, the essential items of equipment are listed and described.

Splicers

No matter what kind of films you want to make or how you intend to make them, a splicer will be your most important accessory, second only to

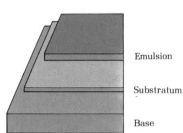

Emulsion

Substratum

Base

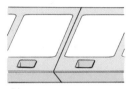

There are two ways of splicing film — tape splicing and cement splicing. The latter involves overlapping the portions of base to which the cement is applied

Above **However, this method calls for the sacrifice of portions of two frames of film and it can also be messy if not carried out with extreme care. Tape is easier and more convenient.**

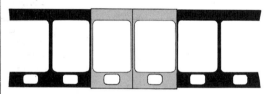

In tape splicing, the film can be joined without losing a single frame. The tape then covers two frames on both sides. Trim the ends of the tape with the cutting bar of the splicer and butt them together.

Press the tape down hard, bring down the pressure plate and then the sprocket hole cutting bar. Lift them up, remove the film and fold the remaining tape over the base side to complete the splice.

First scrape away the emulsion to reveal the acetate base.

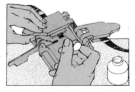

Apply the cement to one of the scraped edges of the film.

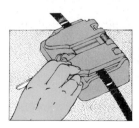

Bring the two pieces of film into contact under pressure for 30 seconds.

the camera itself. There are many different brands available and they are generally cheap to buy. They can be used in conjunction with either cement or tape; the more expensive ones have a built-in scraper to remove the emulsion from the film so that it will take the cement more easily. Be sure to choose one that is quick and easy to use and examine as many different types as possible before making the final purchase.

Many beginners are nervous of splicers, feeling that their use will take them into regions of creative difficulty and complexity. This is not so; a splicer is simply a device for cutting film and rejoining it. Its most ordinary function is to allow the film maker to remove unsatisfactory material, such as an out of focus shot, one that is under exposed or, perhaps, a hand-held shot that is uncomfortably shaky. The splicer enables you to remove such errors at a stroke of its blade.

Splicers, however, also have a much more positive use. While removing the odd bad shot, you will find yourself trimming a few frames off the tail of the preceding shot or from the head of the next. Heading and tailing, as this process is known, is most beneficial; the first and last few frames of most shots are very often weak in content and better removed. From here, it is a short step to lifting out a whole shot and splicing it in somewhere else, or cutting a shot in two and putting something in between. The splicer is thus the key to the art of editing.

The editor viewer

Imperceptibly, from simple heading and tailing, you will discover new techniques that can transform your film completely from its original raw footage. In addition, you will find that the ideas which come into your mind at the editing bench generate an awareness of options that existed at the shooting stage and which you might have taken had you more clearly foreseen an editing plan. Thus, editing helps to sharpen shooting technique and encourages profitable pre-planning.

All this derives from confident and decisive use of the splicer. But, of course, this simple tool is merely the means of cutting and joining. In order to make intelligent and creative cuts, you must be able to decide exactly where the blade should fall. This means viewing the film.

The editor viewer allows you to view your footage at slow cranking speeds or, indeed, one frame at a time. It is the most expensive item needed for editing, but the investment is well worthwhile. It also enables you to make splices without removing the film and, when necessary, to take the film out easily, speedily and without damage.

An editor stands or falls by the simplicity of its film path. The more cogs, wheels, sprockets and rollers the film passes over, the greater the risk of scratching and the more difficult it will be to thread and unthread. Never buy an editor without thoroughly testing it first. Take a spool of film with you to the store, thread it up and wind it backwards and forwards several times at high speed. Then take it home and project it, examining it carefully for evidence of scratching. If the film is unmarked, return to the store and assess other functions. Check that the editor is

Left **Two tape splicers. For general use, tape is preferable to cement. if too much cement is used, the film can stick in the film gate, while frames** **also have to be sacrificed. Tape, however, has one main disadvantage; tape splices can gradually stretch.**

easy to thread 'and that the film path is easily accessible for cleaning. Make sure that it sits stably during winding when one spool is full and heavy and the other nearly empty.

Also confirm how the film is 'marked'. Most editors have some form of punch which dents, nicks or pierces the film to identify the cutting point when it is removed from the editor's gate. Some models, however, do not mark the frame in the gate, but a point several frames removed from it. Others can grossly mutilate the film.

The best marking device is one which punches the edge of the film without touching the picture. This allows you to change your mind and to use 'marked' film regardless after the event.

Sound editors

If you have a sound camera, you may find it useful to also have a sound editor. This is an editor viewer which plays the sound as well as the picture.

Sound viewers fall into two categories. There are motorised versions which can run the film at constant projection speed. These naturally play the sound without any wavering of pitch. There are also hand-cranked models, which are basically silent editors with a sound head added. Which kind you buy will depend very largely on what you can afford. But, as in the silent editor, the most important feature is film transport. Sophisticated audio circuitry can never compensate for a scratched film.

The synchronizer

This is another editing device, consisting of a bank of sprockets which are mechanically locked to each other. It is an extremely useful tool for the amateur, who almost invariably projects his camera-original film, rather than a print of it. Because of this, there is a constant risk of damaging the film at the editing stage through repeated handling and viewing. This is especially the case if the picture is being matched precisely to a complex sound track — where the visuals are cut to the beat of a piece of music, for instance.

The professional strikes a cutting copy from the camera original. No matter what damage this copy suffers, the former is never at risk. Your alternative is to use a roll of white leader tape as a picture guide-roll. You can write on it, scratch it, punch holes in it or stick numbered labels on it. You could even annotate it with musical bar lines and notation. Having marked the leader with whatever cueing information is required, this guide-roll is then fed through the synchronizer together with the film, matched and cut to the guide-roll's visible cues.

Some synchronizers incorporate the features of an editor viewer and most have some form of frame-counting device. Many are designed to match up different media. Super 8 film can be matched with Super 8, Standard 8, magnetic tape or perforated tape, for instance. In addition, they can be fitted with a sound head which is equally able to read different media.

Editing horse

This is simply a rack to carry spools of film. It stands, or is fixed, at the left of the editing table, so that film can be unspooled from it straight to

An assembly of the various pieces of equipment needed for editing. Of these, the editor viewer is the most essential for the basic groundwork, though a projector is also necessary to indicate the true rhythm and timing of the film.

Super 8 editor/viewer

Leader tape

the editor viewer. It is an easy piece of equipment to make; in its simplest form, it consists of two wooden uprights with notches cut into them to support a number of horizontal spool pegs.

Pencils can easily serve as spool pegs. A standard pencil has just the right diameter for a Standard 8 spool to rotate on it smoothly. For Super 8 spools, wooden dowels of just under 12mm/½in diameter are preferable.

The editing horse is especially useful when it comes to making the first rough assembly of the film. The viewer's own feed spool is left empty and film is fed to it directly from the horse — first a shot from one spool and then a shot from another and so on. Apart from film, the horse is also a convenient dispenser for leader tape, magnetic tape and magnetic coated film.

Headphones
With the increasing popularity of direct sound cameras, headphones are fast becoming an exceptionally useful accessory. A simple ear-plug phone is usually supplied to monitor the camera's sound imput, but a proper head set is much better. Headphones can be expensive, but hi-fi ones can easily be adapted to do the job. Make up a short lead with a 3.5mm jack plug on one end and a standard jack socket on the other. A hi-fi store can also be asked to make the adaptation.

Microphones
The truism that you get what you pay for is no less accurate in the case of microphones than with anything else. The microphone supplied with a sound camera or projector is not usually of the highest quality. This does not necessarily mean that you will fail to achieve a first class result, but it is a fact that the more skilled and imaginative a film maker becomes, the greater are the demands he makes on his equipment.

In sound recording, the most important thing is to position the microphone as close to the sound source as possible. The easiest solution is a microphone boom, though you can use a directional microphone which picks up the sound from a predominantly frontal direction. Alternatively, a parabolic reflector can be used. This not only picks up frontal sounds but also magnifies them. It is therefore extremely useful for weak sounds, such as bird song. Finally, there is the personal microphone which hangs around the neck, clips to the lapel, or can be secreted beneath clothing. The disadvantage is that considerable lengths of cable normally have to be used.

Whatever type of microphone you are using, never be satisfied with the length of cable as fitted by the manufacturer. Provided the microphone is of low impedance, an extension cable can often safely be used.

If, however, your subject is extremely mobile, or there is huge distance between subject and camera, a radio microphone is the answer. Here, the subject wears a transmitter as well as a personal microphone; the former beams the voice to a receiver and so into the camera or recorder. Radio microphones, though, are extremely expensive and, in some cases, a transmitting licence is required for their use.

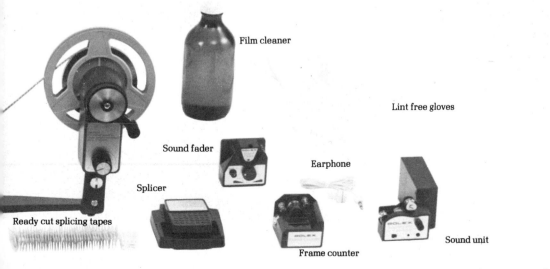

Film cleaner

Lint free gloves

Sound fader

Earphone

Splicer

Ready cut splicing tapes

Frame counter

Sound unit

The reflector

This is a lighting implement which allows you to throw light on a subject when there is no power source available for lamps. Proprietary reflectors are made of specially engineered materials, but, again, improvisation is very easy. A white painted board, a sheet of metal foil, or even a newspaper will do the trick.

One of the chief uses of reflectors is when human faces are being shot in bright sunshine. Without them, the subject's features would be marred by unsightly shadows. This is particularly true with 8mm film stock, so the reflector is an item which should feature in every amateur's accessory kit.

Intervalometer

This is a timing device which causes the camera to expose a single frame of film at regular, pre-determined intervals. It is used, for instance, when a slow gradual movement — such as the opening of a flower — is being speeded up so that it happens extremely quickly on the screen. Though this can be done manually, the use of an intervalometer means that a camera can operate unattended through protracted periods of hours, days and even weeks. It is able to fire a flash gun in addition to the camera.

Titling rig

Every movie maker wants to put titles to his films and the titling rig enables you to shoot titles, photographs, drawings or any kind of art work without fuss or bother. It is easy to improvise, as it is simply a board, with provision for securing the subject being shot, set at an appropriate distance

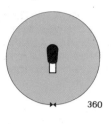

Omni-directional microphones pick up sound over a 360° range.

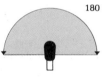

Shotgun microphones are extremely selective, having a 40° effective range.

Cardioid microphones are designed to focus on sound over a range of 180°C.

The parabolic reflector magnifies the sound it picks up, so it is useful for recording quieter scenes.

The best way of monitoring the sound input of a direct sound camera is to use headphones. Special ones can be bought or hi-fi ones adapted to do the job.

and at right angles to a camera platform. The rig sometimes incorporates its own lighting system; the camera platform, for its part, can usually be moved through a range of subject distances, though this is not essential if a zoom lens if fitted.

Filters

There are many optical devices that can be fitted to the front of the camera lens; these are generally described under the general heading of filters. Of the many types available a skylight filter, or an ultra violet (UV) filter is probably the most essential. Though it has little discernible effect on the film image — unless shooting is being done in the mountains, where ultra violet rays break through the atmosphere — its prime advantage is that it causes virtually no light loss. It can therefore be left on the camera permanently and this affords useful protection for the lens.

The polarizing filter reduces glare and reflections on water, glass and most non-metallic surfaces. It also darkens the sky dramatically, mainly in the areas at right angles to the sun. It also causes a severe light loss (one or two stops) and the camera's aperture must be increased accordingly. Self-metering cameras usually make automatic allowance for the effects caused by any filter, but some will not make the correct adjustment for polarizers. In such cases, manual exposure setting may well prove necessary.

The Starburst filter is etched with many fine lines in hatched patterns. It causes point-source lights to radiate spiky flares, whose character is determined by the strength of the light, the aperture and the focal length of the lens. This type of filter does not cause a light loss, but it should be used with caution, as it has a softening effect.

There are many other special effects filters available; choose those suitable for the job in hand. Among the most spectacular are the range of chromatic filters, which produce amazing shifts of colour and spectral distortions.

Left **A proprietary blimp, designed to reduce camera noise and** *below* **a homemade version. Both are equally effective.**

Every movie – whether it is a simple record of a family outing or an elaborate production, involving the use of a set, production team and a large cast – must obey a set of fundamental rules if it is to be a success when it is shown on the screen. This section of the book details the various steps involved from the moment the camera's start button is released to expose the initial frames of the first 50 feet of film to the premiere of the finished movie before an audience.

The first chapter – Basic Movies – explains how every film sequence must be 'filmic' and the steps necessary to achieve this, whatever the subject. The way to avoid jump-cuts, the functions of a cut-away and the development of character, for instance, are all explained in the context of an overall aim – to produce an artistically satisfactory whole from the moment filming starts. Two chapters on sound – one on basic principles, the other on the more complex task of synchronizing sound and picture – make the point that a film should never be seen in silence, while Script, Direction, Production applies the lessons learned in the Basic Movie chapter to more elaborate films. Movie Magic shows how to achieve special effects, trick photography and animation; In Performance covers the whole art of projection. A final chapter, Film and the Future, sets out to explore new developments, including the growth of video.

Basic Movies

Films are made by human beings for human beings. The only qualification needed to make a good film is human awareness — the ability to see the things around you, and the natural desire to share them with others. This qualification is above all others — the non-technical film maker who relies on a camera's automatic functions has just as much chance of success as the expert. A film is judged not by the technical expertise of its maker, but by its own inherent appeal.

The First Fifty Feet

Having bought your first ever fifty feet of movie film, the first thing is to stop and think how to make proper use of it, rather than rush into action. Remember that, unlike the couple of dozen shots you get in a pack of snapshot film, 50 feet of movie film gives you a great many pictures — 3600 of them. Of course, it is not difficult to use them up; eighteen are used every second that the camera is running. But, though any movie film consists of a stream of individual pictures, that is its only parallel with still photography. A snapshot records a single split second of action. Film, on the other hand, records action continuously, not momentarily, for as long as the camera continues to run.

This basic difference emphasizes film's vital and unique quality. It is not so much that it moves — important as that is — but that it delivers a continuous visual experience.

Naturally, this has a bearing on how the first 50 feet, and every subsequent 50 feet, of film should be used. Film is not snapshot material and it must not be used as such. You must try not to make moving snapshots, though this does not mean that you cannot shoot snapshot subjects. Families, holidays, weddings, birthday parties are all highly film-worthy subjects, if only because their human elements are of especial interest to you, and to those who

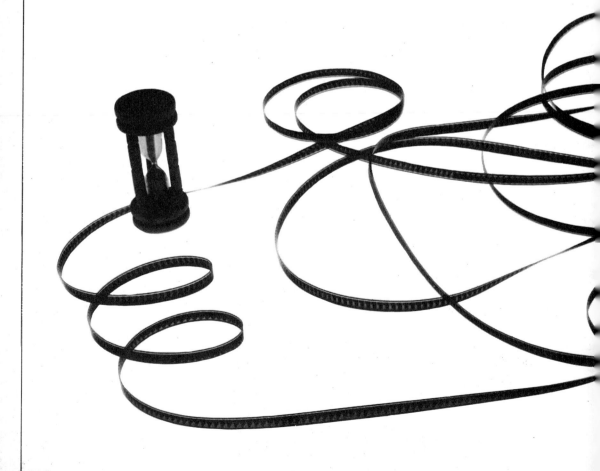

ultimately, may see the film. But it does mean that you must take a little more care than if you were snatching tiny moments with a still camera.

Film language
Whatever subject you may choose for you first fifty feet, you should make some attempt to achieve footage which can communicate to your audience in what is called film language. This term may sound daunting, but its basic principles are very simple and easy to grasp.

The best way of understanding film language is, again, to compare still photographs with movie films. When you show snapshots to friends, they are quite willing to accept the interruption between one picture and another. They will not mind particularly if the photographs are not presented in any logical sequence — say, if you first show them a picture of a newly-married couple eating their

wedding cake and later one of them cutting it. This is because each picture is a separate, isolated experience; each can be viewed individually. Film, however, is very different. Because it is a continuous medium, the audience expects the action within the film to be continuous. Interruptions will not be tolerated so readily, nor an illogical sequence of events.

The technique of achieving this — presenting film images smoothly, and in logical, continuous sequence — is called continuity. It is the fundamental starting point of film language.

The obvious way of achieving perfect con-

Fifty feet of film is the content of a single Super 8 film cartridge, but the lessons learned when shooting this apply to all movies. The most important point to remember is to observe the basic rules of film language from the moment you start shooting.

tinuity is to shoot the entire 50 feet in one long, continuous take. This way, there would be no interruptions, and the action would be seen in logical order — the exact order in which it all happened. However, there are two main objections to this. First, it is very extravagant, and second, extremely boring. Fifty feet gives you 3 minutes 20 seconds of action and most action, if prolonged that long, is protracted and repetitive, as well as a waste of film stock. Take the example of a wedding reception. Devoting all this time to the cutting of the wedding cake is clearly wrong. The sensible thing to do is to stop the camera after the couple have made the first incision in the cake and restart it later, when the next interesting event occurs.

This simple example holds true for practically every film subject. All will consist of some actions that you need and some that you can well do without. This means that shooting is also an editorial process and that the necessary decisions must be made second by second as the action occurs. If you are to make effective use of your first fifty feet, you must know not only when to start filming but also when to stop.

However, this leads back to the problem of continuity, since every time you stop the camera, you cause a break in this continuous action — a cut. It is a common error to think of cuts as a scissors and sticky tape job that takes place on the editing bench, but nothing could be further from the truth. Like it or not, you make a cut every time you stop the camera; the cutting decisions you make when shooting can be just as vital as any that may confront you later.

It is easy to understand that stopping the camera must inevitably cause a break in continuity. When the camera is started again, the action will have progressed; new things will be going on and people will have changed their

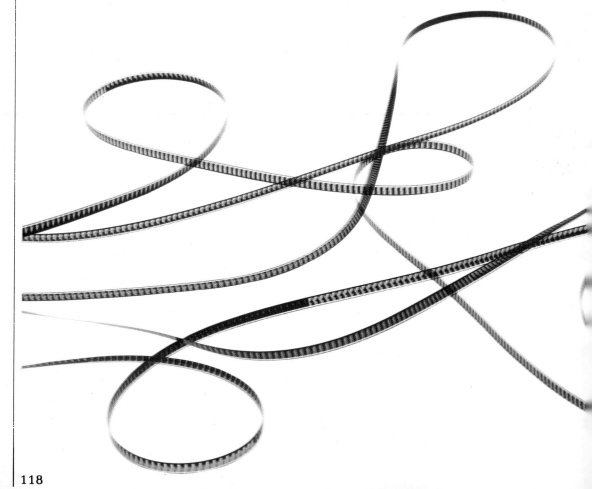

positions. The easiest error to commit is to allow this to become apparent on the finished film. Such a cut causes a jump of continuity and is called, appropriately, a jump cut.

Jump cuts and cut-aways

A jump cut happens when the film maker omits to give the audience an explanation of what was happening between the time the camera was stopped and the time it was restarted. More accurately, it implies that nothing at all happened. Any audience knows instantly that this is illogical. Returning to the example of the wedding reception, jump cutting straight from the couple standing to the couple seated leaves out one obvious fact — they sat down. By jump cutting on this action, you refuse to admit this to the audience. Instead, you insist that there was no such moment — that they returned to their seats by magic. This is a complete misuse of film language.

Film language, however, also supplies the answer to the problems in the form of an insert, or cut-away. In the simplest terms, a cut-away, is a shot of something that can be inserted between the couple standing and the couple sitting to make the audience believe that this happened while they were watching something else. Thus, the cut-away can be a shot of anything that excludes the couple in question. Naturally, the cut-away is far more effective if it makes its own dramatic contribution to the action rather than solely smoothing out continuity.

At a wedding reception, say, there is no shortage of suitable cut-away subjects; the guests themselves make an essential contribution to the action and mood. There is no cut-away so effective as a shot of a person or persons who are apparently watching the main action. The cut-away is obviously a very valuable device: it is common practice in professional film making to shoot a great number of them, so that the editor

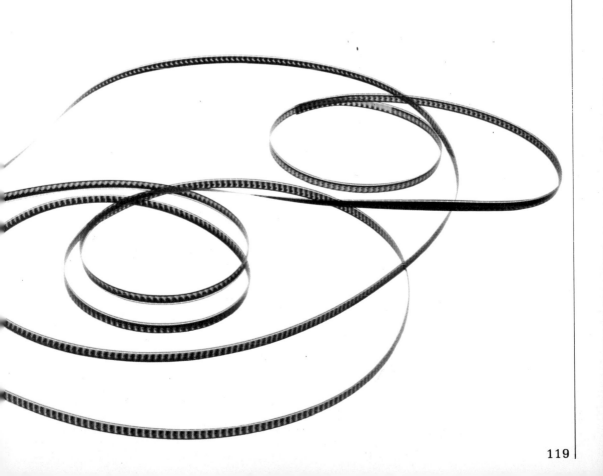

later has the maximum flexibility in cutting. Professionally too, cut-aways are often shot out of sequence in one concentrated session. But it is not advisable for the amateur to shoot cut-aways like this. It is far better to shoot them one at a time, as the need occurs. This is especially important in situations where visual changes are occurring through the time period of the acting. A wedding reception is such a situation. As the party progresses, conditions change; different courses are served and consumed, and the participants become more animated.

If you were to shoot all the main action first, and then shoot a heap of cut-aways later, you might not be able to find enough suitable subjects to use for this purpose. Shooting cut-aways as the need arises means that conditions change naturally and logically along the time scale. And, as an additional bonus, every shot in the fifty foot run occupies its authentic sequential position, which minimizes arduous shunting processes at the editing table.

Out of a simple understanding of the basic principle of continuity a simple but foolproof rule can be derived — never shoot the same subject in two successive shots. Having stopped the camera on the main subject, look around, and if there are people observing the main action, shoot them. If they are observing something else, shoot them anyway, and allow your audience to believe that they were watching your subject. If there is nobody about, then shoot something else — anything at all; but do not return to the main subject until you have first shot that vital cut-away.

There will be occasions, of course, when your main subject is static. In this case, there would be no apparent jump of continuity, and a cut-away therefore would be superfluous. But unwanted cut-aways can be edited out later; cut-aways cannot be inserted if you have not shot them. It pays to observe another rule to be on the safe side — after every shot, look around.

You may begin to worry that, of your precious 50 feet, half will be used up on cut-aways. But this is not so, since cut-aways need not be very long. What matters here is the influence they have in determining the time scale. In this context, you will discover that the cut-away is an even more valuable device than you may have supposed. There are no magic formulae in film making, but the cut-away is the next best thing. Not only does it allow the audience to imagine events that they have not actually seen; it also allows the movie maker to exert tremendous control over what is called the time scale.

Cut-aways and the time scale

Since film is a continuous experience, a graph of any film would show that one axis would measure time. Whatever the subject, a film will invariably depict a period of time much greater than the actual screen time. A wedding, for example, might go on for half the day, yet you could easily depict these events in ten minutes of screen time or even in 50 feet (3 minutes 20 seconds). The ability to move along the time scale — leaving out portions of time, here and there — is an essential aspect of film language.

A lapse of time is engineered by correct use of the cut-away. It has already been seen how an audience understands and accepts that, while they are watching a cut-away, the main subject will continue to exist and move. So they will not be surprised to find that the main subject is in a different position when you cut back to the main action in the next shot. But an audience also accepts that, whatever the main subject was doing during the cut-away, it took time to do it. This is only logical. What is not logical — but something an audience nonetheless also accepts — is that the lapse of time depicted can be much greater than the screen time of the cut-away. A short cut-away can depict a huge time lapse between the two shots on either side of it.

Returning to the wedding example, it may well take at least three minutes to cut up a wedding cake, yet all that time can be effectively lapsed using a cut-away of only three seconds. Brief, snappy cut-aways can lapse much greater periods than this — ten minutes, an hour, and even more. This is what makes the cut-away such a miraculous device. It enables you to insert smooth and acceptable discontinuities into what we have seen to be a continuous experience — motion pictures.

What is even more astonishing is that the cut-away is infinitely flexible in the amount of time it allows you to lapse; you can lapse out huge periods and thereby contract a large actual time to a short screen time. Alternatively, actual time and screen time can be exactly equal. Further, you can even expand the time scale so that screen-time is greater than the actual time.

This last technique is a stock suspense-building technique. If you knew that some rejected suitor, burning with jealousy and determined on revenge, had secreted fire crackers in the wedding cake, you would naturally wish to dwell on the moment when the couple make the first cut. But is is likely that, in reality, this action would last for only a very short time — perhaps ten seconds. However, by breaking this ten second

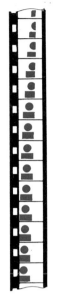

The examples here demonstrate the principle of the jump cut. The term is used to describe what happens when a film jumps illogically from one sequence of events to another. The removal of the section of film indicated here would produce a completely unnatural sequence.

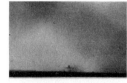

shot into, say, three shots of about three seconds each, and by placing five second cut-aways between them, the screen time is expanded to twenty seconds.

In this case you could not, of course, shoot the cut-aways in sequence, otherwise you would miss most of the main action. You could not shoot them afterwards, either, at least, not if the fire crackers went off! This is a situation in which you would have to anticipate an imminent change of visual conditions (marzipan and icing all over the guests) and, therefore, shoot the cut-aways in advance of the main action.

This example may seem rather extreme and you may be inclined to dismiss suspense building as something totally unsuited to the subject. But this is not so; the explosive-in-the-cake example was chosen deliberately to challenge the notion that suspense is exclusively the stuff of melodrama, with no rightful place in other types of film.

The role of suspense

Suspense has a legitimate role to play in every film. It is not solely the fabric of startling and terrifying climaxes: it is the bricks and mortar of any climax and all films must have moments of climax, however innocuous the action may be. The moment when the bride and groom cut into their wedding cake is such a climax. If it were otherwise, why should the photographers' flash-guns proliferate at this point? Why should you, yourself, wish to film this moment? Why do the newly-married couple regard this as such a highlight of the day? Why do the guests fall silent, and then laugh and applaud? They do so because it is a moment of climax.

There are many more. Examples range from the couple coming out of the church, the rice and confetti, the popping of the first champagne cork, the good luck toast, the farewell, to the departure of the honeymoon car. All these events are climaxes, and they can all be enhanced by being expanded in the time scale to create suspense. A ten second shot of a waiter wrestling with a champagne cork can be extended to an agonising half minute of entertaining footage by using cut-aways of the expectant faces of the guests.

Differentiating time lapses

Having established that a cut-away need not be very long, its function can be examined in more detail. It has been seen that a cut-away of any given length is capable of disguising a hole in the time scale (a time lapse) of any duration the film

Left **An example of a simple cut-away. This is a film device intended to bridge the gap between what might be repetitious main action, if shown in full, and also to disguise any time lapse in the film. In the example shown here, shots of the audience at a puppet show are interspersed between the main action on the stage. Their use adds a further sense of involvement as the film audience can see and identify with the audience's reaction on screen. In this sequence, the film was shot continuously, with the camera cutting from the stage scene to the audience.**

Above **This gliding
sequence demonstrates
a further principle
governing the use of cut-
aways. It is not
necessary to keep the
camera running the
whole time or even to
shoot the cut-aways
during the course of
main filming. The shots
of spectators watching
the glider in flight could
be taken before or after
the actual sequences of
take-off and landing, or
even on a completely
different occasion.**

maker decides. But the actual period of the lapse is depicted not by the cut-away itself, but by whatever lapse seems to have occurred when the camera returns to the main action. If, when the cut-away occurs, the bride has just been seen eating her soup and she is still eating her soup after the cut-away, the audience will think that only a short period has passed. More accurately, they will simply not be conscious of any time scale distortion.

If in the new shot, however, she is now seen halfway through the main course, it is obvious that quite some time has lapsed since we last saw her. The cut-away merely camouflages the lapse; the information is contained in the new shot and it is entirely dependent on the audience's powers of observation, rather than on the length of the cut-away.

Audiences also depend on their personal knowledge to digest time lapses. They know, for example, how long it takes to eat a plate of soup, to have the plates cleared away, and to start on the next course. The new shot, therefore, not only tells them that a period of time has passed, but also enables them to calculate subconsciously the approximate period. Again, the duration of the cut-away does not influence such calculations. It is simply a disguise to patch up the hole.

Thus, if you show the bride eating not the main course but the cake after the cut-away, it is evident that a much longer period of time has passed. Once again, all the information regarding the lapse (its fact, and its duration) is implicit in the content of the new shot — not in the cut-away.

The crucial question is therefore whether a cut-away between soup and -wedding cake should be longer than one between soup and main course. The immediate answer would seem to be that it makes no difference. But, naturally enough, a large gap needs a larger patch than a smaller one, if the repair is to be truly invisible. A short lapse of, say, five minutes can be disguised by a cut-away of a mere three seconds. But a longer lapse needs a longer cut-away period, if it is to be acceptable to an audience.

To be wholly effective, a large lapse requires not just one cut-away shot, but several in sequence. This is called a sequence of cut-aways; for instance, a sequence of three cut-aways, each of five seconds duration, is more effective than just one fifteen second cut-away.

Moreover, a large time-lapse is more readily acceptable if the cut-away sequence takes the

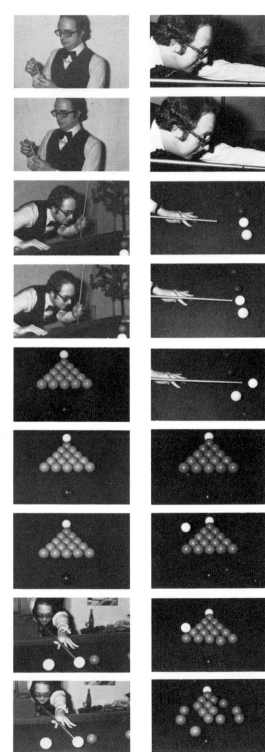

Left **In the simple
sequence tension is
created by cutting from
the player in
preparation — cue-
chalking, lining up — to
the precisely arranged
balls. Because the
audience knows that this
precise pattern is about
to be broken, its
attention is held. Close-
ups of the concentration
on the player's face add
to this.**

**No matter how
scintillating the playing
of the guitarist pictured
here might be, the
audience could soon
grow restless if it was
only given the one
frontal view of the man
in action. Cutting to the
left hand and its speedy
chord changing and to
the strumming and
plucking *right*, make a
much more satisfactory
sequence.**

Above **Suspense is an integral part of every film. Without the moments of climax brought about by the judicious use of this technique, the final version may well seem flat and boring. Here, suspense has been achieved by expanding the time scale to dramatize the progress of a small child through a dark alley. The inevitable moment of release comes at the end of the sequence.**

audience's attention away not merely from the main action (the bride and groom) to the faces of onlooking guests, but to even more remote subjects — say, an exterior shot of the building in which the reception is taking place. A typical sequence might run as follows: Main action: bride eating soup. Cut-away: general view of guests. Cut-away: waiter collecting dishes. Cut-away: exterior of banqueting hall. Main-action: bride eating wedding cake. The most useful cut-away in this sequence is the exterior shot, though the reason for this is almost totally psychological. It is a well-known fact that a longer period seems to have lapsed simply by using an outside shot — even though time actually passes no quicker inside. This is what makes this and other 'remote' cut-aways so effective. When, in the new, main action shot, we see the bride now at the end of the meal, we feel this transition to be much more credible through having momentarily lost sight, not just of her, but of the entire scene.

From this, it is clear that a cut-away can be either long or short, according to need and circumstance. If the cut-away covers a very short time scale, or no lapse at all, it need itself be only of short duration (say, three or four seconds). If, however, the lapse is somewhat more extended the cut-away should be either a little longer itself (say 8 seconds) or, better still, it should consist of a sequence of short cut-aways. Here it is worth noting that long cut-aways tend to slow down the pace of a film; a sequence of brief shots is usually better for this reason. It follows from this that, if the lapse is of a substantial period, not only is a sequence of cut-aways necessary, but it may also be desirable to include a shot not directly associated with the main action.

This, then, is the cut-away — an immensely useful device which miraculously conveys the audience smoothly across the discontinuities which inevitably occur when the camera ceases to turn.

It may seem to the beginner that such subtleties as time-scale are far too complex to be mastered in the first fifty feet. This is not so. Subtle though its effects may be, continuity can be easily managed by anybody. All that is necessary is to remember that every time you take your finger off the button, you have just created a continuity problem which must be immediately solved.

The rule is therefore to look around after every shot. Shoot a cut-away that will not only complement the action and atmosphere of the

The cut-away is a useful device for indicating the passage of time. In the sequence *above* the length of the man's sleep is underlined by cut-aways to a clock face and the rhythmically ticking pendulum.

piece, but, more importantly, will bridge any time gap or change in characters' positions. After that, it is just a matter of counting. If you are forced to shoot a quick succession of shots with no time for cut-aways, count how many times you stop the camera, and remember to shoot the appropriate number of cut-aways later.

If the main action goes into a protracted period of dull inactivity which you think is not worth shooting, and if you feel the time slipping by with tell-tale visual changes occuring, remember that when you do come back to the main-action one single cut-away may not be an adequate time bridge. The longer you take between shots, the more likely it is that you will have to build a sequence of cut-aways or resort to a 'remote' cut-away.

Fifty feet of film offers you the opportunity to present an articulate, continuous experience to any audience. Do not be put off by what may appear to be the complex language; nine-tenths of it is continuity and it has been seen how the simple cut-away can solve almost any continuity problem.

Parallel themes

A wedding reception stands as an excellent example of an occasion where there is a definite main subject (the newly-married couple), and a secondary subject (the guests), whose role is to add atmosphere and to provide cut-away material. But you will often find yourself in a situation where there are two main subjects. By treating these as parallel themes — that is to say as separate but equally important subjects — it is both possible and desirable to move through a condensed time scale by cutting back and forth between them.

Retaining the same example, let us suppose that you are attending a double wedding, with two couples at the top table. You could cut from Couple A eating soup to Couple B on the main course, to Couple A again, now taking the dessert, and so on. All you have to remember is never to shoot the same couple twice in succession. Naturally, you will still want to take shots of the guests, but these shots will now be to give authenticity and mood. Nonetheless, every time you do shoot the guests, you will have put a potential cut-away in the can. This gives you the option of cutting back to the same couple that you last shot or perhaps to a quartet shot of both couples.

It may seem surprising that the cut-away can disguise a gaping hole in the time scale so successfully. If so, the effectiveness of parallel-

Time lapse is the art of communicating to the audience that the main action has progressed, without having to show its every stage and without what is happening on the screen seeming irrational. Here the central theme is children at play and the shots are calculated to show how they spent their time.

theme cutting is even more startling. Here there is no bridge across the time gap; the transition occurs in the split second of the cut. We see Couple A engaged on the first course, and we know that the unseen Couple B are also on the first course. Yet when we cut to Couple B we find that they are on the second course. All the visible evidence suggests the two couples are eating out of phase. Yet rather than believe the evidence of our eyes, we choose to surmise that a time lapse has occurred. There is no logical reason why this should be so, and therefore no logical reason why parallel-theme cutting should work as a time lapse device. But it does work supremely well, and is a ready alternative to cut-aways.

Variations on the cut-away
An essential quality of good camera work is variety and variations of style can be profitably applied to the cut-away technique. Instead of cutting from the main subject by stopping the camera, you can leave the camera running while panning to the cut-away subject. Or you can pan from the cut-away back to the main theme.

Another variation is the cut-in, which is designed to achieve the same result as the cut-away, though in a different way. The cut-away disguises a time-lapse by cutting away from the main subject; the cut-in literally cuts in so close to the main subject that any jump in continuity is obscured from view. Here is a typical cut-in sequence: Shot A: medium range shot of bride and groom eating first course. Shot B: close-up of bride's face. Shot C: medium shot of bride and groom eating second course. A further refinement would be: Shot A: medium shot of bride and groom eating first course. Shot B: close-up of bride's face — shot zooms back to reveal bride and groom eating second course.

In both versions, the cut from medium shot to close-up, and, in the first version, the cut from close-up back to medium shot, is an important feature of the cut-in technique. The sudden change of scale helps to disguise any discrepancy of position, posture or attitude in the moving subjects.

There are many further variations on the continuity theme, but, providing that the basic principle of continuity is understood, you can invent all kinds of variations for yourself. These are just as likely to be effective as any you might pick up from a text book. Without question, you will find that film-making is a continuing process of experimentation and discovery and both

In this sequence of shots the movie maker has treated two subjects — the child playing on the shore and the boats on the river — as parallel themes. Each subject could stand up on its own but by cutting backwards and forwards between them, the movie maker has added depth and interest to his film. In addition, the cut–aways from one subject to the other provide an excellent time lapse device.

begin with the very first fifty feet.

Camera as audience

Continuity is thus largely a matter of knowing when to start the camera and when to stop it. Now we shall consider what happens in between — while the camera is turning. It is then that the continuous stream of images is created; whatever the camera is made to 'see', the audience will see too. In a single phrase, the camera is the audience.

An audience sees precisely what the camera saw — and from the same angle and distance. If you place the camera in the top of a tree, the audience will be transported there for the duration of the shot. If you shoot from a roller coaster, the audience will be shaken about just as much as the camera. If you walk about with the camera hand-held, you force the viewers to walk about in the projected picture. If you shoot with the camera static and tripod mounted, attention becomes fixed.

All this is obvious, but it is very easy to overlook. In every shot, it is most important to remind yourself that your pictures will be seen as a continuous stream of lifelike (and sometimes life-size) images on a large screen in a darkened room. There will be nothing else to look at but the screen, so the audience's attraction to your pictures is compelling and almost inescapable.

This puts you in a position of extreme responsibility. If an audience is shaken about, shocked, or deliberately confused, there should be a good reason for it. So never forget that, whatever you do with your camera, you effectively do with your audience.

Types of picture

The|question| basically comes|down| to| the kind of pictures your audience want to see. More than anything, they want to watch pictures that are easy to look at. These do not necessarily have to be pretty pictures — tulip fields, swans on a lake and the like. The image can be a garbage tip, but the images must be clear and well defined. This is achieved positioning the camera fairly close to the subject and thereby keeping it large in the frame. Just how close is impossible to say, since this depends on the size of the subject. In any case, you will want to vary your camera work by changing the scale — perhaps with every shot. But, as a general rule, remember that increased distance makes a subject more difficult to see, and if you are in doubt, you should move slightly closer.

The more unobtrusive the camera, the more natural the result. By thinking of the camera as the audience, this movie maker has captured a perfectly logical series of shots within the two individual takes.

The importance of stability

Your pictures will also be more comfortable to watch if the camera is held quite still. The best way to achieve this is with a tripod; the result is a rock-steady picture on screen. In the absence of a tripod, the camera can be steadied against some rigid object (a wall or a car). It is sometimes allowable to hand-hold the camera, but the inevitable result is picture shake. This is wearing on the audience and it also draws attention to the camera's existence. So hand-held shots are best used in small doses; reserve them for shots in which you wish to imply that what the audience is watching is a subjective view, seen by a human, moving character in the action. Also remember that the increased magnification of a telephoto lens naturally magnifies the effect of camera shake. Hand-held shots, therefore, should be taken with a wide-angle lens or with a zoom-lens in the wide-angle setting.

Though an audience wants to see a shot for long enough to absorb its content, it does not want to see it long enough to become bored. There are two calculations to be made here. The first is the amount of time required to take in the information contained in a shot. This is fairly easy to calculate when you are setting it up. Look through the viewfinder and count how many seconds it takes you to become fully aware of the scene as a whole and all the relevant features within it. This should seldom take longer than four or five seconds, though, on occasion, it might well be extended if something interesting is going on, or new subjects are moving into the frame.

Mood and time

The second calculation is the amount of time required to give the shot — and the sequence it occupies — a suitable mood. Mood is influenced by many factors, such as lighting, camera-angle and so on, but shot duration and cutting-rhythm are also an important influence. You can create a languorous mood by holding a shot far longer than is necessary to take in the information. Alternatively, an urgent or racy mood can be created by a quick cut. No text-book can help you make this kind of decision. Your judgement will be influenced by many factors — storyline, subject, style, general objective and so on. Purely as a guide, remember that ten seconds is quite a long shot and three seconds is quite a short one. This is not a rule, however, as it can obviously be broken according to circumstances.

Above **The cardinal fact to remember when shooting any film is that the camera is the audience. One character doing something interesting — in this case creating a clown make-up — makes a good subject, provided the action progresses swiftly enough. The points to remember are the time necessary to establish the mood of the shot and to convey its content.**

Panning and tilting

The third point is that an audience naturally wants to look around. If you physically took your audience to the scene in the film, they would swivel their heads about to absorb the widest possible view. You must sometimes do the same with the camera. This kind of swivelling is called panning. A pan shot enables you to show a wide

It is important to judge
the filming distance
correctly, the aim always
being to achieve a large,
clear image. In the child
and donkey sequence
above, your main
concern might be to
capture the changing
expressions on the
child's face, but you
might also want an
impression of the animal
and its particular type of
movement. These aims
will determine the
distances from which
you shoot. You could
also use the parallel
theme technique here.
It would be easy to
diminish the size of the
skater *right* too quickly.
Great care should be
taken to keep such
subjects central and
sufficiently large to
convey the excitement of
movement to the
audience.

subject or scene while remaining relatively close to it, so retaining picture clarity.

Panning, however, can destroy clarity if it is done too fast. This causes a 'strobing' effect. If the camera is panned too fast, it not only covers a lot of ground during each individual picture, but also during the gap between each picture. This means that the image recorded by each picture is substantially different from the following one and the eye is unable to smooth out the disparity.

The result is that the scene moves across the frame in an intermittent, jerky fashion — a most unpleasant sensation which must be avoided. This is done by making sure to pan slowly enough to allow each frame to record a view which is not too different from the one seen by the preceding frame. This should be no faster than one frame-width per five seconds. Put another way, you must allow at least five seconds for a feature entering one side of the frame to pass out on the other side. You will have to make a conscious effort not to exceed this panning speed since, it seems painfully slow when observed through the viewfinder. However, there is no need to be impatient; it looks much faster than this on the screen.

Use of a zoom lens or a number of lenses of varying focal length also means that the panning speed must be monitored carefully. It is no use judging the rate of pan by the speed at which the camera rotates, for the two remain consistent only if the lens' focal length remains the same throughout. A telephoto lens, for instance, 'sees' a smaller area of a given scene than a wide-angle lens and therefore — to observe the five second rule — must rotate more slowly than the latter. A 50mm lens, for example, 'sees' only one fifth of the view seen by a 10mm lens; so, in order to pan at one picture width every five seconds, it must be rotated five times more slowly than a 10mm one.

The problem is further compounded if you decide to zoom while panning. If you start the pan with the zoom lens set at wide-angle, this in turn will dictate the maximum rotation speed. But if, as you continue to pan, you zoom in, you will have to reduce the speed of rotation. The more you magnify, the slower you will have to rotate.

In this case, there is really no alternative method of controlling the panning speed other than by physically counting the seconds. For this reason, it is useful to practise the rotation speed in a dummy run before taking a pan shot.

Panning is the horizontal swivelling of the camera. Vertical swivelling is called tilting. The same principle applies, except that since a frame's height is rather less than its width, the time allowed should be seconds.

Identifying the location

It is obvious that everything happens somewhere, and, naturally, any audience wants to know where you are taking them. You must not depend on their being able to identify the location by what they see in the background. They will be much better informed from the beginning and feel more involved in the action if you start with an establishing shot of the general locality, which tells them precisely where they are. Even if the location is otherwise very obvious — if, say, you are filming your family on the beach — it is more satisfactory if you first show the whole beach, the state of the tide, the number of people on the

Above **To show the full height of a building at close quarters, the camera must be swivelled vertically on the tripod pan head — a process known as tilting. Remember it is important to tilt the camera at a slow even speed. To avoid a jerky effect, about one vertical frame per four seconds gives the best results.**

Horizontal swivelling of the camera to show a wide subject, such as the building illustrated *left,* is called panning. As with tilting, the camera must be moved at a slow even speed to allow each frame to record a view which is not too different from the preceding one; one frame-width per five seconds is the optimum speed for successful results *below left.*
If this speed is much increased, the results will be jerky, producing a strobe effect.

Left and *above* Shots combining panning and tilting. Remember, if you decide to zoom while panning or tilting, the more you magnify the slower you will have to move the camera.

beach and any other information that can be immediately conveyed in a general view. The same principle applies to the wedding film. The first shot is not of the groom arriving at the church, but the church itself, and perhaps the notice board stating the name of the church and that of the minister.

The location can be established either by a single establishing shot or by an establishing sequence of shots. These need not necessarily occur at the beginning of a film. If you wished, you could be deliberately secretive about the location at the start and reveal it to the audience later. This is a legitimate and effective device for grasping attention; nothing is more fascinating than the mysterious. But such mystery must be a part of a deliberate plan and not an accidental omission.

Remember, too, that the audience will need to know whenever you change location within the same film. So you will need an establishing shot for each new location. Once again, it need not be the very first shot. Suppose you wanted to shift from the beach to the holiday hotel. You could cut from a family character drinking on the beach to the same character (or another) at the bar of the hotel. By staying close up in the new shot, you can make the audience think for a few seconds that they are still on the beach.

This is a very good way of changing locations. If you allow the new location to be discovered gradually, there is no single, abrupt moment in which the change occurs. It is also a very neat way of disguising the time lapse. The audience do not know that a time lapse has occurred until the new location is discovered; by the time they make that discovery, they have already been watching post-lapse action for a given number of seconds. By this time it is too late to think about when the lapse occurred.

The location change and the time lapse are very similar, and they require the same sort of treatment. The above example is, in fact, a cut-in. In the new shot, location identity is hidden by staying close in on the character. But a conventional cut-away could equally be used so that the sequence of shots might run as follows: Shot A: family on beach. Shot B: hotel scene excluding family. Shot C: family in hotel garden. Alternatively: Shot A: family on beach. Shot B: hotel scene excluding family. Family walk into frame. Or: Shot A: family on beach. Shot B: hotel scene excluding family. Camera pans to discover family. From this, it should be apparent that, providing the location change is handled smoothly and logically, the time lapse takes care

Above **The first thing any film maker needs to do is to establish the location for the audience. This can be done with one opening shot, but it is better to progress gradually. In this sequence about a botanical garden, this is done by showing the building itself, people going into it and the rare plants it contains. Remember that each new location needs to be similarly established.**

of itself. The information the audience requires in order to understand that a time lapse has occurred is implicit in the change of location.

Location changes, however, need not necessarily be accompanied by a time lapse. You might wish, for example, to cut from the beach to the hotel, not because the family had returned to the hotel, but because the hotel was the scene of a parallel theme. For example, imagine that a member of the party had chosen to stay behind in order to enjoy the company of a group of sun-bathing beauties; you might wish to make an amusing counterpoint between this person and the rest of the family on the beach. In this case it would be a mistake to use a cut-away, or any other smoothing device between the two locations. This would create a risk of the audience mistaking this location bridge for a time bridge and assuming that a time lapse was intended. In order to imply that action is simultaneous, one location must follow the other as quickly as possible. The way to achieve this is with a straight cut.

Establishing the subject

The audience's requirements for information does not end with the establishment of the location. Far more subsidiary information — the time of day and year, who the characters are, why are they there and what are they doing — must also be conveyed. To return to the wedding film, the opening shot of the church establishes the location, the weather, and perhaps the time, if the building has a clock. But it does not establish that a |marriage is about| to occur.|This| may be obvious if the audience is made up entirely of people who attended the wedding, but that is not the point. A good film-maker does not rely on the assumptions and pre-conceived notions of the audience — he or she spells it out. This is very easy to do in the case of a wedding film. If, say, the next shot shows a car decorated with white satin garlands, we know immediately what is happening.

But suppose you decided to film a funeral. Here, the second establishing shot might show the grave digger's spade standing in a heap of earth. If you were making a fictitious film about black magic — or even a factual one — the second shot might show a dead cat nailed to the church door, or a similarly macabre subject.

White satin, a grave digger's spade, and a dead cat — there is a world of difference between the three. Yet each is only the second shot, following exactly the same first shot — the church. The first shot establishes the location; the second

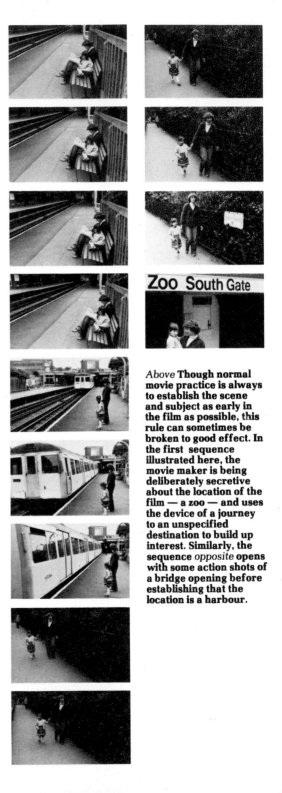

Above **Though normal movie practice is always to establish the scene and subject as early in the film as possible, this rule can sometimes be broken to good effect. In the first sequence illustrated here, the movie maker is being deliberately secretive about the location of the film — a zoo — and uses the device of a journey to an unspecified destination to build up interest. Similarly, the sequence** *opposite* **opens with some action shots of a bridge opening before establishing that the location is a harbour.**

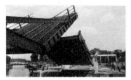

establishes the occasion, or at least hints at it.

Establishing shots can establish much more than the location; the film maker should constantly ask what can be established to help the understanding of the audience. People watching a film involve themselves far more completely if they are well informed. Even if certain information is not relevant to the action, it is still often worthwhile including it. For example, it may be of no significance that the action is occurring in the autumn, but, if a few ripe berries hanging on a bush are shown, this extra information encourages the audience to watch the film more sympathetically and pay more attention to information that is really significant.

The importance of action

An audience also requires action. As stated earlier, a film is a continuous experience, as distinct from the intermittent experience of individual photographs. But, if you are to justify taking thousands of pictures, instead of just a handful, you must give the film action.

This does not mean that film has to be filled with dramatic and rivetting incidents. The simplest everyday occurrences can be profitably committed to film providing you endow them with the action that photographs lack. The essence of action is movement and you must always be on the watch for it.

In a dockyard scene, say, this is easy. There is movement wherever you look: cranes, rail trucks, and vehicles of all kinds. In a country park, it might be very different; there could be a singular lack of movement as far as the eye can see.

You may be tempted to think that in a quiet park there is no need for movement — indeed, that it would destroy the park's inherent calm. In fact, there is every need for movement in a park scene (and all others); the only thing likely to destroy a park's mood is out of character movement.

Movement is the life blood of film. It is what keeps the audience watching. If you find yourself in a situation where there is absolutely no movement, you must ask yourself whether you ought to be shooting it at all. If you badly want the shot, you must ask yourself how you can put some movement into it. It could mean waiting half an hour for somebody to walk into shot, but you will be glad you waited. Even a solitary distant figure is sufficient to bring a scene to life, and, far from destroying the mood of stillness, actually enhances it. Otherwise you might have to find a different camera position, so as to include a stream or a swaying bough. However, if there

Above **Establishing the subject is just as important as establishing the location. In this film about a ferry the location is established in the opening shots, but the subject — the seamen manning the boat and the passengers enjoying the voyage — is developed immediately afterwards.**

really is no action of any kind available, camera movement has to take its place.

Even at the dockyard, you must depend on the scene's own movement to put the film together for you. You are the film maker, and you must decide how to make use of the movement available. Never be content always to show one movement at a time. Try to find a camera position that shows two or more movements simultaneously. This is easy to achieve by zooming from a close-up back to wide-angle, but the increased distance diminishes both the clarity of the picture and the dynamic strength of the moving subjects. Finding a camera position which shows several movements in large scale is not as easy, but the increased impact is well worth the trouble. Three dimensional movement is especially pleasing and powerful. Here, one movement occurs across the frame, while another occurs towards or away from the camera.

It is permissible sometimes to use static shots of completely static subjects, but only for either a very short time or for special effect. As a general rule, movement must be regarded as a vital prerequisite, and you will be well advised to seek it out in every shot.

Variety in the film

Another vital ingredient in any film is variety. The question is what should be varied and the simple answer is everything. You should vary the duration of your shots, your camera angle and height, your continuity devices, camera movements, scale of subject, perspective and zooming speed.

Naturally, it is better if all these functions are varied according to some pattern rather than in a haphazard fashion. But if, when you come to view your shots, you find you have more variety than a consistency of style can support, some of it can always be cut. In any case, variety for its own sake is better than plodding sameness. So if, at the shooting stage, you have no definite plan, or if there is not time to think about an overall style, try hard to ring the changes. This can be summed up as another simple rule: after every shot, think how to do it differently.

Endings

An audience, finally, wants to 'feel' the end. Many amateur film makers end their films simply be screening the last title — THE END. This is not enough, and, in fact, a well constructed film requires no such title. We have no need of an end title to know when a piece of music has ended, or even a good novel. If the film language tells us that

Above **Movement makes your film live. The action can be slow and discreet, or overtly dramatic, but it is the key to your grip on your audience. Also vary the composition given by the camera and its point of view and try to give a pattern to these variations.**

The importance of action is again demonstrated in these shots of children's sports. This is a natural filmic story.

the film has ended, the title is superfluous. If it does not, then the film maker has not learned his craft.

In the feature film '633 Squadron', for instance, a character says: 'How can you justify the waste? . . . . . They've probably all been killed!' The Air Marshal sets his jaw defiantly and replies: 'You can't kill a squadron!' The music swells to a climax and the Air Marshal climbs into his car and drives off down the middle of the runway. This is not the first film in which such a device has been used. But, of course, it does not matter, for by now the film language is concerned only with symbols.

The ending of '633 Squadron' is just as symbolic as the classic 'cowboy riding into the sunset' ending and actually not very different from it. But, like most feature films, it uses dialogue to prepare the audience for the final shots. In silent features — or ones without speech — purely visual language has to be used to end the action.

A useful technique is to repeat the opening, establishing shot, assuming that the action is still taking place there. But unlike the opening shot, which would have been relatively brief, the closing shot needs to be held for a considerable period — perhaps ten seconds or more. Even before the last shot occurs, however, a winding-down process should already have begun. Cutting pace should be slowing, and shots progressively widening towards a general view.

In the wedding film, the last piece of action might well be the couple driving off to their honeymoon destination. But this does not make a good final shot, as there may be many variables over which you have no control. That last word is the key to a successful ending. Try to finish with shots that you can control. For example: after the couple's departure, cut back to the opening scene of the church. Start with a shot of fallen confetti on the church grounds, now silent and still. Cut to a wider view. Finally, cut to an even wider view of the church and its surroundings. Fade out slowly. If the sun happens to be sinking in the west, it makes the perfect conclusion.

If music is being used, it must end naturally in conjunction with the visuals. It is no use switching the music off, or even fading it. Music must end musically. Music, sound effects, and commentary are all very useful for supporting a film's ending (as they are throughout the main body of a film). But they are only supporting devices, and no substitute for visual language. A film is primarily a visual experience and every film must begin, continue and end in visual terms.

Four examples of possible endings. The shots to aim for should be as final as possible, slowing the pace of the film down for the final credits.

Editing in camera

There is an old saying that the camera never lies, but this certainly does not apply to the film camera. Film's essential attribute is its capacity to colour the truth. It has already been shown how it can distort time scale and can execute useful deceptions. That sunset over the churchyard might well be shot at sunrise, before the wedding took place, or three weeks later. In addition to these, there are two creative areas in which the film maker can improve on life. One of these is the cutting room, where shots can be toyed with, and ideas considered in depth before final cutting decisions are made. The other is the slightly more complex process of editing in camera.

The technique of editing in camera is successfully practised by many movie makers. Its immediate advantage is that it is more economical than shooting everything in sight, which often happens when the building up of the film's structure is left until later. More importantly, it is a highly creative technique.

Editing in camera involves the film maker in planning right from the start if the uncut film is to succeed as a piece of language. It is inevitable that a few cuts will be needed at the end of the day, but, even given this, the technique offers one great advantage. It gives you a footage which runs in logical order and shots which were taken with a full awareness of those that preceded them.

All the fundamental features of film language — establishing sequence, succession of action shots, of cut-aways and a final end sequence — can be achieved in camera, provided you have a plan. Naturally, fine details can never be anticipated, but, with forethought, you can speculate on general patterns of action, so that you are not surprised or unprepared. The unlikely and the unexpected are a different matter; if they occur you will have to rely on spontaneous inspiration. Careful planning, however, can provide for almost every eventuality. It is largely a matter of being in the right place at the right time. The more unusual or unpredictable the occasion, the greater the need for investigation and planning in advance.

Pre-planning

The importance of the continuity rule — after every shot turn around — now becomes clear. It is obviously useful to consider before the event what you are likely to see when you turn around. What, for example, are you likely to see when you turn around from the shot of the couple coming out of the church? The answer is probably very little. The order of events in the

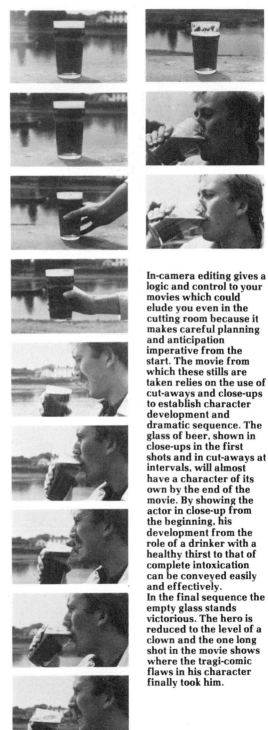

In-camera editing gives a logic and control to your movies which could elude you even in the cutting room because it makes careful planning and anticipation imperative from the start. The movie from which these stills are taken relies on the use of cut-aways and close-ups to establish character development and dramatic sequence. The glass of beer, shown in close-ups in the first shots and in cut-aways at intervals, will almost have a character of its own by the end of the movie. By showing the actor in close-up from the beginning, his development from the role of a drinker with a healthy thirst to that of complete intoxication can be conveyed easily and effectively.
In the final sequence the empty glass stands victorious. The hero is reduced to the level of a clown and the one long shot in the movie shows where the tragi-comic flaws in his character finally took him.

wedding service does not make the film maker's job easy. Normally the married couple are first to emerge, so that the smiling observers you would like to cut-away to, remain inside. So do you cut away to something else, or do you keep the camera rolling until the guests emerge? The latter course could be expensive, as it could be a considerable time before they appear.

So what do you do? How do you get those precious cut-aways? Remember that there are always some cut-aways available, but, to do the job properly, you should plan not only the camera work, but the action itself. It may be possible to persuade the couple to step out of the church and allow the others to follow. Arrange with the couple beforehand to walk out into the church grounds, so that you can film them and their guests before a photographer organises the formal pictures.

This is a good example of how thoughtful advance planning can give you a position of greater control. You could ask the bride and groom if they would mind greeting guests at first in the garden of the reception hall, rather than in some dimly-lit room. Or, after the couple's departure, you might persuade the guests to wave goodbye at the camera as you are driven off by a friend. But even if you are unable to stage manage the action, at least make sure that you manage your own job efficiently.

The basic rules

The first thing is always to make a plan on the following lines: 1 Investigate the occasion beforehand, and note how many locations are involved. You will need establishing shots for each. 2 Pre-plan an opening sequence and an end sequence, and if necessary shoot them on a separate occasion. 3 Find out who the principal characters are, what they will be doing and in what order. Only then can you be sure of being in the right place at the right time. 4 Look out for the action. Remember that the essence of film is movement. 5 Remember also that your audience want to view your pictures with ease, so stay in close and give them big, clear images. 6 Do not pan too quickly. 7 Vary the pace of your in-camera cuts by varying the duration of your shots. 8 Enable your audience to identify with the action by giving them plenty of information. There is more to establish than just the location. 9 Sustain the continuous experience. Do not allow jump cuts. Smooth out the lapses. Do not forget the cut-away. After every shot, turn around. 10 Think before you film. Always remember that your camera is your audience.

Types of film

The marvellous thing about film is the infinite variety of subject material from which you can choose; you can literally make a film about anything. In fact, the beginner is often so intimidated by such a wide choice that he or she does not know where to start.

You can just go out with your camera and take 'pot shots', but this is unlikely to be very productive unless your chief interest lies in experimental editing. It is much better to start with an objective. But where do you start? The first step is to consider the options and assemble them into recognizable categories.

Family films include weddings, christenings, holidays, birthday parties and so on. Inevitably

they feature friends and relatives, and usually they will be screened in front of the same interested parties. This does not diminish your responsibilities as a film maker; family films, in common with all others, must observe the dictates of film language. Viewers should not be expected to tolerate a shoddy structure just because they themselves are featured. Often, for instance, family films will be shot in familiar surroundings, so ensure that your own familiarity does not lead you to omit information that would be essential to an outsider. When making a family film, the most useful rule is to shoot it as though it were to be shown not to the family but to complete strangers. Do this, and your finished film, however ordinary the action,

This jumble of shots from a horse show demonstrates how essential it is to plan before starting to shoot. The sequence here makes no logical sense, because the movie maker has ignored the cardinal rules of film language.

may well be worthy of such a screening.

Documentary film covers all subjects of a factual, informative nature. Of course, the range is limitless. You can make a documentary about your work, your hobby — in fact, any subject in which you are particularly interested or are prepared to research. The greatest danger is that you will turn such a film into a lecture. Many documentaries are based on a continuous commentary with pictures that are sometimes not even strongly related, so try to avoid this. Commentary should be a supporting feature. If it is impossible to say nine-tenths of what you want to say in purely visual terms it is better to say something else.

Mood films are especially suited to the film maker with limited technical resources. No commentary is required — merely a programme of accompanying music and sound effects. But the chief element is the pictures. The objective is to show the audience a succession of images which have no intellectual content, but which establish a mood. These pictures might be of subjects with which the audience are familiar (a wood in springtime) or one with which they are not familiar (a dockyard, perhaps, or a steelworks). The objective could be either to show the subject in its authentic mood, or in whatever mood you choose to impose. You could give the wood a realistic, springtime mood of birdsong and buzzing bees; you could try to create the nocturnal atmosphere of 'A Midsummer Night's Dream'; or you could attempt to create the mood of an enchanted forest — sombre, foreboding and sinister. All three are possible in the same wood — it is up to you, and your camera.

In fictitious films, it is easy to get caught up in the complexities of acting, script preparation and so on. But this is not necessary. A perfectly good fiction film can be made using a couple of imaginative children, or just one reliable actor. The basic rule for the beginner is to keep it simple. Plots based on simple mishaps and misunderstandings are effective: for example, next door neighbours receiving each other's mail. Ghost stories are also an interesting subject, as the great thing about ghosts is that you do not have to show them. Providing you have an actor with a good, expressive face, he need not utter a single word and all you need then is a suitably eerie location. The rest is just mood-inspiring camerawork, with the use of many cut-aways to expand the time-scale and create suspense. Finally, remember that fictitious films invariably feature human beings,

Left **Developments like the Eumig Nautica allweather Super 8 camera bring underwater movies within the scope of any interested amateur. This particular camera is waterproof to a depth of 130 ft; it s use does away with the need for complex equipment** *right.* **Underwater movies make fascinating watching, especially if they include scenes like the one** *below.*

and humans are talking creatures. Steer clear of plots which depend on words and keep the film as visual as possible.

Experimental films allow you to do virtually anything, though, like any scientific experiment, there ought to be an objective. You can meddle with the camera's functions to produce special effects by running the camera at the wrong speed, for instance, or one frame at a time, backwards, or upside down. You can distort focus, exposure, shake the camera about or use masks and filters on the lens. You can present sequences in an illogical order, and intercut them with subjects that seem to be irrelevant. You can understate, overstate or contradict. You can cut the action at an infuriatingly wrong moment, and you can repeat the same action over and over again. You can jump cut. You can bend every rule in the book, or completely discard them.

But you do not have to make an experimental film in order to enjoy such freedom. Whatever kind of film you make, you will find that its success depends far more on your own good judgement than on text-book rules. Remember the fundamentals, of course, but never let them inhibit your own personal style. Your camera is your audience, but your film is essentially you.

Wildlife is another ideal movie theme. *Top* **A movie maker's hide, while** *below* **a cameraman conceals himself behind a tree.** *Bottom* **The results of patience — a close-up of a swan.**

Simple Sound

Sound is a constant companion in our everyday lives. Stop and listen at any time, anywhere, and you will hear a sound of some sort. It may only be the faint buzz of a bee or the low drone of distant traffic, but it is sure to be there. Generally we are not consciously aware of this background noise, yet for some deep psychological reason its presence acts as a reassurance that all is well. Take it away and we become aware of the silence, which acts subconsciously to make us tense and uncomfortable.

Music and amateur film
The amateur film maker can and should make use of music in both silent and sound films. Nowadays it is not needed to drown the clatter of the projector, as in the pioneer days of the cinema. Music is principally used to complement what is being seen on the screen and maximize its effectiveness. Careful editing, plus the addition of the right piece of music will provide extra impact and give an amateur production that final, professional touch.

Most amateurs will probably avoid anything too elaborate with their first films. But, even if the music is only to be used as a general background, it is important to realise that it can greatly influence the way that an audience sees a film.

Though music is one of the most important film accessories, silence can be just as effective. For instance, the tension leading up to some dramatic action can often be intensified by having absolutely no background sound. When the action starts, the contrast of sudden, loud music will considerably heighten the impact.

Choosing the music
Many film subjects readily suggest a particular type of musical accompaniment. For instance, Beethoven's Symphony No 6 'The Pastoral' is an obvious choice for a film about the countryside — as Walt Disney demonstrated in his 'Fantasia'. In general, however, well-known pieces of music should be avoided, because they can distract the audience's attention from the screen and, in extreme cases, they can overpower the visuals completely. Even if this does not happen, a well-known composition is likely to have been used many times before, so that originality and impact will be lacking. Rather than using a very popular piece of music,

Recapture the atmosphere of the first motion pictures and add to the mood and excitement of silent films by adding your own musical accompaniment.

it is preferable to search for something unknown in a similar style. It is the style that is most important, not the specific theme.

Even if the music is only to be used as a general background, it must still be in keeping with the overall tenor of the film. Light orchestral music is normally appropriate for most subjects. In general, anything with a strongly local character should be avoided, unless it relates specifically to the setting. French accordion music may be ideal for a film shot on holiday in Paris, but may not be particularly suitable for a picnic in the country.

Film makers are sometimes tempted to use vocal music as an accompaniment. This seldom works well because the audience tends to listen to the words rather than watch the visuals. If the words are directly related to the pictures, it may be possible to break this rule; but generally this only applies if the film has been planned and shot with the song specifically in mind.

Music on disc and tape

For the majority of film makers, however, professionally played and recorded music generally provides the best form of accompaniment. The easiest way to do this is simply to play a disc or tape along with the film as it is being shown. Discs are very convenient and the range of music they offer is almost limitless. However, since the timing of the music on record and that of the film sequence are

The functions of the ear.
The outer ear funnels
sound waves down a
canal to the ear drum.
These vibrations are
passed on to the middle
ear and three small
bones located there. The
stirrup bone transmits
them to the inner ear
through a fine
membrane called the
oval window. This
membrane is much
smaller than the ear
drum and has the effect
of magnifying the
vibrations. They are
then received by the
cochlea, which turns
them into signals to be
passed to the brain.

The human ear is an
extremely sensitive
instrument, able to
attune itself to sounds
ranging from the buzzing
of a bee *left* to a pop
group in performance
far right. Microphones,
however, are not as
discriminating, so, when
recording any sort of
sound, it is important to
choose the right mike for
the job. The trouble is
well worth the effort, as
the presence of the right
type of sound enhances
the simplest silent film.

unlikely to correspond, some planning and experimentation will be necessary in order to obtain the best results.

The first step is to run the film through and note the timing and mood of each sequence. Working from this basis, a selection of suitable music can then be made. Next, each piece must be played with the appropriate film sequence to see if music and visuals are compatible; the music must always run for at least as long as the sequence. If everything seems satisfactory, the start of the music can be marked on the record with a white chinagraph pencil. This will not damage the disc if it is used carefully, and it can be removed later with a soft cloth.

When all the music has been chosen, timed and marked, the next step is to compile a cue-sheet indicating where the musical changes are to take place. For the sake of convenience and a smooth-running performance, it is best to keep these changes to a minimum. The cue sheet normally consists of a brief description of the first and last scene in the sequence, the approximate running time, and the title of the music.

The show can now commence. Dim the lights, lower the pick-up arm and start the projector. As the title appears on the screen fade-up the music. When the end of the first sequence approaches, gradually fade down the music and quickly change the records. The chinagraph mark shows where the new piece of music starts and, as soon as the pick-up touches the grooves of the record, the sound can be faded-up. Obviously this needs a little practice, but after only a few showings the performance will become more polished; soon only an occasional reference to the cue-sheet will be necessary.

Pre-recorded music on commercially produced tapes can be used in much the same way as discs. Instead of making a start mark, each cassette is wound to the correct place before the show. The music change then becomes a very quick operation, consisting of a fade-down, ejecting the old cassette, inserting the replacement, and fade-up. However, each cassette can only be used once during the film, as it is almost impossible to locate a second piece of music unless a second player is used.

Re-recording a sound track
Apart from the direct use of records or cassettes as described above, the most obvious way to obtain a second track is to use a domestic machine to re-record music from commercial discs and tapes, or even TV presentations. However, this practice is, in fact, illegal. It is an

Music should always be chosen to complement the mood of the subject. The traffic *above left* obviously calls for loud music to indicate bustle and rush; the canal scene *above right* needs soft music to emphasize its tranquility.

infringement of copyright legislation to re-record such material, even if it is intended only for home showing.

Alternatively, there are specially-produced mood music discs on the market. These have the advantage of containing music specifically designed for film accompaniment, as well as offering a variety of sound effects. Their principal disadvantage is that the choice is rather restricted.

Whatever the type of music used, it must be remembered that, although it can greatly enhance a film, the visuals are of paramount importance. Therefore the film maker must always ensure that the music is not too obtrusive, and that its volume is set at an acceptable level.

Adding a commentary

Showing a film almost inevitably provokes considerable question and comment from the audience. This is particularly the case if members of the audience are featured in the film, as is quite likely with home movies of family and friends. Obviously they want to elaborate on the action and talk about what is being shown, both during and after the show. Pictures alone are not always sufficiently self-explanatory; there may be a need for more information than they can convey. The best way to put across essential facts and to add further detail is to add a commentary.

Spoken commentary

The most simple form of commentary is a spoken one, delivered from a written script while the film is being shown. The basic purpose is to give the audience a better understanding of the visuals; but a commentary should never explain things that are already obvious to the audience. It is a common error to produce a commentary that merely describes the action on the screen, rather than providing extra information. For example, a typical line from a family film commentary might be: 'Here's Jenny riding her tricycle'. In fact, everyone in the audience will know that it is Jenny, and the fact that she is riding a tricycle is patently obvious. Much more informative would be a line like: 'Grandma gave Jenny a new tricycle for her fourth birthday.' This contains the additional details that the little girl is four years old, that the tricycle is new, and that it was a present from her grandmother.

Writing rules

Commentary writing can be made much easier

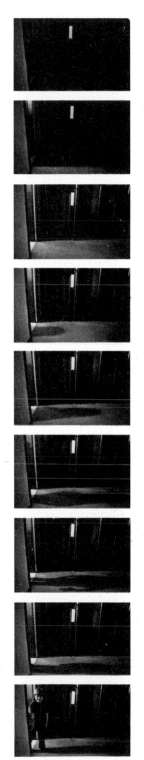

Left **The build-up of tension in these shots would be considerably increased by a suitably sinister accompaniment. Either use a specially-produced effects tape or disc — there are many of these on the market — or choose a piece of music yourself. Remember that the music must be matched as closely as possible to the film; here, it reaches a crashing final chord as the door swings open, with the appearance of the little girl as a deliberate anti-climax. Such synchronization calls for considerable advance planning. The preparation of a detailed cue sheet is essential, while the start of a piece of music must be carefully marked. On records, this is best done with white chinagraph pencil; on tapes and cassettes, the projectionist must rely on the accuracy of the tape counter.**

and more effective by following a set of simple rules. Basically, if the action is self-explanatory, a detailed commentary is not required. Nevertheless, some things may still need explaining. Questions such as who the characters are, where the action is taking place and what the time is, are all fundamental points to consider before deciding on whether a particular sequence needs a commentary. In more complex films the audience may require further information, perhaps of a specialized or technical nature. Possibly some off-screen action may have to be described. But it is important not to go too far and give more information than the audience can absorb.

The film maker should always ask whether the audience really needs to know more about what they are seeing. If they do not, then a commentary is not required. A good commentary can improve a poor film, but a badly-written one can spoil even the best production. The most successful commentaries are the result of careful planning and preparation. This can be a time-consuming process, but the results are well worth the effort.

Before attempting to plan the commentary, the film maker should view the film several times and make a detailed list of the various sequences. The running-time of each one should be recorded and a note made of anything that might be relevant to the commentary. It is sometimes easier to use a viewer to do this, especially if the viewer incorporates a frame counter. This means that sequence lengths and hence running times can be determined. In this case it is important to know the running speed of the projector to avoid miscalculations and consequent lack of synchronization.

Level of information

The next stage is to examine the list of sequences in the light of the basic rules described earlier and try to decide what information the audience needs to know regarding each one. For example, suppose that a commentary is being prepared for a short film about the Tower of London, the White House, or any similar historical and factual subject. There is no question that such a film benefits considerably from a good commentary. The whole story cannot be conveyed by the film alone, so the audience's total appreciation will be enhanced by the additional information. In fact the main problem is likely to be the sheer quantity of information available. Therefore the

These four scenes would all benefit from added sound. In the case of the harvesting picture, either music or a commentary could be used. Crossing the river needs a suitably comic accompanying piece, while the best piece of music for the band would be an on-the-spot recording of the actual composition it is playing.

Live sound is easily captured on a portable cassette recorder.

film maker must be very selective in composing the script and also ensure that the various aspects of the subject are given an equally balanced treatment in the commentary.

Although the visual images for such a subject may be relatively simple, the information in the commentary is likely to be specialized and must be factually correct; someone in the audience is quite likely to spot any errors. It is a mistake to try to cover a lack of actual information by making vague statements: to say 'The White Tower was built hundreds of years ago' actually tells the audience nothing new. Viewers will be far more interested and impressed to hear that the tower was built in the eleventh century by William the Conqueror. Such detail makes a commentary sound much more authoritative.

By analysing the opening sequences of the proposed Tower of London film we can consider the type of information required for the commentary. The film could open as follows: Picture **1** Title 'The Tower of London' (7 seconds); **2** Long shot of Tower from across the river (8 seconds); **3** Entrance to Tower with visitors, several medium and close-up shots, two shots of Japanese tourists, one group of schoolchildren (32 seconds); **4** Long shot of two Beefeaters, one close-up (12 seconds); **5** Several shots of the White Tower from various angles (62 seconds).

Titles obviously need no commentary. Picture 2, the long shot of the Tower, is too short to allow for more than a brief comment. However, the next sequence can include a great deal of information — a lot can be conveyed in 32 seconds. The facts could be of a non-historical nature, in keeping with the visuals. For instance, the annual number of visitors would be of interest, and attention could be drawn to the Tower's tourist appeal. The shot of the schoolchildren might lead to a comment on the educational value of such a visit. The Beefeater section is again too short for much detail commentary but it makes a useful link between the twentieth century action and the following sequence, in which the historical facts relating to the White Tower can be examined at length.

Style and composition

A commentary should normally take only about two-thirds of the total running time of the film; this rule also applies within individual sequences. It is therefore necessary to know the speaking rate of the commentator in order to get the correct length. This can be easily established by noting the time it takes to read aloud a passage of known length. The standard rate is about two-and-a-half to three words per second.

When deciding on the style and content of a commentary, the film maker should take into account the type of audience likely to see the film. An audience interested in history would want a plain commentary full of factual information about the Tower. However, by introducing some humorous element into the composition — perhaps about Henry VIII and his wives — the same film can be given a much more general appeal.

Many home movies involve the film maker's immediate circle; similarly, the audience is likely to include close friends and relatives. If this is the case, the commentary could then be simply an account of a family outing to the Tower, needing few, if any, historical facts. In this case humor could be even more important, and various amusing incidents could be included in the commentary. An alternative approach in a family film might be to produce the commentary from the point of view of one of the participants — for example, a child telling the story of his visit to the Tower. This will prove more difficult and challenging to write, but the results are often highly original.

In the first draft, the most important thing is to write down all that needs to be said about each sequence, without worrying too much about the time involved. When all the information has been included the draft can be adapted to the required length. Each section will probably need to be re-written several times before it sounds natural when read aloud. Try to aim for a natural speech flow, avoiding abrupt changes in pace or subject within a section. When everything seems satisfactory, it is a good idea to put the commentary to one side for a few days and then give it another reading, as the lapse of time may well lead to seeing it in a new light and suggest it needs further alteration. Although the writing process can be very lengthy, involving many re-writes, the results, in terms of a professional finish, will be highly satisfactory.

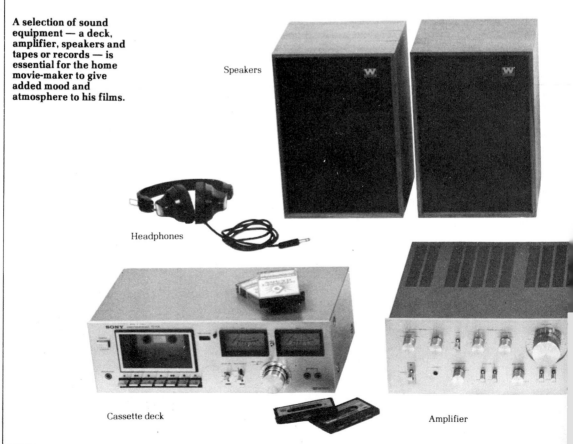

A selection of sound equipment — a deck, amplifier, speakers and tapes or records — is essential for the home movie-maker to give added mood and atmosphere to his films.

Speakers

Headphones

Cassette deck

Amplifier

A chinagraph pencil can be used to mark the section of music chosen for a sequence, without harming the record.

The commentary should be either typed or written in block capitals with double spacing between the lines. Each section should be separated from the others, so that it is clear and easy to read. Next to each section a note should be made of when to read it. These picture cues need only be very brief, but they are important in ensuring that each part of the spoken commentary coincides with the appropriate visuals.

Recorded commentary

Speaking the commentary each time the film is shown can become something of a chore, while any mistakes may well detract from the effectiveness of the presentation. A much more satisfactory way of combining film and commentary is by using a cassette recorder. These machines are cheap, easy to use, and their sound quality is quite adequate for speech. The commentary is recorded with a pause of a few seconds between each section, so that when the film is shown the recorder can be stopped

Reel to reel tape deck

Tuner

Record deck

and started according to the picture cues.

Most recorders now have remote control systems. These enable the film maker to sit in the audience and operate changes in the commentary by a flick of a switch, according to the cue sheet. Eventually the starting and stopping points will become so familiar that this sheet will no longer be needed.

A new cassette or tape should be used for each commentary. It is advisable to wind off the leader material before beginning the recording to ensure the tape always starts from the same place. This can be done by inserting a pencil into the take-up spindle of the cassette, and winding on until the actual tape appears. Even the shortest running cassettes available are quite adequate for most short films; these have an average total length of under four minutes.

Cassettes are normally fitted with a device to prevent accidental erasure; once the recording has been made it is wise to activate this by breaking the plastic keying tag. Another sensible precaution is to label each cassette so that it can be found easily and quickly.

A reel-to-reel tape recorder with the ability to record two tracks or more of sound on one tape is the most useful machine for the home movie maker.

Many cassettes, such as the one pictured *left*, are made with plastic pegs which can be pulled out to prevent the tape being accidently wiped clean.

Apart from records or cassettes the easiest, if illegal, way to make a sound track is to record from commercial records or tapes or from the radio or television. Remember the re-recording of such material is an infringement of the copyright even if it is only for home use.

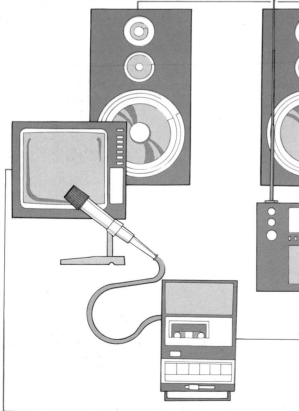

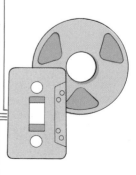

Reel-to-reel recording

An even more satisfactory way to record commentary is to use a reel-to-reel tape recorder. Although these tend to be more expensive than cassette machines, they are more versatile and particularly useful for more advanced and complex soundtracks. The basic requirement for this method is a four-track machine that allows two tracks to be played back together; a stereo recorder offers even more possibilities. Usually two running speeds are provided, of $3\frac{3}{4}$ in and $7\frac{1}{2}$ in per second. Some equipment also works at speeds of 15in or $1\frac{7}{8}$ in per second, but the standard $3\frac{3}{4}$ in is adequate.

A reel-to-reel recorder can be used in exactly the same way as a cassette machine, with the film maker physically controlling the tape with the pause control throughout the film. However, most modern equipment can also work automatically. In this case the tape recorder and projector are linked together, a system of electronic pulses ensuring that they are precisely synchronized.

Making a pilot track

Before recording the actual commentary, it is usual to record a 'pilot' sound track. This enables the final sound track to be produced with greater flexibility and also eliminates projector noise from the recording.

The first thing to do is to run the projector and tape recorder for several minutes so that they can warm up and the speeds become stabilized. The next step is to make synchronization marks on both film and tape. This is done by scratching a clear frame on the leader of the film, and drawing a white cross on the tape with a chinagraph pencil. The tape is threaded on to the recorder so that the synchronization mark is opposite a fixed point. The start and pause controls are depressed, the pause control being released as soon as the clear sync frame appears on the screen. This positioning procedure is repeated each time the film is shown.

It is possible to record the commentary directly by simply reading it from the written script in accordance with the picture cues. This means that it will be correctly spaced out on the tape, but, in general, the results are not very satisfactory. There will inevitably be some projector noise; it is also likely that the commentator will make mistakes in delivery, which may well spoil the end result.

An alternative way of producing the pilot track is to record a spontaneous verbal description of the film as it is being projected. With this method it is also possible to interject cues for changes in the music as well as the commentary. In this case a typical pilot track for a film on the Tower of London might run as follows: 'Now, title appears. Now long shot of Tower across river. Now, visitors entering Tower. First piece of music over all this. Now party of schoolchildren. Now, Beefeaters, change the music. Now, White Tower sequence...'.

Whichever method is used to produce the pilot track, the system of starting with the sync marks must be followed. When the track has been recorded, it should be played back with the film to check that reasonable synchronization is maintained. The tape should be re-wound to the first sync mark and the frame counter set at zero. The pilot track should be listened to carefully and the points at which sections begin and end noted against the counter number. Music changes can be noted in the same way.

The commentary can now be recorded on a separate track, in accordance with the counter number cues. After making one final check on the synchronization, the music can be recorded over the pilot track.

If a stereo recorder is used, the commentary can be recorded in a slightly different way. First, a pilot track is made as described above. The tape position counter is used to compile a list of cue points, but these are needed only as a rough guide. With stereo equipment, headphones are used to listen to the pilot track and locate exactly where commentary is required. This is then recorded simultaneously on the other track of the tape.

These methods of producing a recorded commentary are not always entirely successful — but, even so, the pilot track method is still the most convenient way of making a sound track. The most common problem is synchronization. If the tape recorder and projector do not run quite 'in step' — or at least within an acceptable margin of tolerance — some sort of synchronizing device will be needed. Difficulties may also arise with tape position counters, since these are not always accurate or consistent. However, just as when recording a musical accompaniment, cue points indicating the start of commentary passages can be marked on the tape with a chinagraph pencil or numbered adhesive tags. This method gives a high degree of accuracy and it can be used in conjunction with a tape counter.

Recording the commentary

It is pointless spending time and effort on writing a commentary if the final results are unintelligible due to poor recording.

Remember that the magnetic properties of the various brands of tape on the market differ, so specific ones may require a particular recorder to produce optimum results. Most recording equipment comes with a list of recommended tapes and it is always advisable to use these. Avoid using very thin tape; anything thinner than long play can easily be damaged. It is a good idea to use a fresh tape for each new sound track, but this is obviously expensive. The usual practice is therefore to re-use tapes, but to make sure they are wiped completely clean before use. This will eliminate the possibility of unwanted sounds from old recordings intruding into the new soundtrack.

A good quality microphone should always be used for recording commentary. Crystal mikes, of the sort often supplied with recorders, are not really suitable. It is better to use a moving-coil, or electro-condenser type, microphone. Within this classification, there are two basic kinds — omnidirectional and cardioid. Omnidirectional microphones pick up sound from all directions while cardioids discriminate in favour of sound coming from the front; this makes the latter the most suitable microphone for recording a commentary. Whichever type is used, however, it is important that the microphone is electrically compatible with the recorder.

The microphone should never be held in the hand during recording as this will invariably lead to bumps and crackles on the soundtrack. A support of some kind is essential; the most convenient is a table-top stand. It is a wise precaution to fix both stand and cable in position with adhesive tape, to prevent the microphone being accidentally disturbed during recording. Normally the commentator should sit about 30cm away.

Unwanted noises can be a problem during recording sessions, but most of them can be prevented. The rustle of paper from the script or cue sheet, for instance, can be eliminated by sticking each sheet to a piece of cardboard. This should be planned so that there is no need to change cards during a passage of speech. Creaking chairs, knocks against the microphone table, or loudly ticking clocks are all common sources of unwanted sounds which can be easily avoided with care. A further

Below left **Some film sequences need no commentary at all. A description of the girl feeding the ducks would be completely** *superfluous. Below right,* **however, a commentary is obviously needed to establish the background to what is being shown.**

problem may be mechanical noise from the tape recorder itself. This can be helped by positioning the machine as far as possible from the microphone.

It is also necessary to choose the room selected for use as a studio carefully. Rooms with a very reverberant acoustic are totally unsuitable; the best rooms for recording purposes are those with plenty of soft, sound-absorbent furnishings.

Before actually beginning to record the commentary, a series of tests should be made to determine the setting of the level control and to assess the overall sound quality. If the needle on the recording level meter is allowed to reach the overload position the sound will be distorted. When delivering the commentary, the speaker should always try to maintain a constant level of sound. Some people tend to start in a loud voice and gradually get quieter. Test recordings also provide a good opportunity to rehearse the commentary and practise any phrases which might be difficult to pronounce.

Recording procedure

The recording procedure is a straightforward one. Select the track opposite the one used for the pilot track recording. Align the sync mark on the start position and adjust the counter to zero. Switch the machine to record, but first turn the level control to minimum. Now run the tape until the first cue point is reached. At this point the level control should be quickly turned up to the predetermined setting and the commentary delivered. At the end of each section of commentary the level control should be returned to zero, so that there is no danger of accidentally recording sound between the periods of speech.

If music is to be added to the tape, it must be recorded over the pilot track. However, it is not advisable to use a microphone for this. A much higher quality of sound will be produced if the tape recorder is linked directly with the record or cassette player. This can be done with most equipment, but it is important that the machines are electrically compatible, and also that the correct input and output sockets are connected. If, for example, the extension loudspeaker socket on the cassette player is linked to the microphone socket of the tape recorder, the system may be grossly overloaded and the resultant sound will be very badly distorted.

The same system of cues can be used for both commentary and music. However, all the

Left **Films can be made or marred by the level of the spoken commentary. A good commentary is clear, crisp and to the point. It also contains additional factual information to back-up the pictorial content of the film. It should never repeat what is obvious from the screen. An example of good and bad commentary is given below.**

Good *The raw material for any potter is clay; this potter is using China Clay from Cornwall. Moulding the material on the wheel takes place in stages. The clay is kept constantly moist, while the task of shaping it is made easier by varying the wheel's revolution speed.*

Bad *Here we see a potter at work. He places the clay on the wheel and slowly it builds up to form a vase.*

music changes should be planned to occur during a section of speech. This will make them less noticeable so that they blend in better with the commentary and visuals as a result. Never make direct cuts in the music — always fade in and out by using the recording level control. The former will break audience concentration.

With most recorders it is possible to link the two tracks during playback to produce a composite sound. However, unless a stereo machine is used, the volume levels of the tracks cannot be independently adjusted. It is therefore important not to record the music at such a high level that it drowns the commentary. At the recording stage it is possible to fade down the music as each section of speech comes along. This, however, relies on the cueing system being very accurate, and it is usually much better to keep the music at a constantly low level throughout. The best precaution is to make a series of test recordings to establish the right balance between the two tracks. On the whole, it is better to err on the side of under-recording the music. An inaudible commentary, or one drowned by the music track, is worse than no commentary.

Sound and the projector
Modern sound projectors offer a wide range of devices to enable the film maker to produce highly complex sound tracks. However, it is worth remembering that no equipment can improve the sound if the quality of the original input is poor.

Automatic sound level control is now a very common feature of movie recording equipment. Its function is to prevent overloading and maintain the optimum recording level. The system's circuits will automatically reduce a high level signal, or alternatively amplify a signal that is too low. However, though they are perfectly satisfactory, they are not always sophisticated enough to cope with widely-varying signal levels.

A further problem is that of over-recording the first instant of a piece of music or speech. However, most projectors include a manual over-ride and a recording level meter; if these are used correctly, most of the problems associated with automatic circuits can be eliminated.

During the recording process it is useful to be able to monitor the sound signal by means of an earpiece or headphones. Almost all projectors include this feature; it enables the film maker to spot faults in the signal and rectify

them. Monitoring is particularly important with projectors which allow two different sound sources to be mixed together. Obviously the balance between the two can only be judged by listening to the 'mix'.

Superimposition is a feature now found in even the most inexpensive projectors. This allows a new sound to be superimposed over an existing recording without erasing it; it often also permits the balance between the two to be adjusted. It is even possible to gradually blend the new sound in with the old recording until the latter has faded away. This process of variable erasure allows very polished soundtracks to be produced.

With dual track recording, the balance track on the film is used to record a second channel of sound. Many projectors provide full stereophonic sound, but dual-sound techniques are also advantageous for the production of mono

Before starting to make the sound track for your film it is vital to list and time each sequence of shots to ensure that the commentary is the correct length and about the actual scene on screen at the time.

soundtracks. The two channels can be used and paralleled as with a reel-to-reel tape recorder. With dual track, it is also possible to transfer sound from one track to another, while mixing in a further sound. In this way complex soundtracks can be compiled, using the minimum of external equipment. These facilities are particularly useful if the main stripe has been recorded in a sound camera. With some more expensive projectors it is even possible to pre-programme effects to occur at precisely the right point in the film.

Most of these elaborate features, however, are not essential for the production of a basic soundtrack. If the track has previously been compiled on a tape recorder, a simple projector may be all that is needed, especially if the correct balance between music and speech has already been achieved on the tape. For instance, a music and commentary track can be recorded from tape simply by connecting the input and output sockets in the projector and recorder respectively. The recording level can either be adjusted automatically or operated manually by referring to the level meter.

A more polished result can be obtained from the same tape by transferring the music track first. Both film and tape are then re-wound.

Stills from a film about the Tower of London, made by an American visitor, show the principles of extended commentary. The first sequence — the title of the film — speaks for itself, so no commentary is needed.

The first establishing shots for location and subject — a long shot across the River Thames, gradually revealing the Tower.

Standing on the banks of the River Thames in London, the Tower of London is one of Britain's most celebrated monuments. In its 900-year history, it has been fortress, palace and prison.

A crowd of tourists enter the Tower. This establishes its attraction as a visiting place.

Every year many thousands of tourists visit the Tower. People come from all over the world to view its treasures; the most famous of these are the Crown Jewels.

The tourists progress into the Tower. The film maker has inserted a cut-away of a particular couple to add contrast, strengthen the point of the Tower as a tourist attraction and to disguise what would otherwise be a jump cut to a different view.

The entrance to the Tower today is through the Middle Tower and the Byward Tower. The outer walls were built by the 16th century monarch, Henry VIII. Many of his enemies, however, entered the Tower by another route — the infamous Traitor's Gate.

The film maker has now singled out an individual group to focus on. The aim here was to depict individual reactions to the Tower. This leads speedily on to the next shot, so only a short introductory commentary is necessary.

People of all ages find something to marvel at in the Tower's history.

The film now starts to explore the possibilities of the people best associated with the Tower — the Beefeaters.

The Tower's guards — the Beefeaters — are a living link with the past. Their proper title is Yeoman Warder; their picturesque costume dates back to Tudor times. The Beefeaters were originally a military force; now they are under the command of the Tower's resident governor, spending much of their time acting as guides.

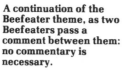

A continuation of the Beefeater theme, as two Beefeaters pass a comment between them: no commentary is necessary.

The White Tower — the centrepiece of this part of the film — is introduced by an establishing shot. This again could be a cutaway, if desired.

The oldest part of the Tower of London is the White Tower, built during the reign of William the Conqueror. Work started on its forbidding walls in 1078 under the direction of a bishop — Gundulf of Rochester. In Norman times, churchmen were also men of war.

A change of angle. The main subject is still the White Tower, but a parallel theme is now introduced. This is the story of the Tower's ravens.

The Tower's ravens have almost as prominent a role in history as the building itself. Legend has it that, without their presence, disaster will befall.

The subject is the White Tower itself again. The commentary picks up the original theme.

Subsequent building made the White Tower the nucleus of a strong defensive system. The Tower itself is 27m (90ft) high. It houses armouries and dungeons; despite popular belief, the latter are not below water level.

The White Tower story continues. The tourists with their Beefeater guide are introduced again, but the camera quickly pans away from them to the object of interest. The commentary here takes up the point the guide is making.

Many notable prisoners have entered the Tower — the majority never to leave it alive. Among them were Henry VI, murdered there in 1471, the two nephews of Richard III — the 'Princes in the Tower' — and two of Henry VIII's eight wives, Anne Boleyn and Catherine Howard.

A final sequence of the White Tower, culminating with the tourists leaving the building. The decision whether or not to have a commentary is optional, as this could either be the end of the film or the build-up to the next sequence on a new subject.

The commentary can now be transferred using the superimposition control to fade out the music and fade in the speech according to the picture cues. The best settings for the controls can be established by carrying out a series of test recordings.

Sound on sound

It is also possible to compile a commentary and music soundtrack without a tape recorder. First, music from a disc or cassette is recorded on to stripe. At each music change, the recording is faded out by turning down the superimposition control to zero. It is left at this setting while the projector is run in reverse for a few seconds. Then the disc should be changed and the projector run forward again; check, however, that it is still in the recording mode. The new piece of music can then be faded in by operating the superimposition control. Ideally, the two pieces of music should blend together smoothly on replay; in practice, though, it is usually best to note exactly where each change is required in order to avoid unintentional gaps in the soundtrack. The superimposition control should again be used to add the commentary. If it is absolutely necessary to record speech directly on to stripe, the microphone should be placed as far as possible from the projector. It is important to rehearse the commentary to

perfection before attempting to record in this way, since a mistake may mean that the music will also have to be re-recorded.

As well as recording music and commentary, sound-on-sound offers plenty of scope for adding sound effects. The order in which the various recordings are done is important; each successive recording slightly erases the one on which it is laid. In particular the higher frequency sounds, such as the treble notes in music, will be slightly 'dulled'. The most important sounds must therefore be recorded last.

For instance, if the commentary is considered to be the most important part of the soundtrack, the order would be music and then effects, with the commentary coming last. This is about the maximum number of recordings that can be superimposed satisfactorily; after more than this, the first sounds tend to become inaudible.

Most projectors include a built-in loudspeaker. This is convenient and useful for checking or previewing sound films. However, internal speakers are too small to get the best out of a sound track; a larger specially designed ciné speaker will give much better results. An extension loud-speaker has the additional advantage that it can be placed near the screen, so that the sound will be associated closely with the pictures.

Script, Direction, Production

Movie reality is, by definition, an illusion. When the audience gives itself up to the film maker's world, it becomes the victim of a deception. In any form, film manipulates everyday experiences in order to reproduce them; the skill of the film maker is measured in relation to the audience's awareness of how far it is being deceived.

In a fiction film, say, the film maker starts from scratch; he must capture the imagination of the audience so that he can fill it with his own images. In a documentary film, on the other hand, the film maker is concerned with removing the audience's awareness of the screen between it and the world being shown.

Types of subject

There are two groups of film subject. Into the first, fall themes which have what is termed an inherent 'filmic' quality; the second group contains subjects which demand all the film maker's skill to make them work once they reach the screen. Filmic subjects usually come as a package. They offer a subject that performs for the camera without the need for any control by the film maker. They also have an inbuilt structure or sequence of events. This means that the cameraman has only to be in the right place at the right time for the end product to have the customary beginning, middle and end.

A stockcar or motorcycle race is a typical example of a ready-structured subject. This could provide the material either for a documentary or the background for a fiction film. The meeting begins, the races progress and, at the end, there is a winner. This natural structure could be extended by showing how an individual contestant prepares for the meeting and this central character could be studied during the event.

The natural structure of an artist painting a

Movie-making is both an art and a science. The skills and complexities have to be practised, and mastered but imagination and ideas are just as important.

portrait could provide a frame within which to study the imaginative processes involved. The film maker allows the development of the portrait to give his film a direction, but is then free to broaden out from it. The result could be a filmic study of the artist's imagination at work.

Subjects without an internal structure are obviously much more difficult to bring to the screen. Take, for example, a short story about a man dying in hospital. He is unconscious most of the time and the story concerns his fears and dreams as death approaches. It is an excellent short story, but the image is not a particularly filmic one. To make it work visually, a more dramatic situation would be needed; the death bed could be replaced with a train crash, say, in which the central character is trapped. This treatment would not only work better on screen; it would also provide an extra element of suspense in the possibility of the hero being rescued. The setting has been changed, but the theme — the important ingredient — has been transferred intact to the screen.

Ideas
All movies stem from an idea and, to a large extent, the film maker's belief in the end product. Except in rare cases, inspiration should not be sought in film or photographic techniques.

Natural filmic subjects have an inbuilt story line and a fair amount of action. Topics as diverse as a visit to a traction museum or a child's birthday party *above* make good movie subjects for these reasons. *Left* A child at play can also provide a natural theme for a film sequence, though, in this case, some direction may be needed.

In theory, a spinning roundabout *left* should provide a splendid film sequence; in practice, however, the technical problem of synchronizing panning speed with the motion of the roundabout is hard to overcome. The two landscapes *right* and *below* illustrate another important point. Though both would be extremely attractive still photographs, they lack the action necessary to make a good film theme.

Movies made deliberately to exploit a piece of equipment or a particular technique are interesting to watch only until the novelty wears off.

It is a good idea to keep an ideas file. A film idea can sometimes fizzle out once it suffers the discipline of being expanded on paper. Parts of the rejected story, however, could well fill a space in a subsequent script.

Telling a story

All films tell a story and, whatever the type of film involved, the story is built up in much the same way. First of all, the characters are introduced to the audience. Next, we learn that the central figures have an objective. It could be marriage or a bank robbery; digging the garden or exposing a government scandal. Whatever it is, the characters in the story must have a clear objective and this must be clearly explained to the audience.

What the author does next is to introduce a few obstacles to hinder the progress of the characters to their objective. Now the story is concerned not only with what is doing to happen, but how. This leads to part four of the story formula — the hero's path to triumph.

The basic story formula is therefore: 1 Get to know the characters. 2 Introduce the objective. 3 Introduce the obstacles. 4 Show how these are overcome. It is possible to amalgamate the second and third stages by making the objective simply the overcoming of the obstacle — a man struggling to escape from a burning building, say.

The usual treatment of the four stages is to have them happen as simultaneous threads within the story. The formula can also be extended by introducing new characters, objectives, obstacles and solutions as sub-plots to the main theme.

This scheme of story telling is the basis of all good film work. Take, for example, a sporting documentary. The subject is one with a natural structure — the attempt of an athletics team to win an important competition. The film maker begins by introducing the members of the team to the audience. They talk about themselves and their sport; from the discussion, the audience learns that they are about to take part in a national final. Their objective is to win and represent their country in world events. There is only one rival and they train especially to overcome this obstacle. Half the screen time of the documentary is taken up by the actual competition, but the lead-up to it follows the basic formula to build a good story.

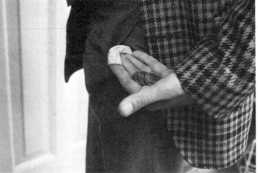

Whatever kind of film you are making, the storyline can be built up in much the same way. First of all there should be some establishing shots of the characters to introduce them to the audience and establish the necessary background details. Secondly, the central characters should have an objective which must be clearly explained. Thirdly, some obstacles are introduced to hinder the characters' progress.

Fourthly, the climax is reached and resolved. In this simple sequence, the hero returns home, only to be confronted by the problem of a locked front door. Though the search for the key proves fruitless, the solution is eventually found — climbing through the window. The story obviously has possibilities for more complex development.

Below and right **These shots of an unhappy housewife illustrate how character can be expanded without the use of dialogue. The first shot shows her arguing on the telephone with her husband; in the second she is washing-up, but obviously in a distressed state; in the third she is shown glaring at a plate; in the fourth, there is a close-up of her fingers letting go of the plate; and in the fifth the plate has crashed to the floor as an expression of her hatred and unhappiness.**

Developing the people

Because film is a visual medium, it is very tempting to allow the story to leap straight from the opening titles into the middle of the plot. Screen people are often seen moving from place to place and doing things to get the plot moving, but without being given the time to build up any character. In other words, they are little more than animated props. Nothing is more fatal, as the audience may well be completely baffled and so lose interest in what is going on on screen.

It is possible to expand character through dialogue — a telephone call is often used — but this wastes the important visual quality of film. Take the situation of a wife who is unhappy with her life at home. To make this point, she could be shown having the standard telephone conversation with a friend. Alternatively, she could simply tell her husband (and the audience) how she feels. More visually, she could be seen facing a pile of greasy washing-up. She picks up a plate, stares at it with hatred and slowly lets it crash to the floor.

Often, however, more subtle points of characterisation need dialogue to make them clear to the audience. An exclusively visual development of difficult character points can completely obscure what the character is supposed to be feeling.

Making your own movie

It may seem a big jump from using your camera

for general family records to making a film with actors and story. The only difference between a carefully-made holiday film and a story film, however, is one of organization. In addition, what appear on the surface to be difficulties are also the main source of enjoyment. It is surprising how quickly you can learn about photography, sound recording, set building, make-up, special effects — in fact, all the aspects of film production — when they crop up in the very practical context of shooting a film.

The following sections are based on the true story of an amateur film production. The important thing to stress straight from the start is that the approaches and techniques demonstrated here could be used for any movie — not just this particular one.

How did you think of that?

In most cases, the actual origins of a story are hard to pin down. You may know where you were when the initial thought struck you, but knowing how it was formed — how all the pieces making up the story came together — is a different matter. In this instance, the story for the film came out of a meeting at a movie club, whose

An ideas' file culled from newspapers, magazines, books, other films or everyday situations, is an invaluable aid for creative film making. It is often difficult to expand an initial concept into a film and it can be time-saving and useful to see if it will first work on paper.

members had decided to enter a competition on the set theme of 'Take A Pair Of Sparkling Eyes'.

The way the problem was first approached was to think of as many situations as possible in which the subjects of the theme could occur. The most popular suggestion was the eyes of a warder in a prison as seen through the spyhole of a cell door. The idea which seemed to appeal the most involved a study of a prisoner's environment, its routine and the fact that escape was an unobtainable dream. The main thread of the plot was to be the dream of escape and the importance of this dream in the prisoner's daily life.

To keep the story simple, it was decided to have the prisoner alone and not to attempt to explain why he was there. For dramatic purposes, only the eyes of the warder were to be seen — and so it was as early as this that a part of the set was designed. As the eyes were the sole visible feature of the warder, it seemed more effective to show them both; the traditional cell spyhole was thus discarded in favor of a split. To emphasize the prisoner's isolation, it was decided that the door to the cell should never be seen open; food and water should be passed through a shutter at the bottom of the door.

This oppressive environment obviously shaped how the prisoner would be made to react. The eyes at the spyhole would have an intimidating character; the prisoner would react with fear whenever they appeared and they would also dictate his routine.

Having established this skeleton, the next step was to decide what would happen to the central character. The first stage was to establish in the audience's mind what circumstances the prisoner was living in. It would be easy to show the grey-walled cell, the prisoner's reaction to the steely eyes when they appeared at the spyhole and the drab food and living conditions. But the important fact that these were all part of a depressing routine would be harder to establish without resorting to a long-winded visual sequence, and it was decided to avoid this. The only alternatives seemed to be thought speech or the prisoner talking out loud to himself.

The second stage in the story was to show the prisoner's reaction to the routine and to introduce the theme of escape. The point being emphasized here was that it was the possibility of escape, however remote, which kept the prisoner sane, together with the thought that, if he attempted to do so and failed, he would have nothing left to hope for. This again posed the problem of how the prisoner was going to discuss the dilemma.

After establishing this, the prisoner would finally attempt an escape. This would involve finding some form of tool to loosen the bars and concealing what was going on from the warder. This end of the story was to be that the escape would fail and the prisoner — now without hope — would slip into insanity.

Outline script

Rather than rush into a detailed version of the script, it is usual to write an outline of the story first. The idea is to trace the development of the story in fairly detailed notes, so that it can be properly planned. As a script is written, new ideas will be occurring all the time. This poses few problems in the first few pages, but a new idea towards the end of a script could require major revisions of earlier sections. Even additions that do not need actual changes to the beginning of a story will often need to have ideas, or even props, laid or planted in the story at an earlier stage.

The business of planting ideas, or physical props, in the story to tie in with later events is a useful device. By making use of this trick, we can prepare the audience to accept fresh lines of story development. Suppose the central character in a story tells lies and the story revolves around the results of one particular

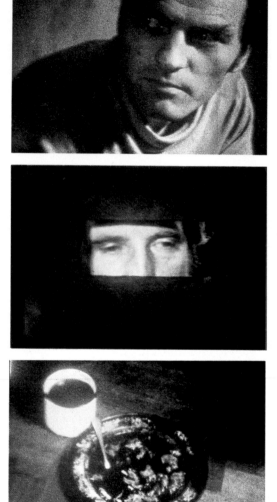

Before shooting can begin it is important to list the main events around which the action will be built. In 'The Prisoner' there are six key shots. These establish the mood of the prisoner, the constant surveillance, the dull routine of prison life, the attempt to escape, the discovery and the resulting despair.

untruth. The story could be presented in such a way that the hero simply tells the big lie and suffers the consequences. By using the idea planting technique, the central character could be shown at the beginning of the story telling a few harmless lies. So, when the really big lie is told, the audience is perfectly ready to accept the way the character behaves; they know what to expect from a constant liar.

As far as 'The Prisoner' was concerned, the first thing to do was to make a list of the major events in the story. 1 Establish routine of prison life. 2 Show relationship between prisoner and

eyes. 3 Explain the importance of hope of escape and the decision to try to do so. 4 Finding a tool to loosen the window bars. 5 The loosening of the bars, including fear of discovery. 6 Attempted escape, failure, insanity. Here are all the elements of the classic story formula — a central character faced with a dilemma, the obstacles to its solution, the solution and a satisfying ending.

The six major events in the story also progress in turn towards the climax of the film. Each event either gives more information about the character or moves the story forward in its development. Now, each part of the story has to be developed and all six parts blended together, so that the film flows, rather than jerks, to its conclusion.

One of the problems of this particular film was solved at this stage — the problem of dialogue. The idea was to have the prisoner in some form of conversation, during which some of the important story points could be explained for the benefit of the audience. The solution was to physically portray the other side of the prisoner's personality — the cautious side of his nature. His impulsive self could consider the possibility of escape whilst his cautious self opposed the idea. The latter could even be represented by a shadowy figure which would appear when the warder was not watching — at least in the prisoner's mind. This would also add mystery to the story and set the atmosphere for the eventual mental collapse at the end of the film.

From outline to detail

In most script outlines, the dialogue — except for major scenes — is only briefly sketched; in this case, however, it was so important to the story that it had to be included in as full a form as possible. Nor does an outline have to be presented in scenes, since it is intended only as a basis for the final script. For the same reason, it need only contain rudimentary camera or stage instructions, the main concentration being on lighting requirements. On the other hand, it is important that the outline mentions any special props or effects that might be needed, so that they can be planned and costed into the budget at the earliest possible stage.

Having accomplished this, the next task is to produce a final version of the script ready for shooting. Here, a lone film maker, as opposed to a club or group script writer, could probably proceed straight from the script outline to shoot the film. The lone worker would use the outline simply as a proving ground for his ideas and to make sure that all the information was in the film

Planning the story line of a film is a slow and time-consuming business but it is a mistake to skimp on this preliminary stage however frustrating it may seem. The first task in film making must always be to jot down ideas for the plot and for a sequence of shots which can gradually be worked into a coherent script.

1. Closed slit in door, close-up to show that the prisoner is unobserved.

2. Awareness of absence of observation, close shot of face.

6. Insert cut-away of eye

5. Medium shot, looking out of cell window prior to escape bid.

4. Close-up hands at work loosening cement.

3. Working on the bars of the cell, long shot.

7. Prisoner reacts to eyes, moves away from window, Tries to re-establish routine.

8. Close-up face. Fear that his escape bid is about to be discovered.

A section of the 220-shot storyboard drawn for 'The Prisoner'. This detailed plan is vital for the organization of a complex film, as it shows how it will appear on the screen.

for the audience to grasp what was going on. His actors would similarly get enough information from the outline — provided that it contained full dialogue — to play their roles and, since there would be only one person working behind the camera, elaborate stage directions would be unnecessary.

As the size of a crew grows and jobs such as lighting, camera work, continuity, props, directing and producing are split between the members of a group, however, the need for a very detailed production blueprint becomes clear.

Script style

A full script also has to be laid out in such a way that all the information needed by the different production workers and the actors is easily comprehensible. While the outline can be a work of literature, the final script is a working document.

The way a script is presented depends very much on the whims of individual scriptwriters, but there is no doubt that the professional feature film format is the best. Besides being actually easier to write, it presents the odd blend of literature and technical information that a film script must contain in about the best possible way. In general, it is a list of what the writer expects to appear on the screen when the film is complete. Specific instructions are given — zoom, track, fade, loud, bright and so on — and dialogue is presented in detail. Settings and exact character movements, however, are only sketched in — unless they are of great importance.

The script provides all the basic information, but it is designed to leave the director free to interpret the words in a visual way. This form of script has evolved in response to the freedom of location filming and modern techniques for shooting dialogue sequences. It is impossible for a writer to describe precisely the sort of wandering, zooming, craning shots that are used by directors, while locations are so unpredictable that they defy the writer's imagination.

Avoid the type of script presentation in which the page is divided into two vertical columns, one for the visuals and the other for the sound. The main drawback to this format is that it is difficult to read and it is hard to relate particular sound and picture sequences.

Two stills from the thriller described in the text. In the one, the two villains are arranging a meeting with their unwilling accomplice, seen with his worried **secretary in the other shot. The pictures themselves look simple, but a detailed script is still required for both actors and production team.**

A modern script format looks like this:

66. INT. PETER ASHBY'S OFFICE. DAY

PETER ASHBY has just put the telephone down. He looks hard at TONY CLARK.

PETER

It's on. He'll be in the car park in ten minutes.

TONY

Good. I think we'd better go.

They stand to leave the office.

67. INT. GEORGE PELL'S STUDY

Close on GEORGE as he thinks about the meeting. SARAH, a tall girl who makes an effort not to risk being a distraction by dressing down her good looks, enters the study. For a 24-year-old she takes her secretarial duties very

Below **Pages from the script of 'The Prisoner', with the director's rough notes in the margin. It is from this raw material that the final film takes shape. The director's** 'shorthand' includes notes of possible camera set-ups, lighting cues and so on, all of which have to be planned in advance of shooting.

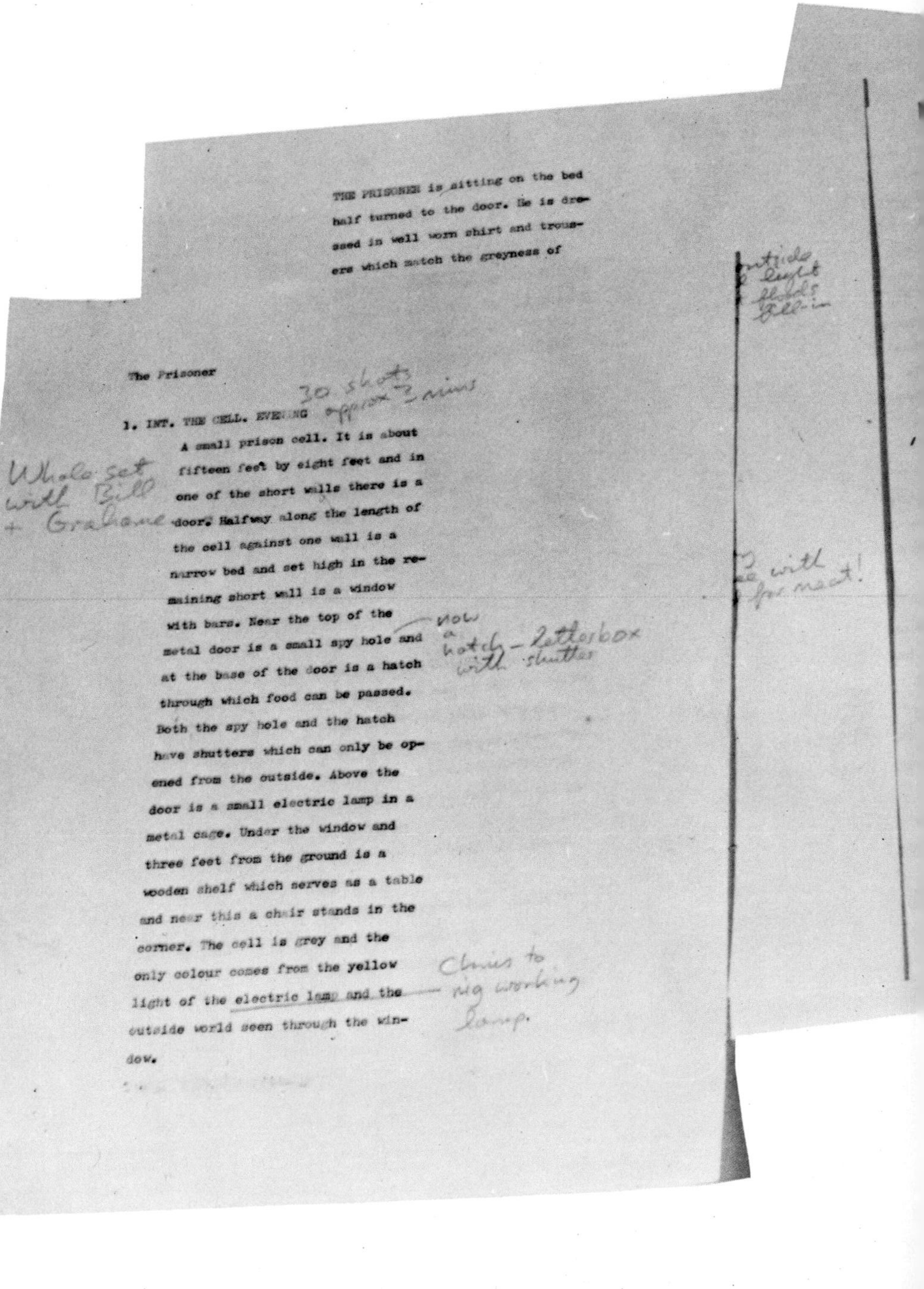

THE PRISONER is sitting on the bed half turned to the door. He is dressed in well worn shirt and trousers which match the greyness of

The Prisoner

1. INT. THE CELL. EVENING *30 shots approx 2 mins*

Whole set with Bill + Graham

A small prison cell. It is about fifteen feet by eight feet and in one of the short walls there is a door. Halfway along the length of the cell against one wall is a narrow bed and set high in the remaining short wall is a window with bars. Near the top of the metal door is a small spy hole and at the base of the door is a hatch through which food can be passed. Both the spy hole and the hatch have shutters which can only be opened from the outside. Above the door is a small electric lamp in a metal cage. Under the window and three feet from the ground is a wooden shelf which serves as a table and near this a chair stands in the corner. The cell is grey and the only colour comes from the yellow light of the electric lamp and the outside world seen through the window.

now a hatch — letterbox with shutter

Clues to rig working lamp.

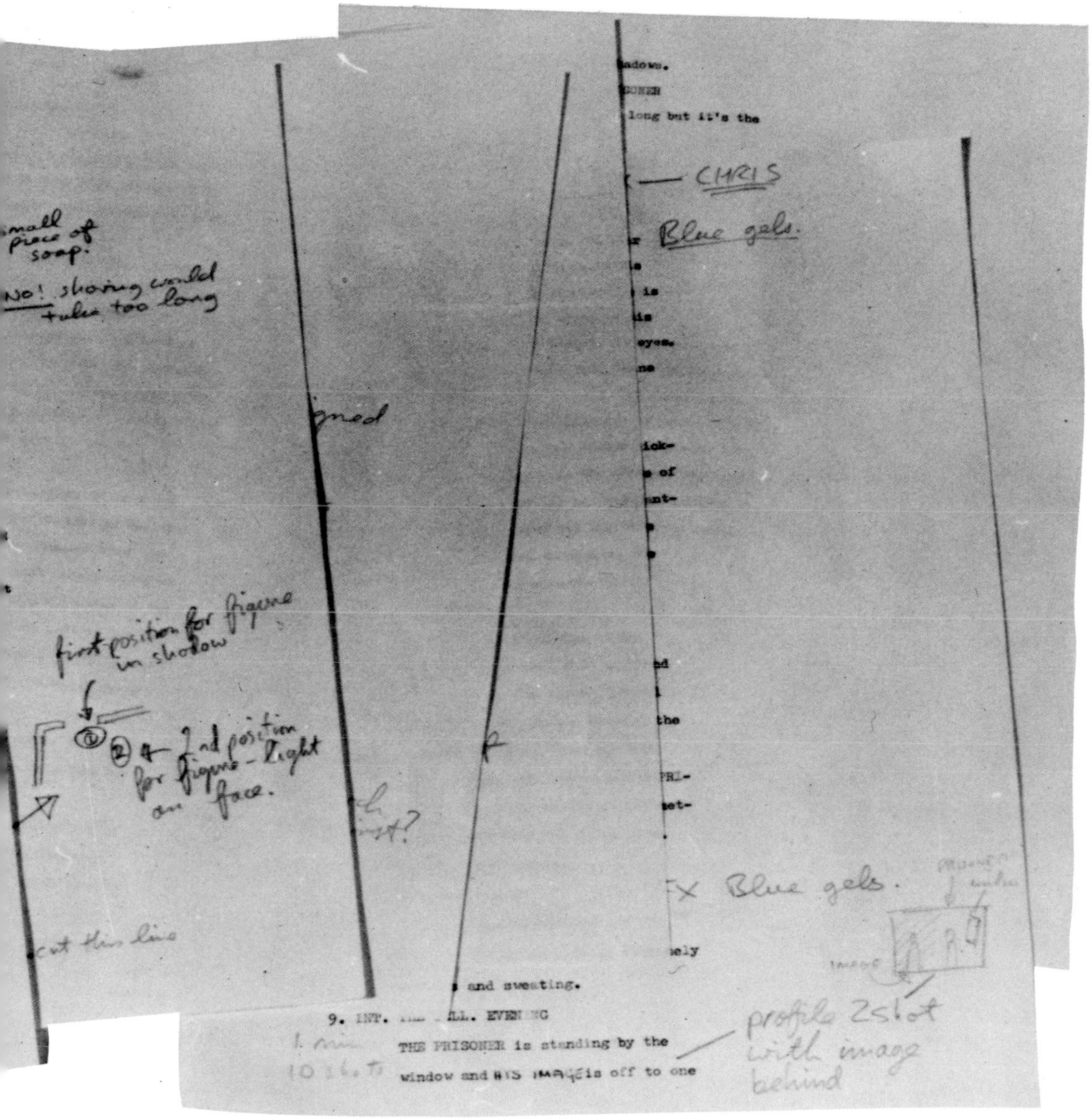

small piece of soap.

No! shaving would take too long

first position for figure in shadow

2nd position for figure – light on face.

cut this line

CHRIS

Blue gels.

X Blue gels.

image

profile 2 shot with image behind

and sweating.

9. INT. ... LL. EVENING

THE PRISONER is standing by the window and HIS IMAGE is off to one seriously.

GEORGE

I'm going out, something I wasn't expecting.

SARAH

You can't, there are two . . . GEORGE interrupts her by standing.

GEORGE

I'm sorry, Sarah. This one's a secret even from you.

68. EXT. A BUSY CITY STREET. DAY

PETER ASHBY and TONY CLARK are seen walking quickly through the crowds of shoppers. They do not talk but TONY looks at his watch.

69. INT. GEORGE PELL'S CAR. DAY

It is an expensive car in keeping with the profits to be expected from the trade GEORGE follows. GEORGE is alone as he drives through heavy traffic.

70. EXT. A BUSY CITY STREET. DAY

Start close on a traffic light showing green. It changes to red. In a wider view of the traffic light, we see GEORGE'S car brake hard in order to stop in time. Horns blare out from behind. At the wheel, GEORGE glances quickly at his watch.

71. EXT. AN OPEN CAR PARK. DAY

We are looking at the entrance to the car park. After a pause, GEORGE'S car comes into sight and enters. Pull back to a high angle wide view of the car park. We see that it is full and GEORGE driving slowly along the rows of vehicles.

72. EXT. OPEN AIR CAR PARK. DAY

PETER ASHBY and TONY CLARK are standing close to a large truck. GEORGE, who cannot see PETER and TONY, is driving slowly towards them. TONY, who has been watching GEORGE, turns to PETER and nods. PETER reaches into his coat and, in a close shot, we see that he has a large calibre revolver.

The difference between this type of script and old format ones is that shot descriptions are not given in great detail and such specifics as 'long shot', 'medium shot', 'close-up' and so on are omitted. Shot types are indicated — the appearance of the gun in 72, for instance — but this is only done when it is very important. The writer wanted a general view of the car park (72) to demonstrate the positions of the three characters relative to each other, so a closer view had to be indicated when the gun appeared.

On the other hand, the close shot of George in 67 is indicated, but the change of shot when the girl enters the room is not particularly important and so there is no need to describe it. The convention of putting character's names in

Before filming starts, it is important to draw up a list of props and clothes, to see what can be borrowed from friends and what you will have to allow for in your budget.

Calculating a budget is a vital factor in home movie making. The most critical factor in such calculations is judging the length of the finished film and how much you will inevitably waste in the process of editing. For dialogue scenes a ratio of 4:1 should normally be allowed; for silent shooting $2\frac{1}{2}:1$.

capitals is simply to draw attention to who does what and when in each sequence. The numbers are for reference to sections of the script; they also indicate each fresh camera set-up that will be needed.

The first line in each part of the script is very business-like. Take, for example, the introduction to section 67. The first time George Pell's study occurred in the story, it would have been described for the reader, but, thereafter, only the brief headline is necessary. 'Int' is short for interior and 'ext' for exterior. The reference to 'day' or 'night' is an obvious one. As with settings,

Below **The director briefs his 'soldiers' in this amateur US Civil War epic, a subject quite possible for an organized team.** *Bottom* **A solo movie maker also working on an American theme; sheriff and prisoner are captured in 16mm. Though not used in this scene, sound headphones are ready for action at the side of the tripod.**

Top right **and** *below* **Two contrasts in outdoor filming, each designed to obtain a specific effect. In the second, the camera is at ground level to get a close-up of the wounded soldier; in the first, the cameraman has climbed a tree to film an overhead shot.**

a character is described in full only on his or her first appearance, unless a costume change is involved.

The freedom this type of script format gives to everybody involved in the production is extremely valuable. The writer is not involved with laborious technical or pictorial descriptions, which would probably be altered by the director in any case; the director knows that the really important story points are the ones described and therefore he is free to interpret the script; and the actor does not have to wade through irrelevant technical information.

Preparing a budget

Film making is an expensive business, so it is essential to make an estimate of the likely cost — especially if the money is coming from your own pocket. In calculating a budget, the most critical factor is estimating how long the finished movie will run and how much film you expect to waste. This last factor is known as the shooting ratio.

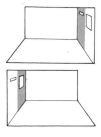

As a guide, shooting a dialogue scene will probably involve a shooting ratio in the region of four to one — that is to say, for every 50 feet in the finished film, 200 will need to be shot. Silent shooting is much more economical; the ratio in this case is something like two-and-a-half to one. In documentaries, you should expect a very high shooting ratio — something like ten to one upwards on unscripted subjects — because of their unpredictable nature.

It is more difficult to assess the finished running time of a film, but not impossible. Section 66 of the feature film, for instance, would probably run for about 12 or 15 seconds. The only way to establish this is to act out the script; after

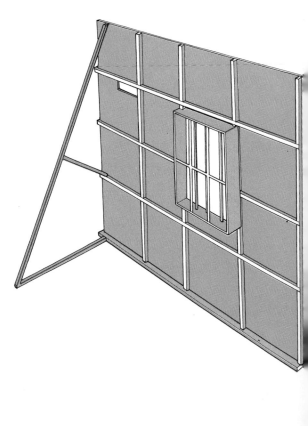

Right **This view of the set for 'The Prisoner' shows how effective the results can be, even if time and resources are limited. With imagination and skilful use of the camera camera, the results can be as convincing as movies costing a good deal more to film. The walls consisted of heavy cardboard nailed to a batten framework. For the window iron bars were set in a weak concrete mix. The back flat was fixed but the side flat could be moved from one side of the set to the other.**

assessing a dozen or so pages, it becomes easier to make reasonably accurate guesses.

The difficult parts to time are those such as 71 and 72, where the action depends on an unknown location. In the case of a scene like 71, a completely abstract timing method is the only answer — allow four seconds, say, on the car park entrance before George arrives; ten seconds for paying the entrance ticket or collecting the time ticket; and about 15 seconds to cover his entry and the camera pulling back to the wider view. This total of 29 seconds could be profitably rounded up to half a minute.

Top **The prisoner begins to free the bars of his cell window. Real iron bars were used for realism,**
Above left **Director and actor discuss moves, working with a model of the set.** *Above right* **The final touches are added to the false windows, pictured here from the back of the set.**

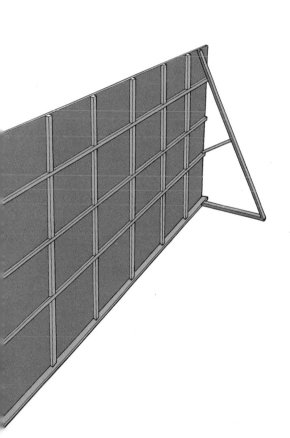

Running speed and film stock

When finished screen time and shooting ratio have been established, the next thing to decide is the speed at which the camera will be run during filming. Fifty feet of Super 8 film will run for three minutes and twenty seconds at 18 frames per second (fps) and for two minutes thirty seconds at 24 fps. If any high-speed filming is planned — to produce slow motion — then a 50 foot reel will give one minute and six seconds at 54 fps.

On this basis, a film with a projected screen time of 10 minutes would need 40 minutes worth of film stock — 600 feet at 18 fps or 800 feet at 24 fps. This will be the largest expense to be accounted for, but there are a number of other items to be included. Among them are: camera and recorder batteries; costumes; recording tape and cassettes; bulbs for lighting units; special props; set construction materials; and payment for use of electricity. Depending on the shooting system, there could be further costs, such as Super 8 fullcoat (magnetic oxide coated film for editing), laboratory charges for processing film and sound and so on.

Set versus location

Because of the expense involved, it is usually preferable to film on location rather than to build a set. For some films, however, a set is essential and 'The Prisoner' is one such example. No location could provide the right combination of door, window and space for a camera, so the only solution was to build a set for the job. This also involved very careful advance planning, as one of the chief difficulties with a set is frequently the problem of storage. It is often impossible to leave a set standing for any length of time.

Shooting schedule

All productions should therefore have a shooting schedule. In the case of 'The Prisoner', this was established at four weeks, with two week-ends for actual shooting. This was inevitable, given the availability of the people making up the crew and the hall in which the set was built. Two problems immediately resulted.

Right **Three shots from the break-out sequence in 'The Prisoner'.** *Top* A **cut-away shot showing the tool to be used; the tool in action** *centre;* **the prisoner wrenching out a bar to make his escape** *bottom.*

The first of these was that it was unlikely that the rushes from the first shooting week-end would be returned from the processing laboratory until after the second week-end. This would make re-takes very difficult because of the problem of finding the time to erect the set and so it became vital to check all the equipment beforehand.

Because the set could not be left in position between the shooting week-ends, it needed to be designed in storable sections. It was therefore constructed as a timber frame, faced with thick cardboard. To reduce the building and storage problems as much as possible, just two flats (a stage term for large pieces of flat scenery) were built, their size being governed by the available storage space. This meant that the two

It is always useful to test the lighting required for different scenes before shooting begins, especially when the time schedule is tight. In 'The Prisoner' both day and night lighting were required. Daylight conditions were first tested with the actor present, then with the empty cell to check the effect of the sky back-cloth; finally the right lighting was found to create the illusion of daylight from the window on the prisoner. For the night scenes the blue filters were used;

the additional effect of starlight was created with perforated black paper illuminated by a lamp outside the window. The lens of the camera was set one stop below the usual exposure setting to make the scene darker.

pieces of scenery could be no larger than 12 feet long and eight feet high.

One of the flats was to be painted as one stretch of wall, while the other was to double as the window end of the cell and the door end. This was accomplished by putting the window and door at different ends of the same flat so that, when it was positioned at one end or other of the plain flat, it could serve as both ends of the cell. As a consequence of this, there was no possibility of panning with the actor, as he walked from the window along the length of the cell to the door. The shooting would also have to be very carefully planned so that the action taking place at either the door or window was all filmed at the same time, regardless of the script order of the scenes. This would avoid continually moving the dual-purpose flat backwards and forwards.

The door was easy to construct since it did not need to open. The window was more difficult, because it needed iron bars set in concrete, which the actor could appear to loosen. The

solution was a wooden box fixed to the frame of the flat and fitted with an opening window frame. The iron bars were fixed into a weak mixture of sand and cement. The whole process took a week from start to finish.

Shooting method

Because so many pre-production decisions depend on the shooting method, the director and crew must settle this as early as possible. In the professional cinema, this is never a matter for debate; there is one world-wide method for shooting, sound recording and editing. The amateur, however, is not so lucky. Whether he works in Super 8 or 16mm, there is little likelihood of standardization.

Sound systems are probably the most non-standard area in amateur films. Shooting synchronized sound and then editing it presents a multiplicity of choices; in effect, the director must also plan backwards, because the decision about editing method is probably more important here

Below **Light from the lamp is bounced from a screen at an angle of 45°, so that it passes through the window at 90° in a diffused state. This helps to achieve the** **effect of daylight.** *Bottom* **The effect of starlight is achieved by shining a light direcly on to a black-painted screen pierced with star-shaped holes.**

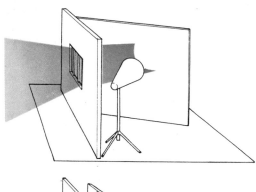

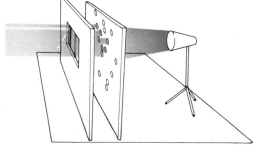

than the shooting one. Obviously, there is no point in shooting a perfectly synchronized sound track if it cannot be edited in step with the film.

In 'The Prisoner', there was only one tiny line of actual dialogue and so lip-sync shooting was not needed. The decision, however, was also made to avoid sync shooting completely — even for the vital sound effects — because of the difficulty in ensuring perfection. Film is a medium of compromise, but the one thing which should not fall a victim is its visual appearance. The microphone either gives way to the camera or it suffers from the effect of locations which do not produce the quality of sound needed. In a documentary, this does not matter so much because the sound is part of the atmosphere, but, in a fiction film, the ear is less gullible than the eye.

This was certainly the case in 'The Prisoner', where it was obvious from the start that a cardboard set could not have the acoustics of a proper prison cell. It was therefore decided to shoot with a silent camera and dub all the thought speech, sound effects and the one line of proper dialogue later. This had the great advantage of allowing the film to be edited as a silent movie, which increased its visual strength. The only area where sound affected editing was in the thought speech scenes. The director had to know how long these sections would run to ensure that there would be enough visual material to cover them.

Test shots

One of the factors forced on the production team of 'The Prisoner' by the very tight schedule was a wide range of tests for the film. The great danger was that any shots which were not right could not be re-shot for nearly two months, the next available week-end in the hall cum studio. The delay would present many continuity problems, but the major hurdle would be storing the set. For this reason, something as seemingly simple to shoot as a figure in the shadows had to be tested in advance. The approach to this was to light the

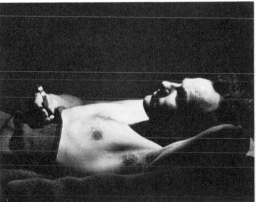

Far left top **Creating the sky; below creating starlight.** *Centre* **An assistant holds a reflector to lighten the shadow under the actor's eyes.** *Above* **A test shot of the prisoner lying in bed planning his escape;** *Left* **the cell window lit for the night effect.**

background, but put no light on the actor so that he became a silhouette. To stop spillage from the background lights falling on the actor, large pieces of black card, known as flags, were fixed on the top of spare lighting stands and placed around the lights to cast shadows on him.

Following the cinema convention that moonlight is blue meant that blue filters had to be tested to give the moonlight scenes in 'The Prisoner' the 'authentic' touch. The filters used were, in fact, the ones designed to match the colour of photofloods to daylight. These are known as 'daylight blues'. With film lights, the camera should be loaded with the right type of

artificial light film; in the case of Super 8 cameras, this means that the built-in filter should be moved out of the light path.

The most awkward problem involving the use of filters over the light source is the damage that the heat produced by a photographic lamp can do to any material placed close to it. A lamp filter needs to be at least two feet square; it must be supported in front of the lamp by either a special frame or another stand. To avoid over-heating the filters, the lamps should be run only for short periods.

An alternative method is to use a filter on the camera lens. This should be the same color as

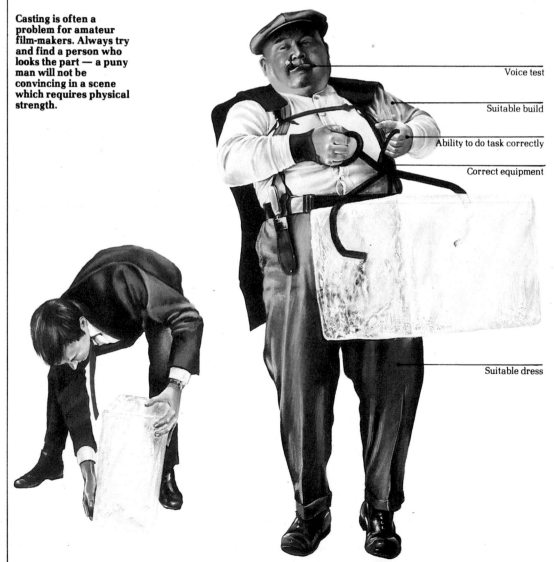

Casting is often a problem for amateur film-makers. Always try and find a person who looks the part — a puny man will not be convincing in a scene which requires physical strength.

Voice test

Suitable build

Ability to do task correctly

Correct equipment

Suitable dress

First stage

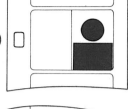

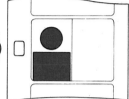

Second stage

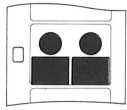

Using the split screen technique to film a double image. Remember to line up the point where the two doors meet with a part of the scene which has natural vertical lines, such as the corner of a room, to hide the join.

Left Casting a double. The only way of avoiding the split screen technique is to use a double. However, it is important not to include the face of both actor and his double in any one shot in case someone spots the deception. *Below* A scene from 'The Prioner' in which a double was used.

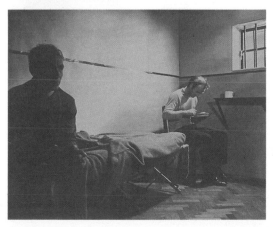

the effect required. In the case of moonlight, the filter needs to be quite strong and therefore exposure has to be increased — one stop in the case of Kodak's CC40 Blue, for instance. If the camera has automatic exposure, it will compensate for this but otherwise the camera must be adjusted accordingly. One way of doing this is to 'cheat' the film speed setting on the hand meter. Every time the ASA rating of the film is doubled or halved, the exposure is affected by one stop — f/5.6 at ASA50 equals f/8 at ASA 100, for example. With a CC40B filter, ASA40 becomes ASA20, and so on.

To go with the moonlight, a background of the night sky complete with stars, as seen through the cell window, was required. A perforated sheet of black paper was hung outside the window of the cell, with a lamp set behind it so that the tiny holes became pinpoints of light. The cell itself was lit with blue filtered lamps and, to give a genuine night time feel, the lens of the camera was set one stop below the usual exposure setting to make the scene darker.

A daytime view was also required, but this was slightly more difficult to achieve. For this, it was decided that a projected color slide would be used, since this would be more realistic than a painted scene. Different slides could also be used to vary the time of day.

Tests were carried out to see if this was practicable. The first thought was to use a projected moving picture, but the problem of ensuring that the camera and projector shutters opened simultaneously proved too difficult to overcome. It would have been possible to film and project only one frame at a time, but this would have meant not including the actor in any of the shots containing a view. Even accepting this, there were still more factors to be taken into account, as experiments proved.

The screen was set up outside the window, so that the projected image could be seen by the camera as it looked towards the window from inside the set. The projector and screen had to be outside the set, with the latter close enough to the window to make the picture big enough. The result was that the projector and screen could not be set up square to each other and so the picture was distorted. Since the view would always be a distant one, the overall distortion could be ignored, but the distortion of the shape presented a problem. The edge of the screen image nearest to the projector was just over half the size of the edge of the screen image furthest from it. When the edge of the screen nearest to the projector was filled with image, a lot of the image thrown towards the farthest edge missed the screen. This meant that overall screen brightness was inferior and the furthest edge was dimmer than the nearer one. For this reason, the method was eventually abandoned.

All these tests were carried out on an improvised set while the actual one was being built. Their exhaustive nature was certainly time-consuming, but went a long way to eliminating the risk of mistakes when actual shooting commenced.

A cast of one

Not counting the eyes at the spyhole, the cast for 'The Prisoner' was one, so casting would seem to have been one of the lesser problems. In fact, this was not so. Because the central character was on screen for every frame of the movie, he needed to be exactly right in both looks and voice. In productions with a larger cast, it is possible to hide individual shortcomings among a crowd.

In amateur film making, the most often faulted area is the acting. Normally, the problem is that actors are too self-conscious so one of the most popular solutions to the problem is to avoid positive selection as much as possible. People usually behave convincingly as they go about their everyday business, but they look uncomfortable when they are shifted into an unfamiliar environment. If you want a dustman in a movie, say, then get one — a real one.

Having found a man who looked the part, the next step was to discover if he possessed the kind of personal confidence that would allow him to perform naturally in front of a movie camera.

Nothing is more likely to kill a performance than an actor who shambles across the screen radiating the impression that he would rather be somewhere else. For this reason, a few tests before camera and lights are essential.

Final preparations

During the week prior to shooting, the set was put together and the props assembled in the hall. The final main task immediately before shooting was the preparation of the cast. This was the responsibility of the director. Since the actor would not be working with anybody but himself, there was little point in having dialogue rehearsals — though these would normally be essential. Preparation was thus limited to working through the shooting of the film, so the director could prepare for any problems and also explain the procedures to the star. In the event, these proved extremely useful because they saved hours of shooting time.

The most important thing the actor had to understand was the method planned for the scenes in which he had to talk to himself. The obvious technique would have been double exposure of the film, known as split screen. In this, a special matte box is fixed securely before the camera lens. In the front of this box are two black doors which fit exactly together when closed. When the actor stands on the left of the scene, the left door is opened so that the camera can film half the scene and the actor. The film is then re-wound to the start, the left door closed and the right one opened. The actor now moves over to perform in the right hand part of the scene

as the film passes through the camera for the second time.

In this way, one actor can appear in the same scene twice. It is usual to line up the point where the two doors of the matt box meet with a part of the scene which has natural vertical lines — the corner of a room, for instance. The camera must be on an extremely solid base, since any movement means that the two sides of the shot will fail to line up correctly.

The problem with this method as far as this particular film was concerned was that the actor needed to react to his double on the other side of the shot. This would have been difficult to achieve, since the actor would have no reference to what was happening on the other side of the picture. The only way this could have worked was through immaculate timing, but there was always the possibility of error.

For this reason, a double seemed the answer. By planning the shots so that the double's face could not be seen in the two-shots (shots with two figures in them), there would be no danger of any clever viewer spotting it. To make sure these shots fitted correctly with the rest of the film, a detailed story board was drawn.

The story board

The function of a story board is to show how the finished film will look on the screen. It also plays an important role during shooting, because the director can see at a glance how many shots need to be taken in each set-up. By the time 'The Prisoner's' director reached this stage, he had a very good knowledge of the story and a definite vision of the finished product. By making a rough sketch of every shot in the film — there were about 220 in total — he was able to show everybody concerned what they were aiming to achieve and explain where each shot fitted into the overall scheme.

A detailed story board also allows a film to be shot completely out of sequence. This means that after shot one, any shots with a similar camera and lighting arrangement can be filmed, regardless of their place in the story. This saves a considerable amount of time, though it does impose an extra strain on the actors.

Continuity

The technique described above also helps solve the problem of continuity. When taking shots at different times, it is vital to ensure that everything is in the same position throughout. A table lamp, for instance, cannot switch itself on; there must be a shot of somebody doing it.

Professional film studios employ continuity girls, whose task is to note all such details down and even take photographs as a visual double-check. Such a system serves equally well for amateur movies. In addition to the kind of information already described, the notes should show what was shot, in what order and on what

One of the most important film making rules is continuity. Every time the camera stops turning, a break in the **action occurs. One of the worst movie faults is to let this show in the finished film.**

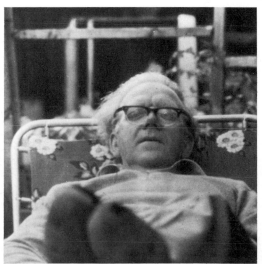

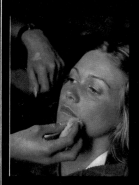

Right **Applying film make-up.** Part of the secret of successful movie making is knowing how much make-up to apply and when. In a documentary, for instance, make-up may well mar the realism of the scene, but in a fiction film its use is essential. Whatever the subject, remember that movie make-up is much lighter than its theatrical equivalent. The first step is to tie back the hair and to apply a thin, even layer of foundation. A sponge will give the best results. Then apply blusher to the cheeks and forehead with a soft cloth. Dark tone is next applied below the cheekbones and a highlight above them to accentuate the shape of the face. Eye shadow goes on the upper lids, followed by highlight, laid down with a fine paintbrush. A darker shade of eye shadow is then used to accentuate the ball of the eye and highlight is added just below the brow. Lipstick completes the first stage. After checking this, more shadow is applied to the lower eyelid to balance the make-up. The lips are outlined with a darker shade of the lipstick already applied, using a fine brush. Several coats of mascara are applied and allowed to dry. The hair can then be untied and arranged as required.

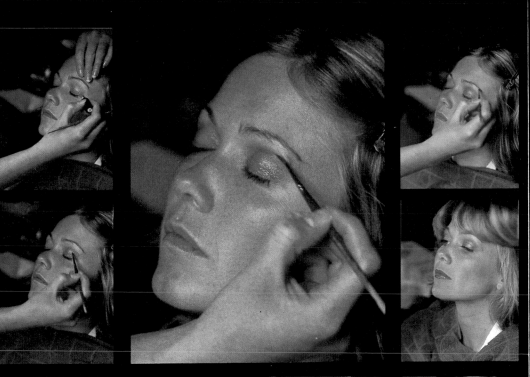

Whether the scene is set in a studio or on an exterior location, the make-up has to be tested under the light before filming can start. Strong lights wash out color, so extra blusher or a brighter lipstick may be needed. In addition, a final dusting of powder is usually added, as make-up tends to run under hot lights.

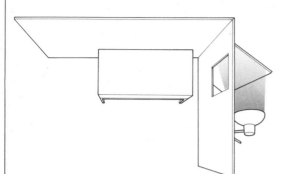

Careful lighting organization before shooting helps its course to run smoothly. The single light above, reflected through the window, simulates daylight. It is complemented by a 500 watt flood above the window, as *below*, along with a fill-in light near the camera and a further floodlight aimed through the window on to white paper to suggest a bright sky.

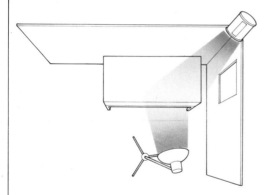

reel of film it can be found. Cameramen should remember to mark each shot with the correct number. This considerably simplifies the task of editing.

Shooting begins

The two complete week-ends of shooting gave a total of 32 hours of shooting time, which meant producing an average of seven shots an hour or one shot every eight minutes. The first thing to do was to organize the lighting, so that the minimum amount of time would be lost.

In all artificial lighting set-ups, the first step is to decide on the mood and style of the lighting. The mood should be apparent from the script and the director's instructions. He may want the scene to look sinister, with plenty of shadow, bright and happy-looking, or stylised to recreate the atmosphere of a particular environment — the artificial light of a large office, for example. It also helps the realism of a scene if the lighting appears to be as natural as possible. To achieve this, the cameraman must decide on the logical source for the illumination in the set and then position his lights to correspond with the way things would appear in real life.

The set for 'The Prisoner' had two sources of light — the window and a small light bulb in a metal cage over the door. In daylight, the light in the cell could be expected to flow softly from the direction of the window, decreasing in intensity as it neared the door. At night, when the small bulb was supposed to be the source, the lighting would be harder and come from high up. It would be at its brightest near the door, with the window end of the cell in shadow.

The lighting equipment consisted of one 500

watt spot light, three 500 watt photofloods and one 1000 watt lamp in a homemade reflector. For the daylight scenes, the 1000 watt light shone into the cell through the window. This produced the correct effect there, but, since it did not reach far into the set, a 500 watt flood was rigged above the window to complement it. It also produced a pool of light on the bed, as well as giving the actor some backlighting as he moved about the set. The second floodlight was placed close to the camera to act as a fill-in light — that is, to lighten the shadows cast by the other lamps. The remaining floodlight was set to illuminate a sheet of white paper positioned outside the window to give the camera a bright 'sky' to film.

For the night scenes, the spotlight was used, positioned near the actual light in the set. This was a working prop; its 150 watt bulb registered well on the film whenever it came into shot. To slightly soften the shadows the spotlight cast, a floodlight was used as a fill-in near the camera — set carefully so that it cast no noticeable shadow of its own in contrast to the main shadow of the spotlight in position. This helped to establish the lighting's overall moody effect.

A lighting set-up like this meant that only the fill lamps had to be moved to any extent. From time to time, one or other of the key lights or the backlight had to be moved a little to stop them casting awkward shadows for the camera, but, in general, very little re-rigging was needed.

The chief lighting effect was the change of lighting in the cell as the sun rose to take over from the small cell light. This started with only the spotlight in position, the prisoner sitting on his bed in the pool of light from the spot. The other lights were in their daytime positions, but connected to a dimmer circuit. To achieve the sunrise effect,

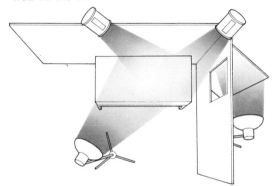

For night scenes, when the cell was to appear as being lit by a 150 watt bulb, the spotlight was positioned near the bulb and shone on to the bed, as shown *left*. A floodlight was positioned near the camera to soften the shadows.

Below The escape sequence from 'The Prisoner'. In this dream sequence, the hero escapes and passes down an alley under cover of night. In search of a safe escape route, he crosses a rubbish tip, while daylight finds him relying on the anonymity of a crowded street.

A director at work. It is common to adopt one of two directing techniques — either to go through moves on the set first or to call directions from behind the camera. Amateurs usually find the former the more helpful.

Below **The prisoner reaches open fields, but the eyes bring him back to reality. On the facing page, the light goes off to re-establish routine and he slips into despair and madness.**

the lights on the dimmer were slowly faded up to full brightness to gradually take over from the single spotlight.

Directing

Shooting is probably the most frustrating time for the director of a film. Before the camera begins to turn, he has his private perfect vision of the finished form of the movie, but, as shooting progresses, this gets mutilated piece by piece. This is the debit side — the profit comes in finding new ideas, as the project is expanded by the suggestions of others.

During the pre-production stage, the director is involved in creating the blueprint for the film (the script) and getting everything organized so that as little as possible goes wrong on the set. At this stage, he chooses alternatives, if necessary, as in the test shot procedure described in a previous section. Where he cannot reach a final choice, he leaves in the luxury of various options.

When the camera and lights arrive and the actors start to perform, the option of choice is replaced by the deadly back-breaking pressure of decisions which cannot be avoided, or, in many cases, changed later. The director must therefore have a complete understanding of the project, so that all the questions he will have to face can be answered within a consistent framework. With enough preparation, all the queries from crew and actors can be dealt with readily and the director will be able to organise and control with authority.

The relationship between director and actors is all-important, though, obviously, it will vary according to the people involved. Leaving this aside, there are two main approaches, depending

on whether non-actors or experienced actors are being used.

Assuming experienced actors have been chosen, the director will have held auditions to select players who offer something which matches the director's own concept of the part. Auditions become a pointless exercise if the actors eventually have to be thoroughly re-rehearsed in front of the camera. The chief test should therefore be whether they can portray the characters in the manner required. This reduces the amount of work the director needs to do to put the characters on the screen, because the chosen actors present a character package which can easily be shaped in the right direction.

Non-actors, on the other hand, need complete direction and therefore come much closer to being purely vehicles for the director's vision. A non-actor will have been selected because he or she is the character, rather than portraying it. The raw material provided has to be moulded by the director to suit the needs of the movie.

It is vital that all actors know what is happening on the set. If they become confused — or worse, bored — it will show in the performance. Since most films are shot out of story sequence, the director's first job is to explain where the current scene fits, what goes before it and what comes after it. The whole scene should then be rehearsed completely, without any reference to how it will be filmed in individual shots. In this way, every action that an actor makes can be slotted into its correct position in the scene, the individual shots when they are made and the whole film. Rehearsing the whole scene first also helps the crew because they will need to know what is going on as well.

The scene can now be fragmented into its various shots, with everybody sharing the director's knowledge of the film and being able to make sensible suggestions for improvements.

Rehearsals should start very loosely and grow in their rigidity as the scene takes its finished form. Over-directed first rehearsals result in making it harder for the actors to respond to later changes; they also mean that the director appears to be uncertain when he subsequently changes his mind.

A relaxed atmosphere produces a relaxed, but competent, performance. Try to avoid false starts and make sure that, when the actors take up position, everything behind the scenes is ready. Any actors not taking part in the particular shot must stay well behind the camera, as otherwise their shadows may affect the picture. Many a good panning shot has also been unintentionally ruined by the presence of an unwanted elbow.

The director's position is a matter of choice, but the best results are usually obtained by actually going over the moves with the actors on the set, rather than calling out instructions from behind the camera. In particular, any tendency to over act should be checked at the start. Screen acting needs to be far less broad than its theatrical equivalent, because characters are projected on a screen many times life size. Dramatic tension, for instance, can be portrayed by a slight movement of the cheek muscles or a tightening of the fist which would be invisible on the stage.

The importance of continuity should also be carefully explained. This applies just as much to the actors as to the position of the props on the set. An unscripted change in make-up or hair style,

say, will stand out like a sore thumb in the finished film.

The director's golden rule is to keep calm, even if things look like going wrong. Remember that much can be taken care of at the editing stage, though it is obviously best if this can be reduced as much as possible.

Editing

Editing can be much reduced in complexity if a thorough story board of the film is drawn. This proved to be the case where 'The Prisoner' was concerned, even allowing for the completely random order in which the film was made. This meant that no editing could be done until every foot of film had been returned by the processing laboratory.

The main editing job was to trim the shots to their appropriate lengths. The aim of the director was to maintain a set pace in the story by a regular length of shot; where the tension needed to be heightened, this was progressively shortened. Shot order, content and image size had been determined by the story board and one side effect of this was a very low shooting ratio of about two to one.

The best way to approach editing is to prepare what is known as a rough cut of the film first. All the scenes are joined together in the right order, leaving in the reference numbers indicating the start of each scene. After viewing, the decision is made as to what to discard. A second edited version of the film is then prepared, tightening up the action where necessary and looking carefully for inconsistencies. Run the film through the projector and then fine cut, inserting the necessary cut-aways. Discarded shots will often provide the material for this. Sound can then be added as described in the two sound chapters.

The basic rule of editing is the more variety in the shots, the more scope for the editor. A sparsely shot film is extremely difficult to edit. Above all, remember that the final version must look realistic on the screen.

The first stage of editing is the arrangement in story order of all the footage. The rough cut, involves taking those frames and sequences which are most obviously superfluous or below standard out of this total assembly to make way for the third stage — the fine cut.

Voice and
Pictures

9
9
9
9
9
9
9

The previous chapter on sound demonstrated how a simple soundtrack, consisting of music and commentary, say, can add a new dimension to silent film. More complex soundtracks — utilizing synchronized speech, for instance — are only slightly more difficult to achieve; with the wide range of equipment available today, the process is a fairly simple one, even for the novice.

How lip-sync works

The real challenge for the home movie maker is the achievement of synchronization between sound and pictures, particularly where speech is concerned. An ordinary tape recorder, used in conjunction with a camera and projector, is not adequate, without some form of synchronizer to keep the equipment running in step, as camera, projector and tape recorder may well not run at their exact nominal speeds. For instance, the nominal filming speed might be 18 frames per second, but the camera could have an actual running speed of 17½ fps and the projector 18½ fps. During filming, therefore, 17½ frames of film will pass through the camera every second and every second of sound recorded will be the equivalent of this. On replay, however, 18½ frames will pass through the projector every second, but each second of tape will still correspond to 17½ fps. After one second, the film will be one frame ahead of the tape; after only three seconds, the film will be three frames ahead — enough for the difference to be noticeable on screen.

Even if camera and projector have been carefully adjusted to run at exactly the same speed, there will still be a discrepancy. The smallest variations in the running speeds of camera, projector and tape recorder will accumulate over a period of time to produce a noticeable sync error.

Simple synchronization

The simplest way to ensure perfect synchronization is to use a camera which records sound on

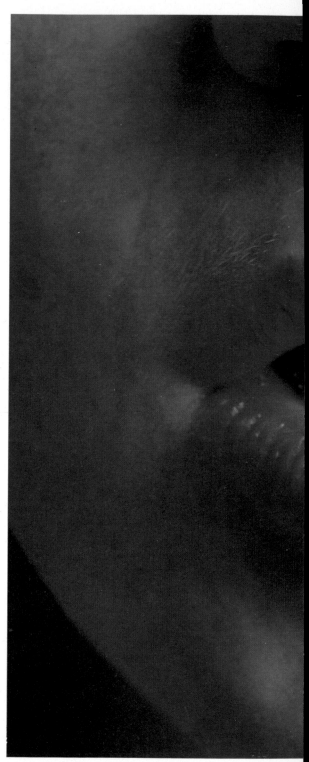

One of the most difficult tasks for any movie maker is to synchronize lip movements with the spoken word. Lip-sync, as it is known, can be achieved in two ways — either by recording sound as you shoot and editing it to fit, or by post-film dubbing.

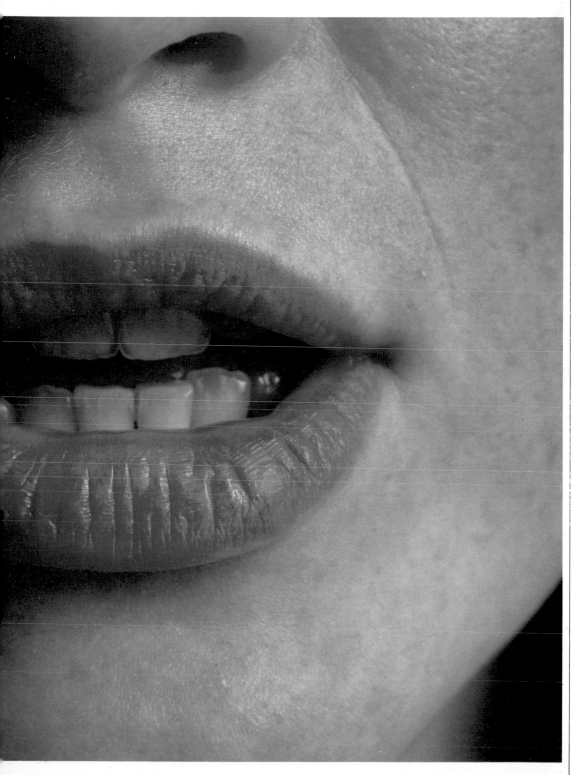

A single system
sound camera, pictured
with a projector, and
right the components of
double system sound.
Unlike single system
shooting, where the
camera records sound
and image directly on to
a single strip of film,
double systems require
two machines — a
camera and tape
recorder, say — and a
means of achieving
synchronization
between the two. The
one most often used is a
pilot control track on the
recorder.

Double system sound means that the sound is recorded separately from the picture. To achieve this, camera and tape recorder must be in sync so that the soundtrack can be added accurately later. This is achieved by means of a sync pulse, a signal between the camera and recorder.

the film itself. This is known as single-system sound. Single-system sound cameras have built-in circuitry to record sound directly on to magnetically striped film; international standards have been established to ensure that the film will replay in perfect sync on any Super 8 projector.

Even if an alternative system is used, sound cameras all have much the same features in common. Basically, they work in the same way as silent cameras, but with one major difference. The jerking movement of the claw pulling the film through the gate has to be neutralized so that the film can flow freely and smoothly over the sound head. To achieve this, the film is gripped between a capstan, powered by a second constant-speed motor, and a pressure roller, while a constant 18 frame gap between picture and sound is maintained by a loop sensor. This is a signalling device; the camera's main drive responds by slightly increasing or decreasing its speed to keep the picture in constant step with the sound.

Other features of a typical sound camera include an automatic recording level control, sometime with a manual override. This is a precaution against the distortion that can result if an actor, say, positions himself too close to the microphone. Some cameras, too, are fitted with suppressor systems to cut out low-level background noise, such as the sound of the motors, which might otherwise be picked up by the microphone. This is particularly useful in confined spaces. A sound fader, sound mixer, quick-start mechanism — this ensures that film and sound start together — and a sync point for tape synchronization are all extra points to look for when making a decision on what type of camera to purchase.

The chief difficulty with single-system sound comes at the editing stage. This is because of the 18 frame gap between the sound and the picture, but the problem is quite easy to overcome if allowance is made for it at an early stage. The important thing is to plan the script in detail, so that, when shooting starts, overlaps can be included at the beginning and end of each shot.

Types of film

These are two types of sound film — optical and magnetic. The former is used exclusively with 16mm cameras in the amateur field, though some Super 8 projectors can replay it. The soundtrack is recorded photographically along the edge of the film. When the film is projected, the track passes between an exciter lamp and a photo-electric cell, generating a series of electrical impulses which are amplified and converted to sound waves via a loudspeaker. However, the system is expensive and the photographic track has to be added by a commercial laboratory.

With the magnetic system, the soundtrack is recorded on a narrow stripe of magnetic oxide, applied to one side of the film. This can be easily added at home — provided that the laminate variety is used — though it is usually more convenient to buy a sound cartridge with the stripe already in place. A second, narrower, stripe along the other edge ensures that the film spools evenly. This is known as the 'balancing stripe'. The magnetic stripe itself works in exactly the same way as ordinary magnetic tape.

Double-system sound

Alternatively, sound can be recorded through a

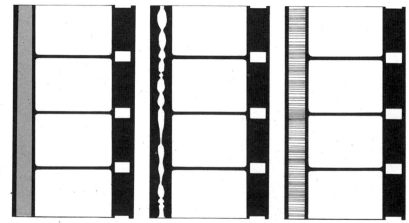

The two types of sound film — **magnetic** *near right* **and optical** *centre and far right.* **Magnetic striped film is coated with two strips of iron oxide, one on each edge. The wider stripe on the left side records the sound, while the narrower stripe on the right-hand edge is a balance stripe to help the film wind evenly on the spool. It, too, can be used for recording music or special effects. In optical film the soundtrack is recorded photographically along the edge of the film.**

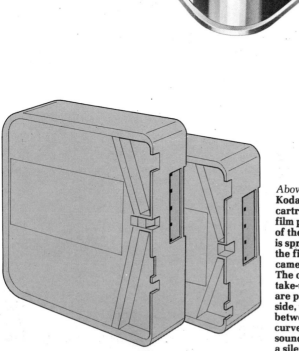

Above **The interior of a Kodak Super 8 sound cartridge, showing the film path and the action of the pressure pad. This is spring-loaded to hold the film against the camera pressure plate. The cartridge's feed and take-up compartments are positioned side by side, the film passing between the two on a curved path.** *Left* **A sound cassette** *front* **and a silent one compared.**

The development of the magnetically striped film used in the sound models has brought sound movies within the reach of every amateur film maker.

A magnetic stripe to record sound can either **be laminated** *below right* **or applied as magnetic paste** *below left* **by a professional laboratory. Professional striping is inexpensive and is often superior to home striping, as the stripe has better contact with the sound heads.**

double system. This uses a tape recorder, together with some form of synchronizer to keep it in step with either a silent camera or a projector. Synchronizers fall into two main categories — those designed to link a projector with a tape recorder for post recording — that is, adding sound after filming — and universal synchronizers, which are used for live recording.

The majority of universal synchronizers are based on the signal pulse principle; for this, the film-maker needs a camera fitted with a once-per-frame contact; a tape recorder fitted with a free head for recording the pulses; a tone generator; and a sync resolver. The principle of operation is simple. A connection is made from the camera's once-per-frame socket to the tape recorder's free head socket, via a small tone generator, which is sometimes built in to the connection cable. When the camera is running, its internal switching causes the tone generator to produce a series of electrical impulses, which are recorded on the tape.

The frequency of the pulses recorded depends on the running speed of the camera. This information is later used by the synchronizer to resolve sync during replay. Some models do this automatically, but the majority merely indicate the state of sync. This is then resolved manually by adjusting the running speed of either the

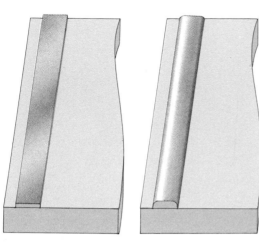

A home-striping machine adds a flat magnetic stripe to film to record sound. With care a good result can be achieved, but it is not easy to apply the magnetic paste evenly and in addition the film can easily become buckled and damaged in the machine.

An optical track can be
regarded as containing a
record of a lamp's
variations in brightness,
where these variations
were originally
produced by sound
waves of varying
intensity. When light is
shone through the track
on to a photocell, the cell
produces an electric
current, the intensity of
which varies in
accordance with the
original frequency of the
sound. This current is
played back through
loudspeakers.

projector or the tape recorder.

The crystal sync system works on a similar
principle to the signal pulse method, the
difference being that the reference signal for the
tape recorder is provided by an extremely
accurate quartz crystal oscillator. A duplicate
crystal provides a corresponding signal, which is
used to control the running speed of the camera.
This system eliminates the need for any physical
connection between the recorder and the
camera, but the latter has to be specially
modified to do the job.

Another system in which the camera motor
speed is controlled is known as Optasound in the
USA and Perfectsound in the UK. This system
uses a special perforated tape, which can be
played on any standard ¼ inch reel-to-reel
recorder. When the tape is running, the
perforations are 'read' by the synchronizer unit
and converted into a series of electrical impulses.
These, again, control the motor speed of the
camera. The pitch of the tape perforations
depends on the running speed of the tape
recorder and the desired filming speed. If the
recorder runs at 3¾ins per second and the
desired filming speed is 18 frames per second, for
instance, then the tape must have 18 perforations
every 3¾ ins.

Choosing a tape recorder

With double-system sound, selecting the right
tape recorder is obviously vital. For location
work, a battery-operated cassette is ideal, but,
for studio work and master soundtrack
compilation, a ¼ in reel-to-reel recorder should
be used. This should have the following features,

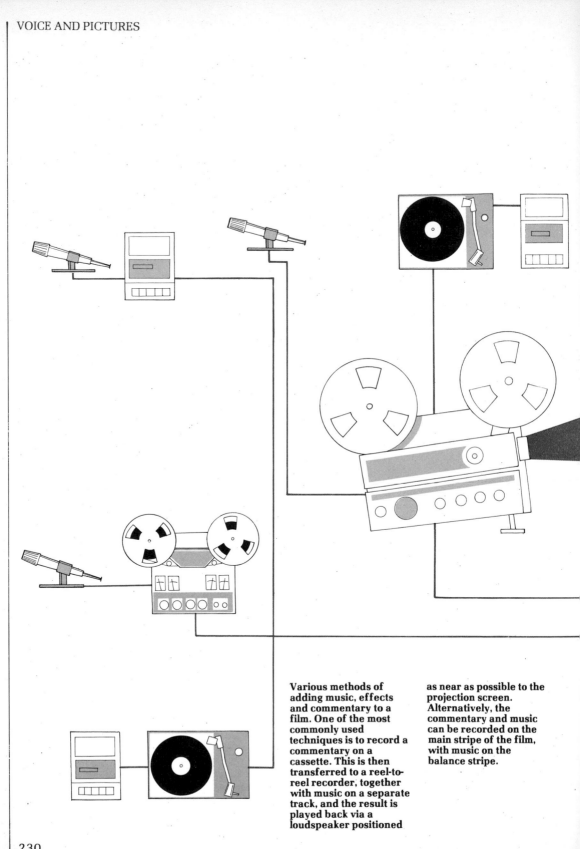

Various methods of adding music, effects and commentary to a film. One of the most commonly used techniques is to record a commentary on a cassette. This is then transferred to a reel-to-reel recorder, together with music on a separate track, and the result is played back via a loudspeaker positioned as near as possible to the projection screen. Alternatively, the commentary and music can be recorded on the main stripe of the film, with music on the balance stripe.

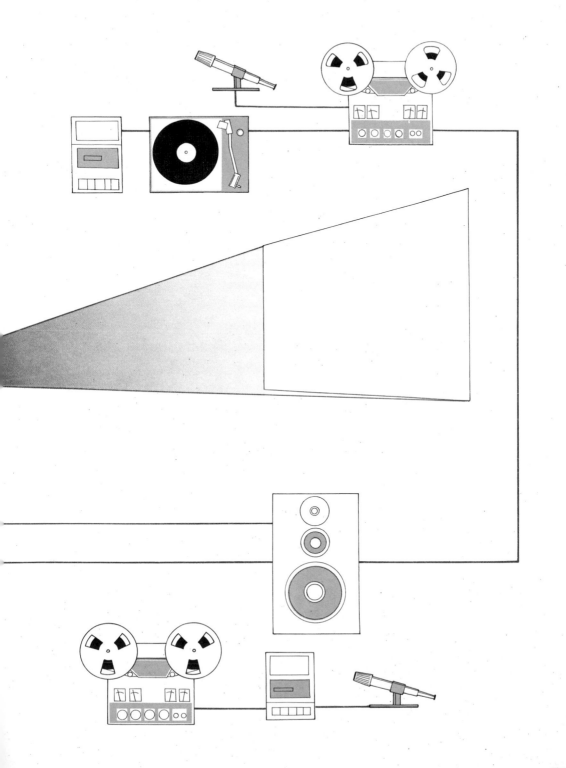

Super 8 recorders produce a soundtrack directly on to Super 8 magnetic film and they can transfer sound to such a film from sync sound tape or cassette recorders. They can synchronize with any Super 8 sound projector, thus allowing transfer of sound from edited magnetic film to the magnetic edge strips of a release print.

all of which are essential.

Firstly, the recorder should be four track, with the capability of replaying two tracks in parallel. Parallel playback allows two independently recorded tracks to be replayed simultaneously. Thus, one track can be used for live recording and the other for background music, commentary or extra sound effects. Secondly, the machine should have a lockable pause control. While in 'pause', some recorders allow the tape to be inched by hand backwards and forwards over the magnetic heads. This makes it easier to cue the tape. When the pause control is released, tape travel should begin instantly, without any noticeable 'wow' — sound distortion causing an inconsistency in pitch.

An accurate tape counter for quickly locating parts of the track is also extremely useful, while a running speed of at least 3¾ ins per second is vital. Many machines have a range of speeds; the higher ones produce better sound quality, while off-beat sound effects can be created by recording at one speed and replaying at another. The machine should also have a headphone socket, so that the quality of the sound being recorded can be monitored. Nearly all modern recorders have some means of monitoring the input signal, while more sophisticated models are frequently fitted with a separate playback head.

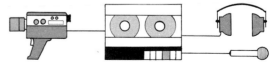

Above **For location work a Super 8 sound recorder will record in sync with about 40 sync sound cameras.**

Below **If sync sound is being transferred, frame rate information has to be passed by means of a sync signal.**

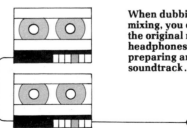

When dubbing and mixing, you can listen to the original material on headphones while preparing an extra soundtrack.

This enables the operator to compare the quality of the input signal with the actual recording at the flick of a switch — a facility known as A-B monitoring.

Finally, it is important to be able to adjust the recording level manually. Some tape recorders are fitted with automatic level control (alc) — also known as automatic gain control (agc) — and this is normally perfectly adequate. However, the system cannot distinguish between wanted and unwanted sound and will therefore adjust the level to cope with the loudest sound present. In the absence of any predominant sound, it will increase the gain, recording quieter sounds, such as a ticking clock, at an unnaturally high level. Manual control avoids this problem.

On location

Whether indoors or outdoors, the first and most important task on any location is to choose the right microphone for the task in hand and to make sure that it is positioned correctly. Preparing the camera is simple; with single-system sound, this can be set up ready for action in just a few moments. Check that the inside of the camera is clean and that the batteries are fully charged. Insert the sound cartridge and close and lock the film door. Switch the camera on, plug in the microphone, check that the batteries are giving full power and that the sound meter on the camera is 'reading' the sound.

Microphones can be omnidirectional — picking up sound from all directions equally — or cardioid. The latter is so-called because its heart-shaped response pattern tends to reject sound coming from the sides and rear of the microphone. In other words, it is unidirectional. Most of the microphones supplied with cameras and tape recorders are omnidirectional, but cardioid models give better results.

Other types of microphone include hyperdirectional 'rifle' or 'gun' mikes, which have an even narrower angle of acceptance. They are extremely useful for picking out a single speaker in a crowd and are often used by film reporters for this reason. However, any microphone can be made more directional by mounting it in a parabolic reflector. This gathers

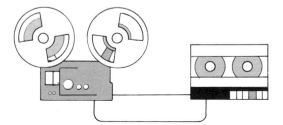

Left **When screening, sound on magnetic tape can be run in double-system with any projector equipped with a 1/F contact switch. Synchronization of projector and recorder is achieved through a PhotoStart, which reacts to a flash frame in the picture leader.**

For multi-track sync recording *below* **you can use several magnetic recorders in sync or use each track of a four-channel machine, syncing three tracks to a control track.**

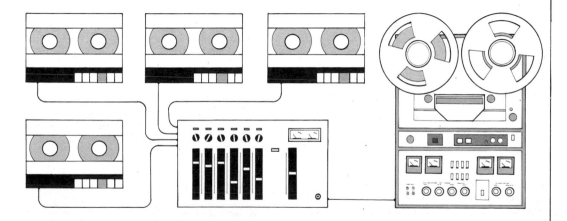

sound from a very narrow angle in front of the unit. In addition, there are bidirectional microphones, which have a figure-of-eight shaped response pattern. As their name implies, they are used when the sound is coming from two opposite directions.

Microphone placement

Normally, the best position for the microphone is as close to the subject as possible. This means that the recording level can be kept at a reasonably low setting and so the risk of picking up any extraneous noise is minimized. The two main objections to this are, firstly, that the subject may move away and, secondly, the microphone may appear in the shot.

One solution to both these problems is to use a cable microphone, concealing the cable under a carpet and the microphone itself behind some object in the scene, such as a vase of flowers. However, this device is somewhat inflexible, because such an object may not be present in every scene — certainly not outdoors — and the speaker's movements are severely restricted. The best solution is usually a microphone fitted into a telescopic hand or overhead boom. The microphone can thus be kept immediately above the subject's head, just high enough to keep it out of frame, while the boom can follow an actor's movements extremely easily.

Alternatively, a small microphone can be

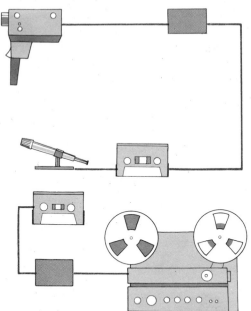

Above **Two of the ways in which a double system can be operated. In the first, images produced by a camera are synchronized with the sound recorded on tape. This can be done either by recording a control tape on a suitable tape** **recorder or, with Super 8, by using a special magnetic film recorder. Similarly, recorders of both kinds can be linked to a projector to produce the sound required — a mixture of music and speech, for instance.**

Right **A detail of a Synchrodek system. Systems like this are designed to control synchronization when the projector is used for editing in conjunction with a film recorder. A single pulse is produced for every projected frame and this later keeps sound and picture in step.**

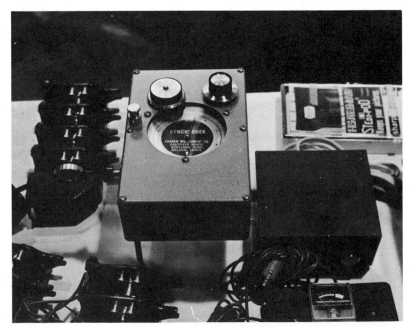

Left **Linking a projector, recorder and synchronizer to build an effects pilot track. The principle behind this is the same as that of ordinary double system recording, only in this case additional effects are required on the finished film. These have to be synchronized in a similar way to the initial sound if they are to run in sync.**

concealed about the actor's person. Lanyard and tie-pin mikes are available for this purpose, but this still leaves the problem of concealing the cable. There is also the additional problem of coping with the noise of the cable rustling every time the actor makes a move.

Even with a boom, the mike can pick up cable rustle or other handling noises. These effects can be minimized by winding a length of cable tightly round the boom and by gripping the boom handle firmly with the hands. Particular care should be taken to ensure that the recording level is satisfactory and does not alter appreciably as the boom follows the actors' movements. Avoid pointing the microphone towards any hard, reflecting surface, such as a bare wall, which will tend to reduce the effectiveness of its directional character. In interior shots, it is a good idea to drape such surfaces in soft, sound-absorbent materials, provided that they are out of camera shot.

The lone cameraman, however, can also use a boom. Several makes of camera have booms fitted to their tops, though the resulting sound will be of lower quality than that produced by a conventional microphone on the set. The only exception is when shooting close-ups. Here, it is important to check that the boom's shadow is not in shot; if in any doubt, it is best to shoot a test film first.

Some microphones, too, have a remote control switch, which either activates both sound and camera from the microphone position or completely independently. This can be extremely useful if, say, the cameraman wants to appear in the scene himself or if his presence is obtrusive — as when shooting wildlife.

Exterior locations
The problem of extraneous noise is much more difficult to solve when shooting outdoors. To start with, background noise is always present, however carefully the microphone is positioned. It is important, therefore, to ensure that all outdoor shooting is done with the background noise at a roughly similar level. Otherwise there may well be problems with the sound continuity at the editing stage. This makes delay inevitable, so the shooting schedule should always be planned with this in mind.

Right **An Uher 4400 Report Stereo IC tape recorder. Such machines are ideal for recording sound and for compiling a master soundtrack for use in the double system. All tape recorders used for this purpose should be four track and be able to replay two tracks simultaneously. In addition, they should have a lockable pause control, an accurate tape counter, a running speed of at least 3¾ in per second, a headphone socket so that the sound imput can be monitored and a manual means of adjusting the recording level. Used in conjunction with a silent camera, the double system produces good results; however, it is far more complex than the single system. In this, a sound camera *far right* records the sound directly on to magnetically striped film.**

Another problem is wind noise. On most occasions, this can be reduced to an acceptable level by fitting a foam plastic windguard over the receiving end of the microphone. If, however, the wind is particularly blustery, the only alternatives are to wait for it to die down or to dub the soundtrack later.

Shooting with sound

Before shooting actually starts, check that the camera is set at the correct filming speed — usually 18 fps — the sound level is satisfactory and the microphone is properly positioned and out of shot. Place a sound proof cover — this is known as a blimp — over the camera to prevent any running noise being picked up by the microphone. Then, start the sound, start the camera and mark the shot.

Shots are marked by means of the clapper board — a device familiar to all movie fans but understood by very few of them. Basically, it serves two purposes; it identifies individual shots

and provides a clear sync reference point for double-system filming. The board itself is a type of blackboard, with a hinged top section. It is shot at the beginning of each take, with a member of the crew closing the clapstick to make an audible 'clap' on the soundtrack and following this by calling out the information on the board. This identifies the scene, the shot and the take.

Sound editing

Sound editing is one of the least glorified aspects of film making — and also one of the most important. Since it is expected to be unobtrusive, only the technical flaws will be remembered by the listener. Sound editing is an integral part of film editing as a whole; it must be regarded as part of the creative process, not as merely the creating of background noise. Whether or not the listener is aware of it, the sound of a film exerts a subtle influence on the emotional attitude of the audience and on its enjoyment of what is appearing on the screen.

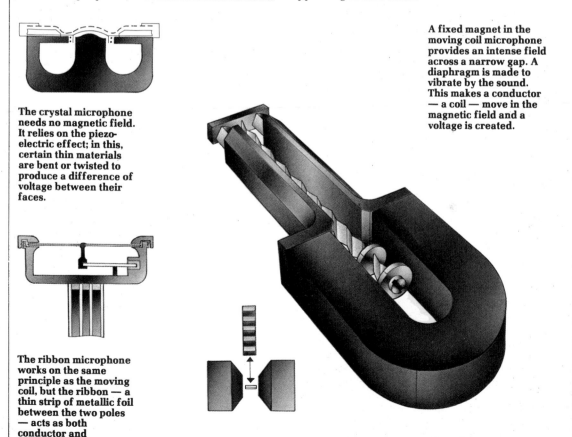

A fixed magnet in the moving coil microphone provides an intense field across a narrow gap. A diaphragm is made to vibrate by the sound. This makes a conductor — a coil — move in the magnetic field and a voltage is created.

The crystal microphone needs no magnetic field. It relies on the piezo-electric effect; in this, certain thin materials are bent or twisted to produce a difference of voltage between their faces.

The ribbon microphone works on the same principle as the moving coil, but the ribbon — a thin strip of metallic foil between the two poles — acts as both conductor and diaphragm.

There are three main ways in which single-system footage can be edited. The striped film can be edited directly, making the necessary allowance for the 18 frame gap between sound and picture. Alternatively, the sound can be transferred to perforated tape. This enables the editor to edit the sound and picture on a frame-for-frame basis. A two-way synchronizer transports the film and tape simultaneously during editing; this can be used in conjunction with an editor/viewer and sound reader to provide simultaneous monitoring of sound and picture.

A third method is to transfer the sound to a special magnetic material, known as fullcoat, which has exactly the same physical dimensions as photographic film. Mechanically, fullcoat editing is much the same as editing with perforated tape, but it has two additional advantages. Firstly, because its edges are not perforated, sound and picture can be edited on a length for length, as well as a frame for frame,

Top **An omni-directional microphone, as its name implies, picks up sound from all directions, so recordings made using it frequently have the problem of unwanted background noise.** *Centre* **The cardiod's heart-shaped response pattern makes it much more directional, while the bi-directional microphone** *below* **is useful for recording dialogue.**

basis. Secondly, fullcoat can be cut and joined with an ordinary adhesive tape film splicer, though the tape should never be allowed to cover the magnetic oxide surface. But its disadvantage is also a big one; it cannot be played on a conventional ¼ in tape recorder and this keeps it from being widely adopted.

Editing direct

Direct editing is undoubtedly the quickest of the three methods and it is the one normally used by amateurs. The equipment required is simple; only an editor/viewer fitted with a sound stripe reader is needed. The technique is very similar to the basic concept of cutting on action, only now the editor is cutting on sound. First, the film is run through the editor and a cutting point at the end of the first shot is chosen. The frame is marked in the picture gate with a chinagraph pencil. The editor then advances the film by 18 frames, so that the chinagraph mark is positioned over the sound reader. The film is then run backwards and forwards a few times and a note is made of what the sound is at the point.

Next, the editor laces up the second shot and finds the corresponding point in the duplicated section of sound at the beginning of the shot — in

Below **Shooting for sound outdoors. Exterior sound is without question the most difficult subject to shoot adequately, as so many external factors can affect the final quality. The thing to strive for is sound continuity; this means watching the background noise carefully, so that extraneous sound is kept to a tolerable level. If it is unacceptable, the alternatives are to re-shoot later or dub the sound.**

Right **Shooting for sound in the studio. The microphone boom on top of the camera, though a boon to the lone movie maker, does not produce as good a result as the hand-held boom. This is the best set-up for general-purpose filming, as the alternatives frequently involve concealing cable or limiting movement on the set.**

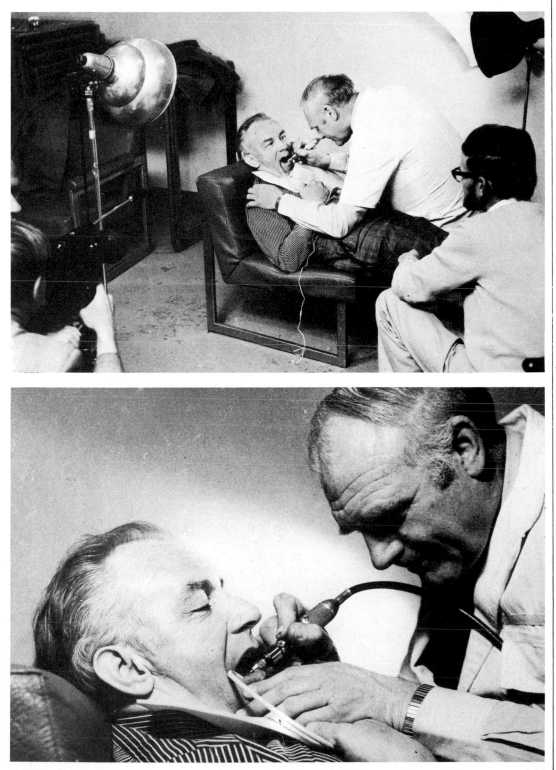

other words, the corresponding point in the overlap. This time, the mark is made at the sound head. The editor now cuts the two pieces of film at the marked frames and splices them together.

This method works best if due allowance has been made for the 18 frame gap between sound and picture when the film is planned; however, unplanned footage can also be edited in this way. In both cases, the basic rule remains the same — edit for sound.

The reason for this seemingly complicated process is simple. When film is transported through the camera, its motion is not continuous because each frame is held for a fraction of a second in the picture gate during exposure. If the sound recording head were to be placed alongside the picture gate, the intermittent motion of the film would produce 'flutter' on the soundtrack. Separating the sound head from the picture gate allows the intermittent motion of the film to be smoothed out before recording takes place. This creates the separation, which has been standardized at 18 fps for Super 8 film.

This means that the sound lies 18 frames in advance of its corresponding picture, so that when a cut is made at the beginning of a shot, the first 18 frames will be lost. Conversely, when cutting at the end of a shot, the editor gains 18 frames of sound from the next piece of film. By shooting overlaps, the film maker covers these gains and losses — the last 18 frames of sound from the preceding shot cover the first 18 frames of picture of the next.

Two types of clapperboard. This simple but invaluable device is like a blackboard with a hinged top section or clapstick.

Shooting begins. Each shot must be marked audibly and visibly by a clapper board to identify individual shots and to provide a clear sync reference point for double-system filming.

Sound discipline

The use of sound imposes its own discipline on the film maker at the same time as extending his or her scope and opportunity. Even at the shooting stage it is necessary to 'think sound' until this becomes second nature. At first it is tempting simply to film someone standing and talking in front of the camera. However, unless he or she has something very interesting to say, this is boring and a waste of valuable film. Used intelligently, live sound will enhance almost every subject. The fun and excitement of a child's birthday party for example, will be captured all the more vividly with a sound camera. Similarly, a documentary will come to life it the participants can recount their experiences directly.

The best films usually result from following a script or plan, and this is even more true of live sound. Of course, this does not mean that spontaneity must be abandoned, or that a detailed script must necessarily be prepared. By following a few simple rules, it is possible to avoid many of the pitfalls of shooting in sound.

A film of a parade serves as a good example to illustrate some of the most frequent difficulties. With a silent camera, the process is simple. First the band is shot approaching the camera, then perhaps the operator switches to a shot of the spectators. By the next shot, the band will be marching away. This basic three-shot sequence has a certain inbuilt continuity even before it is edited.

With a sound camera, the approach must be different. Although the pictures will appear continuously, just as before, the same will not apply to the soundtrack. At the end of the first shot the band is cut off in mid-note; the music of the second shot will not follow on, and the third will again be unrelated. The final effect will be totally disjointed, like listening to three separate snatches of music from a gramophone record.

This problem can be overcome in various ways. One method is simply to film the band passing by in one continuous take, omitting the shot of the spectators. This would provide sound continuity, but it is merely a compromise

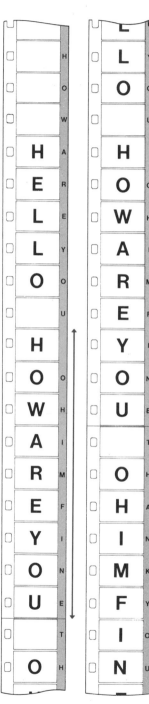

On single-system sound film, shot at 18fps, sound is recorded 18 frames ahead of the picture to which it belongs, so for each cut the sound continues for a second after the picture. If you film for a second longer than you need at either end of a shot, you can edit as *above*.

solution. The best results would probably be achieved by taking the shot of the spectators later, and inserting it into the sequence.

Before attempting to use live sound in a serious film, it is a good idea to shoot a few test cartridges in a variety of circumstances. The results of these tests can then be analysed critically to see where the technique could be improved. Typical things to check are the microphone position, the quality produced by a boom mike and whether a better sound perspective could have been obtained by controlling the recording level manually. Only through a constant process of examination will the film maker reach the goal of the best possible sound movie.

Dubbing

Dubbing, or post-sync recording as it is also known, is the name given to the process of recording the sound after the film has been shot. As far as music and sound effects are concerned, this is relatively simple, but the successful dubbing of lip-sync dialogue is much more difficult. This should therefore be avoided whenever possible, but it may become essential if poor sound conditions — traffic noise, say — or equipment failure make it impossible to record adequately during shooting. The technique involves making a synchronized recording of the actors speaking their lines while they follow their lip movements on the screen.

Loops of film, running anywhere in length from

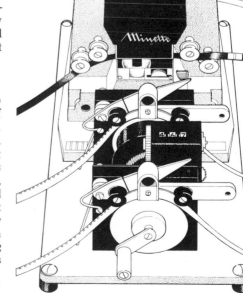

a few feet to a hundred feet long, are prepared for each sequence to be dubbed. Short sequences are extended by splicing in a length of white-coated leader (blank film). The original recordings are played over repeatedly to allow the actors to thoroughly familiarize themselves with their lines and the way they were delivered. The actors should pay particular attention to intonation and timing.

The film loops are then projecting continuously, giving the actors the chance to make several attempts at matching their lip movements. As with filming, the microphone is positioned as near to the actors and as far away from the projector as possible. The recording should be made on synchronized magnetic tape; it can later be transferred to the film stripe.

Adding music and effects

Music and special effects are an essential part of any sound film. They can create, enhance or even break the mood of a scene and are therefore a vital back-up to straight dialogue. Sound can also suggest things that are not visible but are part of the mood of the scene — clashing swords as the screen shows the deserted battlements of a castle, for instance.

There are three ways to add music and effects to live sound. The first is to use the 'Tric' or superimpose facility which is now a standard feature on most projectors. This involves partially erasing the original recording and making a new one over the top. The process is a straightforward one, but also risky. One mistake permanently ruins the original recording.

Alternatively, several modern projectors — some of them stereo models — allow the balance stripe of the film to be used as a second track. This

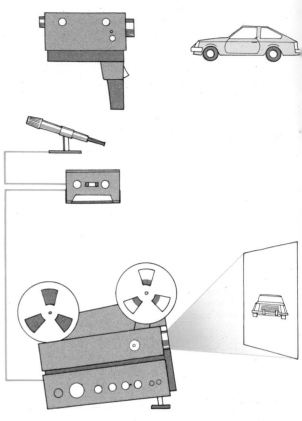

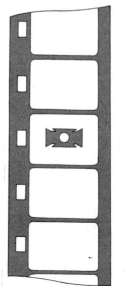
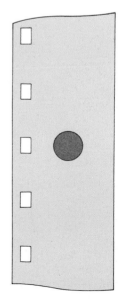

Top right **Dubbing is an extremely useful technique as it means that film and the accompanying sound can be matched up at different times. The sound is recorded on to tape and then transferred to the film via the projector. Even in such a simple sequence as the one illustrated, however, synchronization is** **critical. This involves the use of sync marks on both tape and film** *left* **and** *right*. **These reference points enable the operator to start film and tape from the same point every time they are run. The marks can be lined up at convenient points, such as the gate of the projector and the tape sync mark at the playback head.**

Left **Adding a commentary to 16mm film and** *below* **a semi-professional dubbing studio. Dubbing is frequently used when local conditions make sound recording on location impossible or unsatisfactory. If actors are involved, this involves careful rehearsal, so that the recording matches up with their lip movements on screen.**

can be used for recording music and effects, leaving the original 'live' recordings intact on the main stripe. The two stripes can be replayed in parallel. The only disadvantage of this method is that the soundtrack cannot be reproduced in full if projected on a conventional, single-stripe, machine. A third method is to lift the live sound from the stripe and copy it onto one track of a synchronized ¼in magnetic tape. Music and effects can then be recorded on the second track and both tracks transferred back on to the stripe.

The final method is probably the most convenient one for the majority of amateur film makers. Either a mechanical or a pulse synchronizer can be used to compile the music and effects track; the former is usually the better, as the projector and tape recorder can then be stopped and re-started as often as required without loss of sync. The film and tape can also be run either forwards or backwards in exact synchronization. This is known as a rock-and-roll facility. After the music and effects track has been compiled, the final transfer — together with the 'live' track — can be made back on to the stripe. A simple mixer unit is used to control the balance of the two tracks during the transfer.

Right **A typical sound projector. One useful feature of any sound projector is a variable speed control. This means that if, say, a sound camera runs two per cent slow, then the projector can be adjusted for accuracy. This drive is also a specialized feature. In most sound projectors the combination of a sprocketless drive with a servo system means that only one motor is required, as opposed to the two of the sound camera.**

Take-up reel spindle ——

Rear leg ——

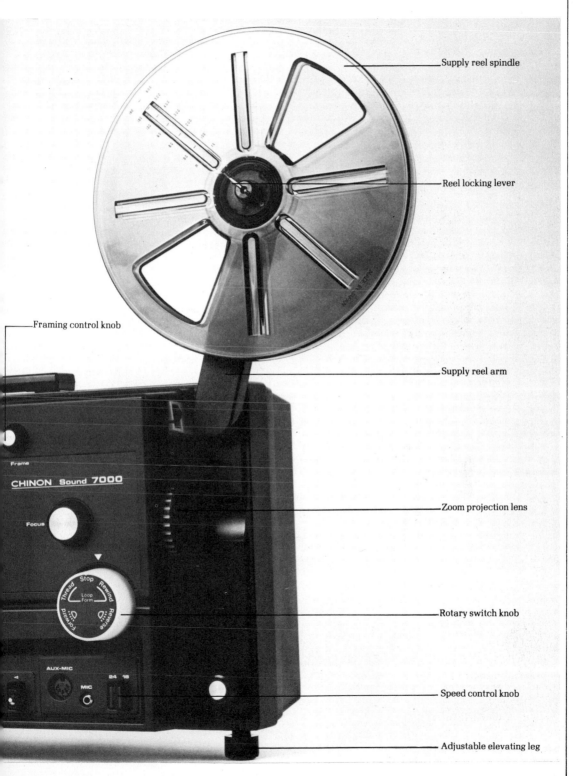

Supply reel spindle

Reel locking lever

Framing control knob

Supply reel arm

CHINON Sound 7000

Focus

Zoom projection lens

Thread Stop Rewind
Loop Form
Forward Reverse

Rotary switch knob

AUX-MIC

MIC 24 16

Speed control knob

Adjustable elevating leg

Sound effects

Even the simplest sound effects can work wonders in transforming a film from the humdrum into an effective and exciting production. A film of a speeding car, for instance, is considerably enhanced by the sound of squealing tyres on the soundtrack; if the final shot is a car smash, it will appear far more realistic if the sound of the crash is heard by the audience before they see the shot of the wrecked car.

There are various ways of obtaining such effects. One obvious method is by on-the-spot recording. For this, you need a good battery operated tape or cassette recorder, headphones and a directional microphone. Either a cardioid or hypercardioid (rifle) mike can be used, either on their own or fitted to a parabolic reflector. This improves sound pick-up, but is only really suited to recording high frequencies.

However, it is not always possible to be at exactly the right place at the right time, so other methods of obtaining effects frequently have to be used. Commercial effects discs and tapes can be purchased; alternatively, effects can be ordered from a sound library. If a large number of effects is required, this is probably the simplest and most convenient way of obtaining them. The library must be told how long the effect is to last — high or low — whether it is to have a repeating chime and so on. The tape speed and the track configuration must always be given.

Sound effects, however, can easily be created at home. The illustrations below show how to make some common ones.

recording the sound made when a piece of card flutters against an electric fan.

The effect of rowing can be achieved by co-ordinating the noise made by a creaky door and the splashing sound made by rhythmically dipping a piece of wood into a bowl of water.

The effect of a large bird in flight can be achieved by flapping two pieces of bamboo in front of a microphone.

To simulate the sound of water lapping, fill a large plastic bucket with water, stir it briskly and record the sound of the 'waves' lapping against the sides of the bucket.

The noise made by a small bird's wings can easily be produced by

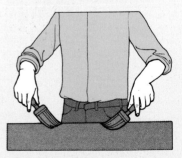

The sound of waves can be created by sweeping two brushes across a sheet of metal in opposite directions.

Artillery fire can be simulated by making a short sharp sound into the microphone.

sandpaper and rubbing them together.

To create the booming sound of a ship's siren or fog horn, half fill a bottle with water and blow across the top. The deeper the sound, the less water is required.

A roll of thunder can be simulated simply by breathing gently on the microphone. Remember, however, not to use an expensive ribbon microphone as it may get spoilt.

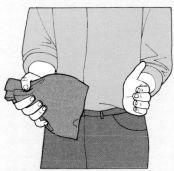

Apart from making a short sharp noise into a microphone *top,* the sound of a single shell shot can also be achieved by bursting a paper bag. For the most convincing results, the effect should be recorded at 15 inches per second and played back at 3¾ inches per second.

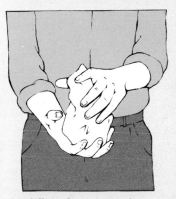

Footfalls in the snow can be simulated by rhythmically crumbling a bag of flour.

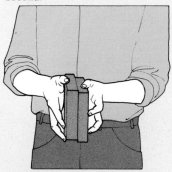

If the puffing noise of a steam train is needed — say, for a comedy sequence — a realistic effect can be created by covering two wooden blocks with

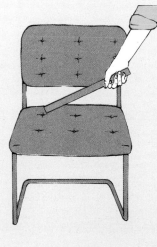

An effective gun shot can be achieved by hitting a solid object, such as a table or a leather chair, sharply with a ruler or stick.

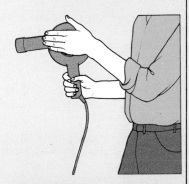

The scream of a jet plane can be simulated by recording the noise made by a hairdryer or vacuum cleaner, first placing a hand over the 'exhaust' to restrict the air flow.

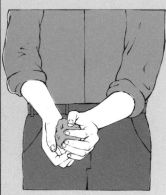

Fire can be simulated in several ways; crushing a piece of cellophane before the microphone is only one of several alternatives. A matchbox can be similarly crushed, or the sound of sizzling fat can be recorded.

The sighing of wind in trees can be achieved by shaking a handful of old recording tape in front of the microphone.

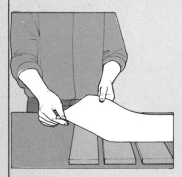

The sound of wind can be simulated by pulling a piece of

silk across two or three wooden boards. By varying the amount of drag, the strength of wind can be varied to produce effects ranging from a light breeze to a gale.

A method of simulating a telephone voice, other than using headphones is to speak into a small china or plastic cup.

Simulating the sound of a telephone conversation is a useful device. One way of creating the sound of a telephone voice is to plug headphones into the microphone input and speak into them.

To simulate the sound of a horse's hooves, two halves of a coconut shell can be struck together or drummed on a hard surface at varying speeds to achieve the desired effect.

A second method of simulating rain, is to record the noise made by a constant trickle of castor sugar being poured down a paper chute. Remember to place the microphone directly beneath the chute for best results.

One way of creating the effect of falling rain is to roll about 20 dried peas backwards and forwards in a fine-meshed wire sieve directly above a microphone. The effect is most realistic.

Movie Magic

Tricks and effects can add a touch of magic to almost every movie film. The transition from one scene to another, for example, is often improved by the use of a dissolve or fade, while some scenes themselves benefit from special techniques, such as slow motion and reverse filming. However, all such effects should be used discreetly and be closely linked with the subject matter of the film.

Stop motion

Stop motion is one of the easiest movie effects for the beginner to master. All that it involves is the correct use of the single frame release button on the camera. This does exactly what you would expect it to do — exposing one frame at a time rather than the 18 or 24 frames per second of normal filming.

The technique can produce some extremely interesting results. Suppose, for instance, you

wanted to film the sun setting. Normal filming would involve the use of a great deal of film stock and could be somewhat boring, even though various stages of the sunset were filmed at different angles. Using single frame exposures, however, you can make the sun set in just a few seconds. Set the camera up on a tripod, select a good viewpoint of the evening sun, check the exposure and then film one frame. Take another single frame a few seconds later and repeat the process until the sun finally disappears. When the film is screened, the sun will appear to speed across the sky in a fascinating curve; the speed will depend simply on the frequency at which the separate frames have been exposed.

Single frame filming can be used to produce all sorts of cinematic tricks. For example, you might decide to give the audience a hair-raising car ride around a town at 200 miles per hour. For this, you

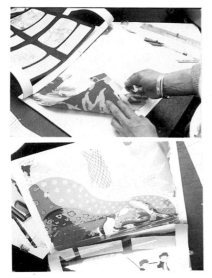

An animator at work on the US TV series 'Fangface' by Ruby Spears Productions Inc. The base material for such animation is transparent plastic sheets, called cels. These carry the final illustrations, after the rough form of the story has been worked out with model sheets and a story board. The central piece of equipment is an animation disc — a light box with a rotating glass surface. There are pegs on opposite sides, which can be moved sideways in either direction. This means that a cel with a figure can be attached to the bottom pegs and moved on the spot, while the background is attached to the top pegs and moved sideways. The back of the cel, as well as the front, is used. The different layers of film are placed one on the other.

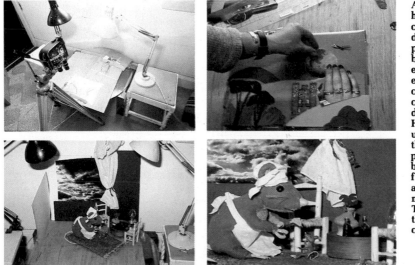

A suitable set-up for home animation. The camera shoots downwards on to a pegboard, fixed on to a base board. The lights on either side must be of equal intensity. Either cut-outs or puppets, say, can be arranged as desired under camera. Household spotlights are used, with cardboard for the windows, a photograph for the sky behind, curtains made from an old nightdress and puppet clothing made from old sheets. The final picture shows the scene through the camera's eye.

Single frame shooting can be used to create many different effects. In action shots, such as a car sequence, it is important to keep the **camera still** *(above.* **On the** *right,* **single framing enables the little girl to 'ride' her rocking horse over the jump.**

just need your camera, a cartridge of film, a tripod and a friend to drive the car. Sit in the front passenger seat and set up the tripod carefully around your body to ensure that it will move as little as possible. Put the camera firmly on the tripod and check that the lens is pointing straight ahead, without any of the windshield surround being visible. Now ask your friend to drive through the town at a fairly slow speed, stopping at crossings and changing direction as often as possible. As he drives, you must operate the single frame release as quickly as possible — the optimum rate is about two frames a second.

When the film returns from processing, the results will be electrifying, especially when the car stops and pedestrians cross the street. The car will appear to be zooming around at a frighteningly dangerous speed and, if you add motor noise, some fast music and assorted tyre screeches to a soundtrack, the result can be extremely entertaining.

Another comedy technique based on stop motion is to 'film' somebody putting up a deckchair on the beach. Ask him to take as long as possible over it and to get into all sorts of tangles. While the action is taking place, operate the single frame release just as you did when filming the car ride. The result on screen can be very amusing.

Stop motion, however, can be used for far more than comedy. You can make traffic speed along, people and objects move unnaturally, plants blossom on screen and generally play around with movement for extremely dramatic effect. Action, for example, stands up well to the contrasts given by imposing this kind of treatment.

Diffusion and distortion

Both these techniques have their uses when the appropriate special effect is required. Diffusion, for instance, gives a scene a misty, romantic atmosphere. Special lens attachments can be used to produce the effect, but it is far cheaper to make a diffuser of your own. Stretch a piece of gauze, or similar material, over a frame and hold it about half an inch away from the lens, increasing the exposure slightly to compensate for the loss of brightness. Cutting out a shape in the gauze means that the effect can be localised.

Distortion comes in useful if, say, a drunken

Below **Star ship in flight. In this shot, this realistic model is being filmed against a star background; it is supported by a 'blacked off' stand. The ship's basic framework is balsa wood and plastic, the external features coming from proprietary** airplane and tank kits. Total cost was $40 (£20). *Left* **Touching up the paintwork and** *above* **the Earth from space. This effect was created by painting on a glass globe and filming against a black background. The camera is panning to cover the surface.**

scene is being filmed from the point of view of the participants. Any form of uneven reflecting material can be used; metal mirrors are ideal. Position the camera at a suitable angle to the subject and simply move the surface in front of the lens to produce the required effect.

Night scenes are almost always faked. The trick here is to take an under-exposed film in daylight so that the sun looks like the moon. Three stops down from normal is sufficient for color film, though black and white may require slightly more. The scene should be backlit, if possible; figures and shapes then show in outline and shadows run forwards and not backwards.

Dissolves
A dissolve — merging the last shots of one scene into the opening ones of the next — is a common and extremely effective method of changing scene. Some cameras are equipped with an automatic dissolve mechanism; others, however, require a degree of physical skill from the operator to achieve the desired effect. The crucial thing is to overlap the scenes correctly. Otherwise there will be a visible lack of density at the mid-point of the dissolve.

The only cameras which can carry out this technique are those equipped with backwind or reverse running and a frame counter. Super 8 cameras can be fitted with a separate accessory unit to achieve this. At the end of a scene, run the camera on for an extra three seconds, reducing the aperture at the same time down to the minimum. Then re-wind the camera for four and a half seconds. Set up the new scene, start the camera and fade-in to reach full aperture after three seconds.

The technique must be carried out over a range of at least six stops to be effective. This can sometimes cause problems — in bright sunlight, say — when the camera is already too stopped down for this to be achieved. The solution here is to use a fader attachment, a neutral density filter or a cross polarising filter.

Reverse action
This is a favourite comedy technique and can be achieved even if your camera does not have a

To achieve a misty, romantic atmosphere *left,* the home movie maker can buy a special lens attachment. Alternatively a perfectly effective substitute — a piece of gauze stretched over a frame *above* — can be used.

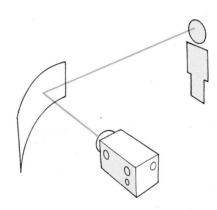

To give the effect of a scene through a drunkard's eyes *right,* the shot can be taken from the reflection in a strategically placed mirror joggled about to give the desired effect *above.*

reverse filming capability. All that is necessary is to film the scene in the normal way, but with the camera turned upside down. The eventual image will appear reversed left to right, so the scene should be carefully arranged to conceal this from the audience.

After the film has been processed, the relevant scene is cut out, turned the other way up and back to front, so that the perforations all run down the same side. Extra care must be taken when splicing, as the shiny and matt (emulsion) surfaces of the film have to be firmly joined together.

The one disadvantage of this method is the loss of sharpness during projection because the image is on the wrong side of the film. The only way to overcome this is to re-adjust the focus for the scene and, for this reason, extended reverse action scenes are usually preferable to short ones.

Simple animation

It is a common misconception that animation involves thousands of drawings and months of work. This is obviously true as far as full-scale features are concerned, but the simpler forms of animation are not at all difficult, not time consuming and well within the scope of the amateur. It is not even necessary to have a talent for drawing; all kinds of things can be animated

The way to produce a dissolve — a standard method of changing scene — is to merge the last shots of one sequence into the opening ones of the next. The effect is a simple one to achieve on cameras fitted with the necessary automatic mechanism; alternatively fade-out and fade-in to produce a similar result. Dissolves can be produced mechanically without an automatic mechanism, but only by backwinding the film in a special light-proof device.

without a pen being put near a piece of paper. Animation is also economical as far as the use of film is concerned and you can work at your own pace. Moreover, you do not have to rely on weather conditions or on having other people to help you.

One good way of tackling animation is to use flexible models and toys so that limbs can be moved easily. As with stop motion, the camera is used to take single-frame exposures, the object being moved a little between each one. To take an example, suppose you were animating a flexible toy — perhaps a little dwarf — which had to raise its hand to its head and remove its hat. The scene is set up, with the camera firmly supported by a tripod and lit with movie lights to give the correct exposure. Next, work out how long the sequence has to last. This particular example might last for ten seconds; this would mean that 180 separate frames of film have to be exposed and 180 separate movements of the dwarf's arm. In effect, however, this work load can be considerably reduced by double framing (taking two frames for each movement) and by a close-up, perhaps, at the start and end of the shot.

The actual section with the hand going up to the hat, lifting it and bringing it down again, might last for only four or five seconds, which means 90 frames (45 if you double frame). Once you have set up the scene and calculated the timings, you simply make the desired movement — bending the toy's hand up slightly, say — shoot a couple of frames, move the hand a little further, shoot another couple of frames and so on until the sequence is completed.

Naturally, toys are not the only articles you can animate. You can give life to all sorts of materials. Plasticine is one favorite, but grains of rice (moving around in attractive patterns), sticks of chalk (which become soldiers on parade), boiled sweets (dancing in formation) and checker counters (staging a battle), are all good subjects.

If you decide to try your hand at animation by drawing, the first essential is a simple rostrum. This need only consist of a support for the camera, a baseboard for the drawings, with two dowel pegs to locate them, and supports for two lights — these could even be a couple of baking tins holding photoflood lamps. Arm yourself with a packet of felt-tipped pens and large pack of white typing paper and you will be ready to start.

Start by experimenting with one cartridge of film, trying out simple ideas. For instance, you could draw coloured shapes that change size, move around the screen and then change shape, adding a piece of lively music on a soundtrack to

Right **Reverse action is a particularly effective movie technique, particularly in comedy sequences. Many cameras have a reverse filming mechanism, but a lack of one does not mean that the technique can be used. The same result can be produced by turning the camera upside down and filming with it in this position** *below.*

accompany them.

Say, for the sake of argument, that you wanted to start with a blob shape and enlarge it until it fills the screen completely. Calculate how long you want the effect to last — in this case, it might well be three seconds — and work it out in animation time. If your projector runs at 18 frames per second, this means that you multiply 18 by 3; in other words, 54 separate drawings will be required, or 27 if you are using double framing.

Place the first piece of paper on the baseboard and draw a tiny colored blob. Take two single-frame exposures and then put a second piece of paper over the first. Draw a second blob in the same position as the first — you will be able to see this through the paper — but slightly larger. Then remove the first sheet of paper. Take two frames of the second blob and then put another sheet on the baseboard. Draw a third blob in the same position, making this slightly bigger than the second. Remove the second paper and then take two frames of blob three. Carry on in this way until the sequence has been completed. If you keep the pieces of paper and film them in reverse order, the blob will start by filling the screen and then diminish.

Using this simple technique, all kinds of images can be created. If you wanted a triangle to travel sideways across the screen, you would start by drawing the triangle on the left side of the paper and expose two frames. A second triangle on another sheet would then be drawn slightly to the right, two frames taken of this, and so on. If the triangle was required to cross the screen in nine seconds, you would only have to make nine drawings and double frame them.

Experimenting with drawn characters tends to be more of a specialist task. To whet your appetite, experiment with very simple story lines that do not require a great deal of drawing. For example, try drawing a fat comic worm that sticks its head above the ground and then spots a huge spider which tries to catch it. The first drawings are of the worm pushing its head above ground. The ground is just a 'line' across the screen, with the worm gradually moving its head upwards and rolling its eyes around. In the arrival of the spider, the web would firstly drop down to the ground over two seconds (18 drawings). In this case, however, it would not be necessary to change the sheets; you can just add to the line with your pen prior to the next two frames of the sequence being shot.

Next, the spider slides down the web. For this, every drawing would have to be on a separate sheet of paper. The spider's eyes revolve and he sees the worm. He then scuttles across the screen in pursuit. Here, it is not essential for the drawing to be true to life. A series of drawings of the spider with his legs in different positions would be quite adequate at this stage and would probably get more laughs.

Animation is one of the most fascinating branches of film making; part of this lies in the fact that all kinds of craziness can be brought to life through it. It is worth perservering to improve your technique, as you are limited only by your imagination — not by your ability to draw. If you do not want to draw on paper, paint the baseboard with blackboard blacking and make your drawings with coloured chalk, which can be rubbed out between drawings. Alternatively, cut-out shapes, colored paper and even felt could be used. Whatever you choose, however, keep the scene and plot simple until you feel competent to tackle something more ambitious.

Titling movies

Titling is another creative area in which the amateur can develop his own ideas and style. Prepared titles can be bought, but these are normally limited to stock general themes. It is easy and much more fun to make your own than rely on the bought-in variety.

Titles fall into two categories — the main titles at the beginning and end of a film and sub-titles within individual scenes. Good camera work usually makes the latter redundant and their use should be avoided when ever possible. By far the widest range of title letters is available in the dry transfer format, such as Letraset, though other materials, of course, can be used. Movable letters made from plastic, felt and cork are all available; their chief advantage is that they can be re-used. Whatever form of lettering is chosen, the style should remain the same throughout the film and should be chosen to suit the subject.

It is easiest to shoot titles in a titler designed for the purpose. This can be very simple; the rostrum described in the previous section is perfectly adequate. Alternatively, position the title board on a level floor and set the camera up over it, using a tripod. Lighting should be flat and angled to avoid reflections. Above all else, always check through the viewfinder to make sure the title is straight before shooting it.

To make titles move, use a roller. The base for this can be a large tin, with the titles themselves pasted round its outside. Either rotate it gradually while filming or move it forward little by little in conjunction with single shots. To make a title bigger or smaller, use a zoom lens.

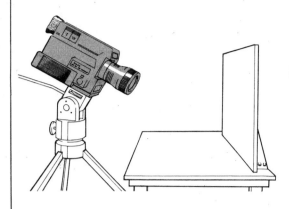

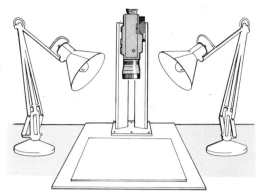

Above **Taking a background shot which will eventually be used as an animation cel and** *right* **a simple titling set-up.**

The sequence of shots here shows the application of the simple rules of stop-frame animation. Remember that this technique can be varied — double framing, for instance, can be used — as long as the results are suitably realistic. The important thing is to calculate how many shots you will need to produce the desired effect.

For a first attempt at animation, it is a good idea to use one of the many toys whose limbs can be bent into different positions in which they remain stable. If you shoot one limb position, stop, move the limbs slightly in the right direction for walking, waving or whatever movement is required, film again, and so on, the results will be most convincing.

262

Below **The various cels pictured here are all drawn individually and eventually brought together to create the animated action seen in the strip right.**

Animated titles

As an alternative to introducing a movie with static lettering on a plain background, animated titles can be used. Only a minimum of extra equipment is needed, it does not take very long and it is not at all difficult to do.

The rostrum previously described can be used as a titler, together with photoflood lamps. Although these have a relatively short life, they give excellent illumination and your titles will thus be bright and full of contrast. Obviously, it is important to focus the camera carefully; check that the model you own does not require a supplementary lens for close-up work. The camera should be high enough above the baseboard to give a reasonable field of view without showing the edges of the background sheet. The lamps should be angled carefully so that the illumination is bright and even.

Some bits and pieces from a local art store will

also be needed: half a dozen brightly-colored sheets of cartridge paper for backgrounds, some sheets of thin colored card for making flat 'models', pins for holding the backgrounds in position, a tin of rubber gum, and sheets of dry print lettering. Rubber gum is ideal for holding down art work under the heat of the lights; in addition, it will not mark the backing sheets since it can be simply rubbed away after use.

You will also need a sharp pair of scissors or a craft knife for cutting through the card. A pencil, eraser and a pair of compasses will come in handy too; probably the best idea is to invest in a child's geometry kit, which contains a number of useful items.

Suppose, for instance, that you have been for a holiday in Holland and made a film about it. One obvious idea would be to use windmills in some way for the title. The windmill is cut out from a piece of brown card, with a small black door

An assortment of the equipment needed for home titling. Dry transfer lettering is the most essential material, together with adhesive, paper and a sharp pair of scissors.

painted on it. The four vanes are cut as a complete section and mounted in position with a small nail or pin, so that they can revolve round it as a unit. The background could be light blue, with a piece of green paper fixed down behind the mill with rubber gum to represent the land.

The final effect could be as follows. As the scene is faded in, the vanes of the windmill start to revolve. As they pick up speed, small cards with the title letters in position appear at the side of the vanes and then form themselves up beside the mill to reveal the full title.

Most movie cameras have a fade-in button or variable shutter lever to achieve the fade, but their absence does not pose an insuperable difficulty. Run a small length of film with the lens cap on and switch to manual exposure. Film three frames at aperture f/22. Open the aperture by half a stop and film another three frames. Open another half stop and do the same, continuing the

Encyclopaedia
Encyclopaedia

Above **An example of a good and a bad homemade title and** *right* **the way to ensure success. The first step is to draw faint, but accurate, guide lines on the card on which the title is being mounted. A metal ruler is the best tool to use.**

The letters for the title — Letraset is being used in this instance — are then laid carefully in position and burnished down.

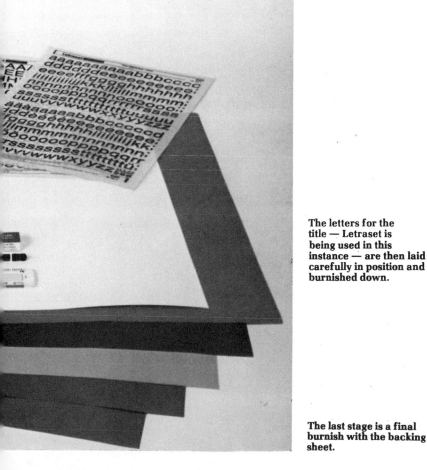

The last stage is a final burnish with the backing sheet.

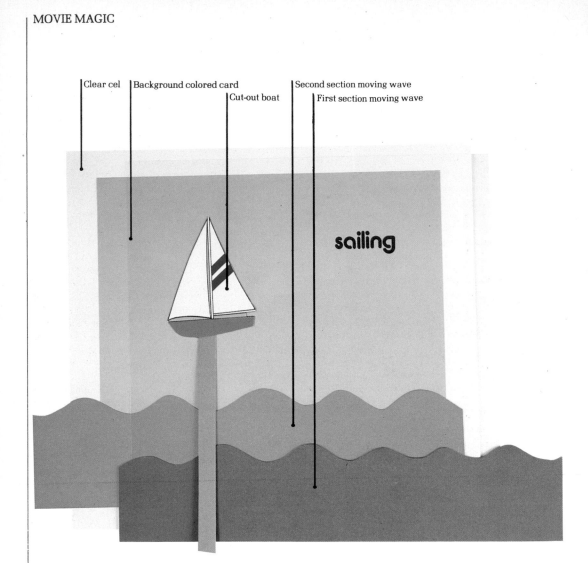

Clear cel | Background colored card | Second section moving wave
Cut-out boat | First section moving wave

sailing

Above **The various components of an animated title board for a sailing film. The coloured car at the back forms the sky, the boat is a cut-out shape, while two sections of card form the waves.** *Right* **and** *far right* **Two of the stages showing how the waves and boat can be made to move by single or double framing.**

sailing

process until you reach the full correct exposure for the scene. This is very easy to establish. Before starting the fade-in, switch to automatic exposure for a moment and see what f/stop the camera is reading from the scene.

Run the camera for about three seconds to establish the scene. Now revolve the vanes, calculating how many single shots will be needed for each movement. If, say, you want the vanes to revolve once each second, you will need to shoot 18 separate frames for one revolution, moving the vanes clockwise slightly after each frame. In practice, it would be quicker to use double framing; this means you would make nine separate movements, shooting two frames after each one. If you required the vanes to revolve for four seconds, for instance, 36 double frames would have to be shot.

Once this has been filmed, the title letters are placed on the vanes, four at a time. The revolving cycle is continued and, as each vane comes down to the right, the letter balanced on it is moved to the right of the mill until the complete title — August in Holland, say — is spelled out. The scene is held for a couple of seconds more and then faded out in exactly the opposite fashion to the way it was faded in at the start.

You can, of course, have several things happening on the screen at the same time. Suppose, for example, you had made a short comedy about somebody learning to drive. You could introduce the theme — and the comic element — with a couple of little cut-out cars. First of all, one of the cars could flash across the screen from left to right. Say, for instance, that this took half a second. In this case, there would be no point in double framing; the car would simply start at the edge of the sheet, one frame would be exposed, the car would be moved an eighth of the way along the 'road' — a black line with a bump in it — another frame exposed, and so on.

Once the first car has travelled across the title, a couple of seconds (36 frames) of film would be exposed before introducing the second car, travelling in the same direction. The whole sequence could be repeated once more before bringing the cars in towards each other from opposite directions. They could then bump into each other, spin around and the wheels fall off before the main title is lettered beneath the road and filmed for several seconds with the cars stationary.

A film of a family outing to a zoo, say, can also be given an entertaining start with an animated title. Here, one idea might be to animate an elephant's trunk and the 'buns' it pulls from the food bin. The elephant's head is glued to the left side of the background sheet, the trunk being made separately out of a number of small

sections. The buns have the letters of the title on them.

Firstly, fade in on the scene and then animate the trunk up and down as if it were searching for food. Remember to move all the trunk sections into a slightly different position after each frame. After about four seconds, the trunk can be slowly animated towards the food bin. Next, the trunk comes out of the bin with a letter bun at its tip, which it deposits towards the centre of the screen. The trunk goes down again and removes the next two buns — and so on.

Any animal could be used for a similar effect. You could, for instance, have a seal with a revolving ball at the end of its nose. Once the ball has rotated a couple of times, the title could then suddenly appear across it. This simply means making two identical balls, one with the title lettered on it and one without. At the point where the title has to appear, change over the two balls, making sure to put the second ball into exactly the same position as the first one. Otherwise the new ball will appear to have 'jumped' slightly when you screen the result.

For a sailing film, it would be a good idea to create the impression of moving water as well as having the yacht travelling across the screen. The 'sea' is made from two pieces of card, one blue and one white, with 'waves' cut from the top of each. The yacht rests behind the pieces, the blue part being fixed down at the bottom corners with a couple of drawing pins so that the white piece can be moved around without disturbing it.

Once you have everything in position, with the yacht at the left of the background, start to fade up the scene. To make the 'sea' move, move the white card slightly to the right after three frames. Continue doing this for a couple of seconds after you have reached the correct exposure. Then start moving the boat. In other words, the sequence is to film three frames, move the boat fractionally forward, move the white card slightly to the right, film three frames, move the boat and so on.

When you have used up the waves on the white card, move it back to the start position so that you can continue the cycle. Once the boat has passed the centre of the screen, You can pause for a moment and letter the title of the film neatly on the left side of the picture before continuing the animated action.

The two card idea can be used to create other effects. You might, for instance, have filmed your family at Christmas and need a very quick and simple title for the film. The top half of the title background could be filled with Christmas decorations, with a candle flickering on the left of the screen and the title on the right. The candle itself would be stationary, but the flame would be interchangeable with three others, all of slightly different shapes. Two frames would be filmed and a different candle flame substituted and so on. If the candle was required to flicker for five seconds, 90 frames would be needed.

It is a good idea to keep the end titles in a similar style to the ones opening the film, although they can be much shorter and do not necessarily need animation. With the zoo idea, the end title could just show the same scene again, with the words THE END lettered on the food tub. To finish the Holland film, the vanes of the windmill could slowly come to a half before the final title appears

It is not necessary to film titles in the studio. They can be filmed on location at any convenient point in the schedule.

In Performance

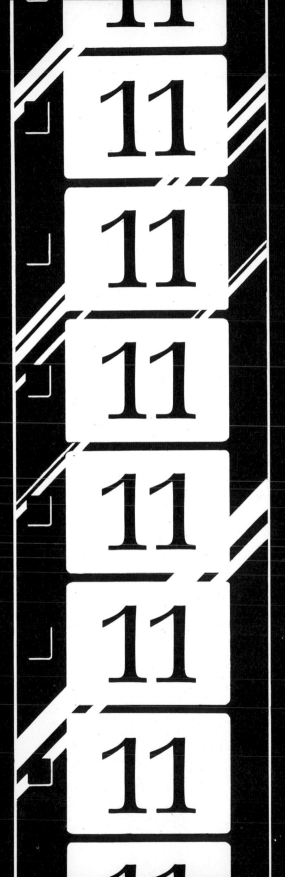

Showing a completed film to an audience for the first time can be just as demanding as actually making it. Right from the start, you have been working towards this moment and, to a great extent, your reputation as a film maker will stand or fall on it.

As with everything in film making, technique is all important in achieving a satisfactory result. However, this must be combined with the right equipment; the best technique in the world is of little use if the projector, say, is of substandard quality.

Choosing a projector

A projector should be chosen as carefully as the camera; it is pointless to buy an expensive camera and then compromise on the quality of the projector, for the quality of the film the audience sees will look inferior, even if the actual film itself is of the highest standard. However, the same argument applies in reverse; an expensive projector cannot improve the images taken by a camera of lesser quality.

What you should basically look for is a machine that will give a steady picture, good sound quality (if sound is required) and get the best out of the film. Compactness and portability should also be taken into consideration. With these guidelines in mind, the final choice can vary, depending on what accessories you have in mind and what you can afford. There are many models to choose from; the basic ones are relatively inexpensive, but the most sophisticated projectors can be very costly indeed.

How a projector works

In the simplest terms, a projector consists of two spools — one to hold the film and another to take it

A Eumig RS300 projector with a built-in screen. Despite the enormous advances in sound projectors, the problem of hum has still not been solved. When screening the original film most audiences will not notice the noise; however, problems can arise when prints are made, as the hum will be built into the copy.

Two views of a
sound projector to show
the lens, the film and
light paths, the motor
drive and the
soundheads.

Camera and projector mechanisms are essentially very similar. Both work on the principle of advancing film frame by frame, holding each frame steady in the optical section for a fraction of a second, and exposing or projecting it. In each case a shutter passes between light source and film during the film advance phase.

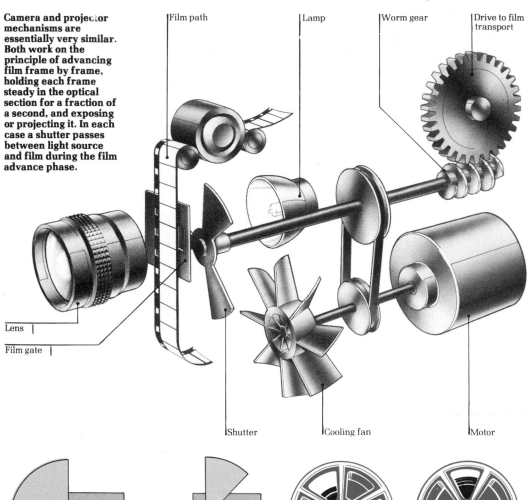

Film path

Lamp

Worm gear

Drive to film transport

Lens

Film gate

Shutter

Cooling fan

Motor

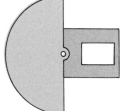

Camera shutter

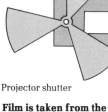

Projector shutter

However, the camera has one shutter blade, the projector three. One of the projector shutter blades prevents exposure of the moving film. The other two each interrupt the projected frame, so that each frame is shown three times. If you have filmed at 18 frames per second, then you will view at 54 frames per second.

Film is taken from the feed spool by the rotating feed sprocket wheel. It is received by the gate assembly which consists of a spring-loaded pressure plate and a fixed aperture plate with spring-loaded side guides. The pressure plate pushes against the film and, with the side guides on the aperture plate, helps to keep the path of the

film straight and steady. The claw pushes the film through the gate one frame at a time. A take-up sprocket wheel then takes the film from the gate area to the take-up

reel. Because the movement of the sprocket wheels is continuous and that of the claw is not, there is a loop between each wheel and the gate.

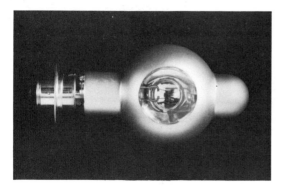

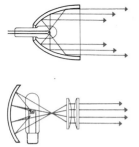

Top **A projector lamp. These must combine the highest possible degree of illumination with the lowest possible heat. The condenser lenses in the lamps** *bottom* **concentrate the light to a pin point. New designs** *centre* **combine a reflector with a lower voltage lamp and so need no condenser.**

small and to give a very bright light. On most modern projectors, the light source is a small filament, low voltage lamp allowing light to be concentrated efficiently on to the gate. These lamps have built-in mirrors, with a 'dichroic' coating. This reflects the light well but allows most of the heat generated by the lamp to escape rearwards; thus keeping the film as cool as possible.

A projector will take only the type of lamp designed for it, so take care to choose the right replacement. If there is any uncertainty, it is best to take the old lamp into the store for an expert check.

Most modern projectors have an automatic threading mechanism, which considerably simplifies the business of actually setting up the film. All the projectionist has to do is to place the reel of film on to its extended 'arm', set the projector in motion and push the trimmed film into a slot. Many projectors, too, use one or more sprockets, whose teeth engage in the perforations and help transport the film through the mechanism. These sprockets turn at constant speed so that loose loops of film are formed between them and the gate. This counters the intermittent motion of the claw.

Smoothing out this action is all important as far as sound projectors are concerned. This must be done before the film reaches the sound heads, which are used to record on, or play back, the magnetic stripe at the edge of the film. In some ways, the sound projector is like a tape recorder and silent projector all in one. The projector contains an amplifier and usually a small loudspeaker. Thus, it can be operated as a completely self-contained unit, though better results are usually achieved if an extension speaker is used.

Lenses are of two kinds — fixed focal length and zoom. In the first case, the projector or screen has to be moved physically to alter the size of the projected image; in the second, this can be done by simply adjusting the zoom. However, it is important to check the quality of image this produces. Some lower price models can give poor image definition, especially around the edges of the picture.

Choosing a cine screen
Theoretically, you can show your films on a white-washed wall or a white sheet, but this certainly will not do justice to them. If you decide to build a permanent screen in your own home, an extremely serviceable one can be made from hardboard painted with several coats of white

up — some form of transport mechanism, a lamp to illuminate the image and a lens. This is made from several pieces of curved glass, each of different thicknesses and optical properties. Light from the lamp shines through the image on the film and the lens enlarges, inverts and focuses it on to the screen. The film comes off the feed reel and is threaded on to a guide path through the gate mechanism — between the lamp housing and the lens — and so on to the take-up reel.

The gate is thus one of the most important parts of the projector. It is here that each frame in turn is stopped for an instant to allow the shutter to open and the light to pass through. Basically, the gate consists of a fixed plate with a rectangle cut out of it; as the film is guided through the gate, a spring pressure plate presses it against this aperture.

The pressure has to be enough to ensure the film lies flat; at the same time, the spring controls this, so that that there is no danger of the film being scratched.

The film is moved on to the next frame by a claw. This is a small pin, which, when the shutter closes, enters a perforation on the film, pulls it down quickly and withdraws as the shutter opens again. The whole process happens 18 or 24 times every second, depending on the running speed of the projector.

Projector lamps are specially designed to be

emulsion and a generous matt black border. If, on the other hand, you purchase a manufactured screen, it is very important to choose one with the correct screen surface. There are several types, which reflect light in different ways. Some give a very bright image at the expense of being somewhat directional — that is, they are dim when viewed from one side; others offer a less bright image over a wider area.

Glass-beaded screens are fairly expensive and need to be handled carefully as the surface is delicate. They are very directional and give a very bright image to those sitting near the projection beam. However, the brightness appears to diminish rapidly at wider angles, so this kind of screen is best suited to long, rectangular rooms. There are two drawbacks; with some screens, the glass beads are visible if viewed closely and others can give a slightly unnatural, 'grainy', look to color film. The optimum viewing distance is about eight feet.

Matt white screens are not directional, but the image is not particularly bright. Given the good light output of most modern projectors, they are perfectly satisfactory for home use, but it is essential to ensure that the room is blacked out carefully. This is because any stray light falling on a matt screen can seriously affect the quality of the image.

Though expensive, lenticular screens are probably the best all-round buy. They offer a sharp, bright image over a fairly wide area and are not as sensitive to handling as other screens. They can also be cleaned easily. Their characteristic 'ribbed' appearance comes from the ridges and indentations on the surface; these ensure that the light is well reflected. As with beaded screens, the best viewing position is therefore a few metres away.

Preparing for performance

When you are planning to have friends round for a film show, most of the hard work is done before they arrive. If the viewers are to enjoy themselves, they should be seated in comfort, so make sure that the chairs are positioned so that everybody gets the best possible view of the

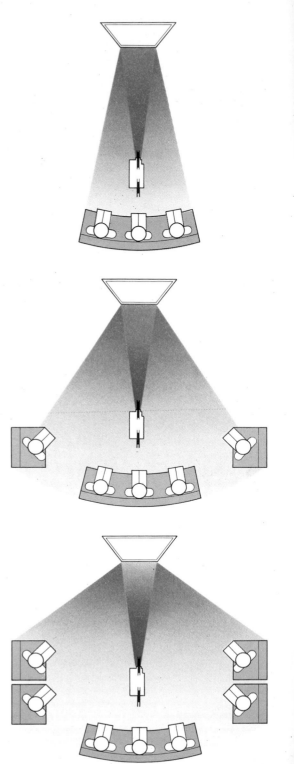

Different types of film screen have different directional properties. The glass beaded screen *top* **is extremely directional; this means that the image can only be seen well from a narrow angle in the** front. **The matt white screen** *centre* **is less directional, but the image is not as bright. The lenticular screen, though expensive, is the best buy. It gives a sharp image and has a wide angel of view** *bottom.*

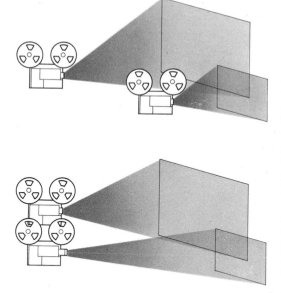

To vary the size of
the image used to
involve physically
moving the projector *top.*
Today, however, zoom
lenses mean that the size
of the image can be
increased or decreased
far more easily *bottom.*

A projector stand, such
as the example *right,* will
help you avoid the risk
of an intruding head
getting into the image, as
well as providing a
handy storage place for
essential spare parts.

screen. Ensure that nobody will have to strain his
neck or peer round somebody else.

If at all possible, the seating should be
arranged so that the projector beam can shine
down the middle. The projector should be
positioned as high as possible off the floor. Even
though it appears as though the projector beam
will be well out of the way, there is always the risk
of somebody's head getting into the picture.
Check for this by sitting in each of the chairs in
turn, with the projector lamp on. Sometimes, you
may find it helpful to rearrange the furniture so
that you are projecting diagonally across the
room, with the screen in one corner. This gives
the beam a longer 'throw'.

Projector stands are useful accessories. They
are inexpensive and, with a little care, will last
virtually forever. They are extremely compact
and easy to store; they also often have an extra
built-in shelf to hold boxes of film, spare lamps
and a gate cleaning kit.

The audience should be seated as far away
from the projector as possible, but, since modern
machines are very quiet, nobody should be
unduly distracted by the slight whirring noise
they make. If you have an older type, muffle the
noise by placing a felt or rubber mat underneath
it.

Position the extension speaker near the screen
and slightly above the heads of the audience, so
that the treble is radiated properly. Do not place
the speaker too close to a corner, or the bass notes
will tend to be accentuated. If the sound track is a
little bass heavy, this will make listening to it an
uncomfortable experience. Stand the speaker on
a firm shelf, or somewhere equally solid, and
angle it towards the audience.

Take infinite care when lining up the picture on
the screen. It must be exactly right, with careful
use of the zoom, so that any debris collecting
around the gate aperture during projection is
hidden by the masking. When zooming the picture
to the right size, be sure not to enlarge it to the
point where the light leaks round the outside of
the border on to the wall behind. If this happens,
important parts of the titles may be cut off.

Checking the projector

Before fitting a film to try out the projector, give
the equipment a quick service. Remove the side
cover and carefully clean out the film path with
one of the special brushes purpose-made for the
job. Use a blower to remove any dust, paying
particular attention to the gate. On some
projectors, the gate sections can be taken out
entirely, which makes them much easier to clean.

On other machines, the lens and part of the gate swings away from the body of the projector; here, again, it is a simple matter to ensure that there are no hairs or dust particles present which would be likely to degrade the picture.

Remove the lens and clean the elements with a cloth and a proprietary lens-cleaning fluid. Take care when replacing the lens because lenses on newer machines are sometimes somewhat awkward to engage with their focusing linkage. It is actually possible to push them back too far.

If the projector you are using has removeable sprockets, flip back the guards, pull the sprockets off and clean and polish them. Make sure they click back into place correctly. If you have a dual gauge (Standard and Super 8) sound projector, make sure that the sound head is correctly switched across for the type of film you are showing. It is all too easy to give your machine a thorough service, put the side covers on again and then, when the film is running, discover that there is no sound. This is especially important with projectors which have three sound head positions — one for main stripe, one for balance stripe and one for main plus balance. If you are showing somebody else's film in the programme, check which stripe has been recorded on or whether both have been used.

Use the materials *right* **to remove emulsion build-up and other dirt from a projector. The gate and sound head are most prone to collecting this debris. Sparingly dampen the cleaning implements with denatured alcohol.**

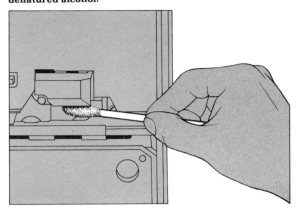

The disadvantage of a one-motor sound projector is that the motor has to both advance the film through the gate and draw it over the magnetic sound head. Because of the intermittent motion this involves, a degree of background noise is inevitable. The two- **motor system reduces this by having one motor for sound and another for the picture. Manufacturers claim that this produces a reduction in wow and flutter of between 0.4 to 0.2 per cent. Though this seems small, it makes a marked difference to sound quality.**

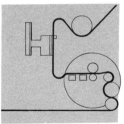

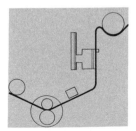

The materials needed for cleaning a projector. Cotton swabs, a soft flannel cloth and denatured alcohol are all useful.

Make sure that the lamp is in good condition and fitted into place properly. With the older type of lamp (without the built-in reflector), there are usually two little levers inside the lamp housing; these should be adjusted to align the lamp correctly and so obtain maximum brightness. If the lamp shows any sign of blackening at all, take it out and throw it away. Even if it does not blow in the middle of the performance, it will seriously degrade the light output of the projector.

It is worth taking the trouble to conceal as much cable as possible — either under the edges of the carpet or around the sides of the room — since it is very easy to trip over one in the darkness. A chair moved slightly during the performance can tension a cable which has not been tucked out of harm's way. Loudspeaker plugs and sockets can be troublesome at times, tending to part company if, say, they have been used to lengthen a speaker cable. To strengthen plug and socket links, wrap a piece of masking tape around them or tie the ends together in a knot. You can then project without worrying throughout the evening.

When you are setting up the show, run the first film in the programme through the projector and sit in all the seats in turn. Watch the picture, listen to the sound and judge how things are going to appear from the viewpoint of each member of the audience. As far as sound is concerned, remember that the level needed will change once the room is full of people, as more of it will be absorbed. The treble will need to be boosted as well.

Find the approximate level of sound you will need, so that the volume control can be turned to the position smoothly and quickly once the performance is under way. A good projectionist stands beside the machine throughout the performance anyway, making minute adjustments as and when they are needed. Remember that an audience will notice even a slight change in focus; that is why the first movie should be sharp from the first frame. An audience, however, is less quick to notice small changes in sound level during a film.

Planning how long a performance should last can be a problem. The maximum is probably about 90 minutes, with a short intermission half way through. Keep your best films for the second half. Never keep the audience waiting between movies while you rewind. Use the empty spool from the first film as a take-up spool for the next and so on. Keep a few spare spools handy on the projector stand in case a film splice breaks or you need a larger spool to accomodate the next film.

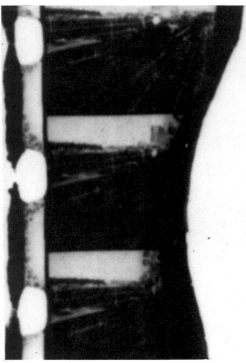

Burns

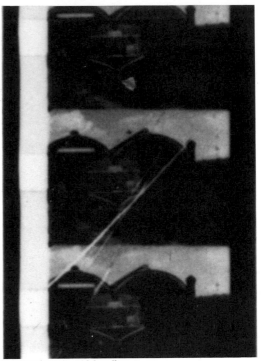

Scratches from rough handling

Scratches from projector or camera

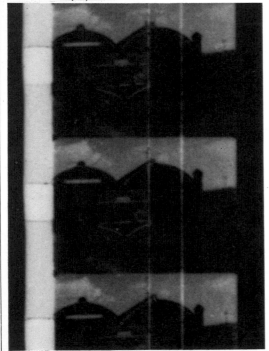

You can cut down the likelihood of scratches by keeping the gate area clean. Make regular checks for cleanliness by running a few feet of black leader through the projector and examining it closely afterwards. One of the most common causes of wear and tear on sprocket holes is the automatic threading mechanism found on most Super 8 projectors. If yours is automatic, make regular checks to see that all is running smoothly. In addition, check the splices on the film — badly spliced film can easily get caught up in the mechanism. If your lamp gets too hot, or your film gets too close to it, then the film will be damaged by the heat. Minor damage can be repaired by cutting and splicing, but it is also important to check the gate area for debris and damage.

Defects in the projector feed mechanisms can cause the film to bend and the emulsion to crack.

The extent of the damage to film when the feed mechanisms fail depends partly on how quickly you notice that something is going wrong. This soon becomes a matter of habit; any change in projection noise should bring instant action. If the film is tangled and bent, it is often preferable to make one cut, rather than try to untangle it. This may be a lengthy business and can result in further damage.

If you have time, run through the films on an editor viewer to check that the splices are sound and that there are no torn sprockets. Also check that the take-up spools are not bent or narrowed at any point; otherwise the film will not be taken up and it may snake all over the floor.

Never be caught out without at least one spare lamp and preferably two. Keep the spare comfortably to hand, together with a small pair of nail scissors, a gate cleaning brush and some scraps of masking tape. If a lamp has to be changed in the middle of a performance, remember that it will be extremely hot.

During the showing of a film, it can happen that a hair gets caught in the gate, where it will be magnified out of all proportion. Do not be tempted to lick your finger and thumb and then touch the film where it is about to enter the gate in the hope that the moisture will remove the obstruction. This is a common mistake. Though it might work, it can also mark the film with a flock of tiny saliva speckles which will be baked hard by the heat of the lamp and become very obvious at every subsequent showing. The next splice travelling through the gate will probably take the hair with it.

Dimming lights
Avoid the temptation to switch on the room lights between films as this can be very disturbing to the audience. Far better to buy a proprietary dimmer unit, which is the same size as an ordinary wall switch and can easily be fitted in place of it by connecting a couple of wires. Another solution is to mount a pair of colored 60 watt light bulbs in sockets at the ends of a wooden bar about a metre long. Conceal this behind the screen. The lights can have their own dimmer control unit, placed conveniently by the projector.

Interval music
Recorded background music between films enables the audience to sit and enjoy themselves while the next film is being laced into the projector. It is also useful while people are settling into their seats before the show starts, for the interval and, of course, for 'playing them out' at the end of the performance.

Obviously, your between-film and interval music should complement the content of the programme. Using different kinds of background music for varying kinds of show helps to give your programmes an individual flavour and audiences will be impressed by your attention to detail. They are far more likely to praise your films if you put them in the right frame of mind before you switch the projector on. For this reason, a box of

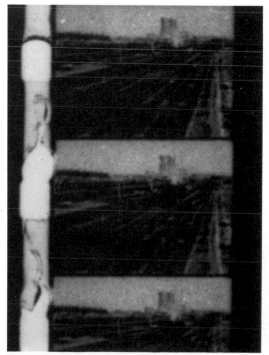

Torn sprockets

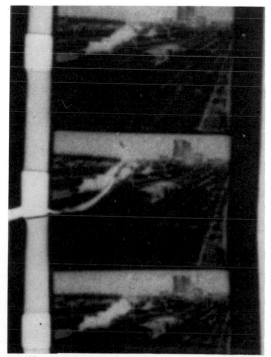

Torn film

assorted tapes or cassettes, containing music for every occasion, is best. One cassette might feature a mixture of movie themes, another light guitar solos, a third classical music and so on.

Integrated screens

Nine times out of ten, you will have sufficient time to set up your equipment before the audience arrives. But on that tenth occasion, you might be asked to show a film in the middle of a general social evening. On this kind of occasion, you need to arrange things very quickly and here a screen with built-in speakers can be an enormous advantage. You certainly will not have the time to wander around positioning an extension unit and trying it out first.

There are several screens on the market with built-in speakers and stereo or mono sound. Naturally, since the speakers are not very far apart, the actual stereo effect is somewhat limited, though the sound quality can be extremely acceptable. In setting up, you merely connect a cable between the screen and the projector's speaker socket.

If you are lucky enough to have a room which is permanently available for showing films, you may well decide to build your own permanent

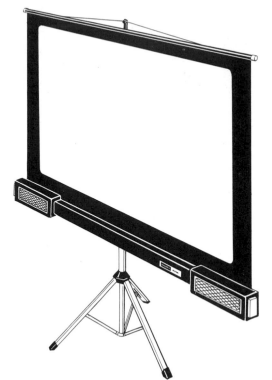

Integrated screens, fitted with their own loudspeakers, come into their own when you need to set up the equipment quickly and have no time for careful positioning of extension units. Purpose-built integrated screens can be bought, but it is easy to build one at home.

The best picture, combined with top quality sound, is the goal of all home movie makers. Chose the best screen you can afford; the investment will be well worthwhile. When selecting speakers, remember that some projectors do not provide enough output for hi-fi ones to be satisfactorily used.

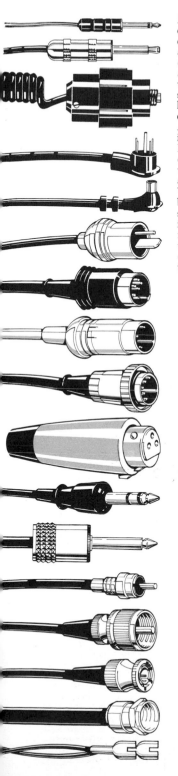

Left **A selection of common cable connectors. These are an essential part of every movie maker's accessory kit, to be used with camera, projector, speakers, microphones, headphones and tape or cassette recorders. Always use the one intended for the task in hand; forcing a connector into a socket will only damage both it and the equipment. When connectors are being used to link cables snaking along a floor, it is often a good idea to reinforce the connection with insulating tape, in case some one catches their foot in the cable.**

screen. In this case, it is advantageous to actually build the speakers into the borders of the screen itself. The speaker units can be bolted behind the screen edges and then holes drilled to let the sound through. A piece of grille cloth pasted over each set of holes adds an attractive finishing touch.

Cine speakers and amplifiers

Choosing a speaker for your film shows can be more complex than it might appear. This is because a loudspeaker which sounds good in a stereo hi-fi system does not necessarily sound as good with a film soundtrack. In the early days of magnetic stripe sound, the frequency response was poor, especially at the treble end of the scale.

Today, however, the picture is completely different. Given a reasonably careful hand at the recording stage, stripe can be little short of superb. It therefore demands a good extension speaker. Top projectors today have transistorized amplifiers producing an output of anything up to 20 watts. This, together with a correspondingly wide frequency response, means that hi-fi speakers can now be matched up with projectors quite successfully.

There is still the need to experiment, however; as many loudspeakers as possible should be tried out with the projector before a final choice is made. Remember that different speakers impose different characteristics on the sound from stripe.

Nowadays, more and more manufacturers are producing speakers especially designed for stripe sound and one or two are complementing these with cine amplifiers to match. If you own an old projector, a cine amplifier can be extremely useful as it not only improves the quality of the sound but also offers you the chance of refining the tone produced. Newer projectors are usually fitted with their own tone control. This is a valuable bonus, as it enables you to get maximum clarity from the all-important treble region.

Points to remember

The basic rules for successful cine projection can thus be summed up as follows. Whenever possible, set up the equipment completely before the audience sits down. Test and check everything and make sure the first film is properly focused, filling the screen. Check the loudspeaker positioning and tone adjustment.

When the audience is seated, fade down the lights slowly and fade up the music slightly. Dim down to darkness and start the projector motor to run the section of black leader into the gate.

Switch on the projector lamps. Fade the background music completely and immediately the first title hits the screen, check for sharpness. Fade up the film soundtrack to the right level. While the film is running, slip the interval music into the recorder. As the film ends, start the recorder, turn the projector sound down and switch off the projector lamp immediately the end title fades. Turn up the interval music.

The final point to remember is that it is just as important to check the film regularly as it is to carry out maintenance checks on the projector. Always, if possible, inspect the film before projection, repairing it if necessary. The points to look for are the physical state of the film — it should be clean, not dirty — and the condition of the splices. A long leader should always be attached to the start of a reel and a trailer at the end. The former helps to protect the first few feet of film from being accidentally scratched or torn during threading-up; the latter protects the film from the damage it might suffer during rewinding.

Film should be stored in light-tight, dustproof cans. If cleaning is necessary, use a recommended movie cleaner. The lubricant in this will help eliminate jumpy projection as it helps the film to pass more easily through the projector. Storage places should be dry and cool.

The first, obvious, but all too frequently broken, rule of good projection is to make sure that your audience can see well and without discomfort.

Film and the
Future

Modern developments in the cine industry have made the old distinctions between amateur and professional movie maker ever more blurred in terms of the quality, if not the scale, of the product being produced. It is not unknown, for instance, for professionals to use Super 8 — formerly regarded as an amateur gauge — rather than 35mm, if the circumstances demand it. Similarly, it is quite possible for an amateur film maker to have shots of a newsworthy event accepted for use by a local, or even national, TV network, provided, of course, that he or she is lucky enough to be in the right place at the right time.

Below **The assassination of US President John F. Kennedy in Dallas in 1963 was captured by an amateur filming in Super 8. The resulting pictures were networked by television stations throughout the world.**

Super 8 has proved its versatility in many different circumstances. *Right* **British yachtswoman Clare Francis filmed her round-the-world voyage on this format;** *far right* **two Nizo 136KL cameras mounted to a catamaran boom.**

Nor is this the only advance affecting the whole movie-making business. The increasing use of video — both professionally and in the home — is challenging many established film concepts. Some film makers see the challenge of video as a threat to the survival of the older format; others, however, believe that its increasing popularity will serve to expand interest in film.

News and film

Occasionally, film makers find themselves in the ideal position to record an event of high news value. In such cases, television has no reservation about using their film — no matter what the gauge or the status of the film maker. One celebrated example was the assassination of President John F. Kennedy in Dallas, Texas, in 1963, which was filmed by an amateur in 8mm as it happened. These, the only pictures of the event, have been shown on TV throughout the world. Even local events, with a more restricted appeal, may still be welcomed by a news programme, possibly even for a fee.

In fact, the low cost of Super 8 film makes it popular with small TV stations all over the world. This professional use of the format is particularly widespread in the USA and Japan. Here, Super 8 is used for daily news coverage. In Europe and on network TV in the USA, Super 8 does not have a regular daily role; it is usually reserved for shooting in special or difficult circumstances. The simplicity and portability of the equipment make it ideal for such purposes; Super 8, for instance, was the format chosen by the British yachts-woman Clare Francis when filming her experiences for British television in the 1977 round-the-world yacht race. It was also used by the balloonists Cameron and Davies in their unsuccessful 1979 attempt to fly the Atlantic.

Super 8 also makes it possible for a news cameraman to film controversial or prohibited

subjects. In 1977, for instance, ABC-TV networked a series of three Super 8 documentaries shot in Rhodesia, while Britain's Granada television used Super 8 to film an exposé of conditions on the tea plantations of Sri Lanka (Ceylon). Hence, the smallest film gauge is extending the 'eye' of television to cover places, situations and people that would otherwise be inaccessible.

Access to television

With the increasing use of Super 8 professionally, there is an increasing likelihood of amateur film being accepted, particularly in the TV field. Here, acceptable results can be produced quite easily; the television camera is simply lined up with an ordinary projection screen and the film run as usual. British TV, for instance, now runs an annual awards scheme for amateur film makers undertaking special expeditions. The winning entries are shown on national television.

In many countries, too, the demand for more public access to television is growing, as a reaction to the exclusive control of the medium by a few powerful bodies. One suggestion has been the setting-up of an Open Broadcasting Authority. This would collect and relay films and information from many different sources; if this happens, the Super 8 amateur will play an essential part in its operation.

Video systems

The other recent revolutionary development from film and television is video — film on cassette. The first home video recorders were introduced on to the market in the late 1970s; since then, they have greatly increased in sophistication and are now extremely popular.

The first manufacturer to release a video system was Philips, with its VCR. This model was relatively unsophisticated and had an extremely complicated cassette, with only a short playing time. Simpler, longer playing, versions were hence devised by two Japanese companies — JVC

Above **Filming in the Matterhorn and** *right* **filming in Snowdonia in the UK. The professional movie maker here is using 35mm; today, however, Super 8 is frequently used in such situations, because of its compact nature.**

and Sony — independently. These three systems form the basis of video today. However, the individual equipment is incompatible and this remains one of the chief problems, as more and more manufacturers bring out versions of their own.

Another disadvantage is that, unlike film, video recordings cannot be easily exchanged between countries. This difficulty arises because different nations use a variety of television standards. In North America and Japan, for example, a television picture is made up of 525 lines, with 30 complete pictures a second. Europe, Australia and South Africa use a 625 line system, with 25 pictures a second.

The problem is further complicated because color coding also varies between the systems. The 525 line standard is usually based on the NSTC system, while the 625 line one uses the PAL system. A few television networks even use a combination of the two.

An almost limitless supply of pre-recorded material, however, is available in cassette form. This includes feature films, foreign TV programmes, pop concerts and specially recorded variety shows. Major distributors now sell video cassettes or offer them for hire. This market is particularly well-established in the USA, where the very latest films and shows are obtainable almost as soon as they are

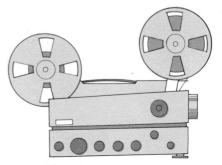

Film projector

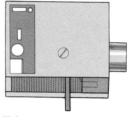

Slide projector

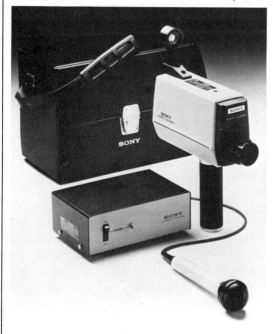

Left **A Sony video camera. Until recently, one of the chief disadvantages of video cameras was their expense and their cumbersome nature. Now cheaper lightweight models are coming on to the market.** *Right* **The many uses of the video cassette in schematic form.**

commercially released. This, in turn, has given rise to the problem of piracy, or illegal copying.

Film and video

Video is often seen as a challenge to conventional film. Its chief advantage is that recordings can be conveniently viewed on a small television screen or monitor, without the need for elaborate or

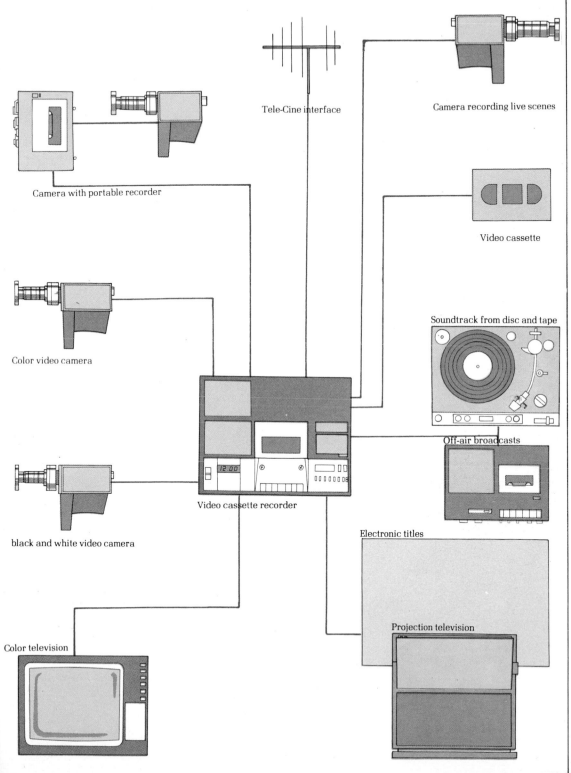

Camera with portable recorder

Tele-Cine interface

Camera recording live scenes

Video cassette

Color video camera

Soundtrack from disc and tape

12:00

Off-air broadcasts

Video cassette recorder

Electronic titles

black and white video camera

Projection television

Color television

cumbersome projection equipment. A further advantage is that it offers the possibility of instant replay. However, at present, most portable video cameras are expensive and heavy, while, in addition, color facilities are limited.

Film and video can form an ideal partnership. A film can be shot on Super 8, using relatively cheap and simple equipment, and then transferred to video cassette. The film should be edited before the transfer is made; the soundtrack is compiled separately and dubbed straight on to the video tape.

Specialist companies exist to provide this service, with the added bonus of exposure and color correction. Only the larger ones, however, have the necessary technical expertise and equipment. It is best to avoid small back-street enterprises, which, however cheap, cannot achieve the same high standard. Alternatively, it is possible to achieve acceptable results at home. All that is needed is a simple proprietary attachment to enable a standard movie projector to project film into a video camera to be recorded. Tele-cine machines, designed to play film directly into a TV set or video recorder, are also available.

Filming television

Even if you do not own a video recorder, it is still possible to record from TV by using an ordinary movie camera. The best results are obtained at a filming speed of 18 frames per second (fps), using a low light XL camera mounted on a tripod. It may also be necessary to use a fast film.

The room should be in darkness and the TV adjusted to give a good quality picture with neutral color balance. The main problem with this method is the difficulty of synchronizing the camera shutter with the TV frame frequency. If a

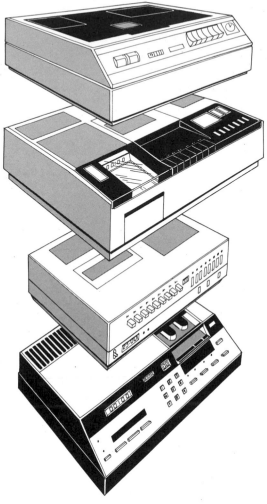

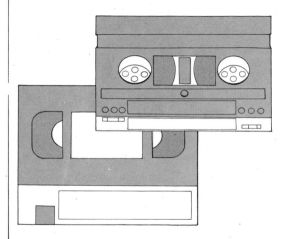

Above **Four video recorders — the Philips N1500, top, Sony Betamix, JVC HR-3300 and the eight hour Philips 2020. The cassettes** *left* **are designed for the JVC and the Philips 2020. Video is fast increasing in popularity and more and more equipment is coming on to the market to meet the demand. Over the next few years, it is probable that development will concentrate on the camera field.**

'strobing' effect is to be avoided, the camera must run at the precise identical framing frequency and the shutter must be open for the total scan period. In practice, this is virtually impossible to achieve without specialized equipment.

Projection TV

Another disadvantage with video is that, however high the quality, the end product usually has to be viewed on a small television screen. It is possible, however, to obtain a 50 inch picture by using a projection TV. This type of equipment uses a modified TV tube and a lens system to project the image on to a directional screen.

Though the system is undoubtedly attractive — especially to video enthusiasts — it is as yet too expensive for the average film-maker. Undoubtedly, an ordinary movie projector is the cheapest way of viewing films.

Video discs

The latest innovation on the pre-recorded video

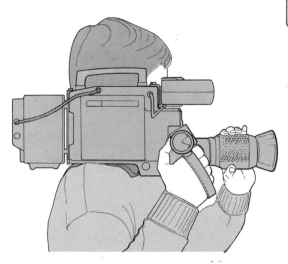

Video cameras range from lightweight models, suitable for amateur use, *top left* **and** *centre,* **to fully professional systems** *bottom.* **The advantages of video over film are considerable. Takes can be replayed immediately, while the video tape can be wiped and used again.**

However, the cheaper machines cannot shoot in color and the quality and size of the final image is inferior to that of film. *Below* **A detail of the VR 2020 recorder, showing recording and playback heads. These make use of a new self-correcting technique.**

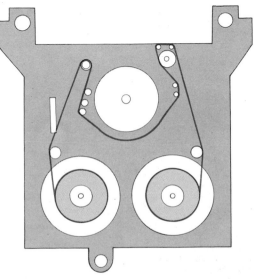

scene is the video disc. In the simplest terms, this is a sort of sophisticated gramophone record capable of receiving and storing color pictures, together with sound. Among the many rival systems under development, two seem particularly commercially viable, since they are planned to be relatively inexpensive. They are produced by Philips and RCA respectively.

In the Philips system, information is recorded in the form of indentations cut into the highly-reflective surface of the disc. These modulate the light from a laser beam and the resulting reflections are converted into a video signal by a detector. The RCA alternative relies on variations in electrical capacity between the surface of a suitably indented disc and a detector to produce the video signal. Both systems are incompatible; equipment designed for one cannot be used with the other.

Looking to the future

Over the next two decades, film is not likely to be the subject of any radical developments, so there is a strong possibility that some of its present-day functions may well be taken over by video. Certain changes in the nature of film are possible. Perhaps the most likely will be the development of a new film emulsion which would not use silver as its basic material. This would obviously reduce costs. Another possible and exciting innovation would be the development of a movie hologram, producing three dimensional, apparently solid, images.

Progress in the video world is even more

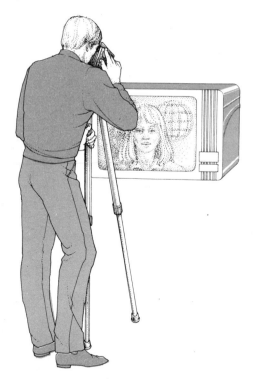

Above **One way of recording a television programme is to use an ordinary movie camera in a darkened room. The best camera to use is a low light XL model, filming at 18 fps and using fast film. However, video results are far superior.**

Below **This cut-away view shows the main features of a cathode ray tube. The electronic signals from the video recorder are converted** **here into images on the screen. One of the chief advantages of video over film is that it is possible to wipe it clean and use it again.**

Trinitron Plus filter screen

Aluminium film

Aperture grille

Trinitron filter screen

Electrostatic focusing lens

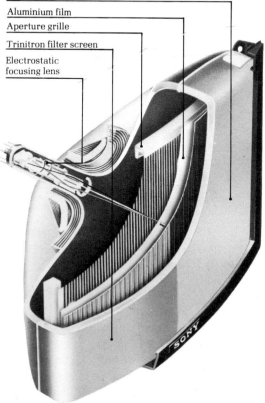

Screen
CRT
Dichroic mirror
Projection lens
Speaker
Reflex mirror

Left **How a video projector works and** *below* **a production model. The system was designed to overcome one of the chief handicaps of video — the small area of the image. However, so far its expense has made it impractical for general use.**

dramatic. Cassette formats and recording systems are being constantly revised and improved. Future possibilities include a combined camera-recorder — perhaps the most important possible development — a mini-cassette with digital recording and a purely electronic recording system based on silicon chips.

One of the first video players to reach the market was the Kodak Supermatic VP-1. Designed for use with Super 8 film — whether reel or cartridge — the machine turns the movie image into a television one. It does this irrespective of whether the film is black and white or color, sound or silent, or whether it is filmed at 18 or 24 fps. All the work is done inside the player; the only external connection is a simple hook-up to the television set's antenna input.

The player works in much the same say as an ordinary tape recorder. The film is automatically threaded and then fed through the machine at the desired speed. There is no intermittent mechanism, as on the conventional projector; neither is there a lens. Instead, the film is scanned by a moving point of light, generated by a cathode ray tube. This light passes over each frame hundreds of times, as though it were engraving it, and the information it gathers on color and density are analyzed electronically by transducers. These convert it into the appropriate form to be passed to the television set. The system is known as flying spot scanning.

Most of the controls are the same as those of an optical projector, but there is one unique feature. This is a steadiness control to ensure good registration of the image. Instead of a claw pulling down the film, the leading edges of the film perforations are scanned to register each frame.

Below **a video disc player. This new development has considerable advantages over the traditional cassette format. The discs are cheaper to duplicate, are unlikely to wear out and make it easy to find any part of their contents. Any one of, say, 40,000 frames can be displayed as a still picture. The playback equipment has slow and repeat motion facilities; on the whole, it is cheaper than the cassette equivalent.**

Glossary

A

Aberration Faults in image formation by lenses, which tend to degrade the image.

AC Alternating electric current, used for household light and power, and also the form of most audio signals.

Academy ratio The 'normal' taking and projection aspect ratio of roughly 4:3 (or 1.33:1), originally standardized by the Academy of Motion Picture Arts and Sciences in Hollywood, USA.

Accelerated motion Speeding-up action on the screen by running the camera at a lower speed than normal.

Acetate Film Slow-burning 'safety' film base, made of cellulose di- or tri-acetate, or polyacetate compounds.

Acoustics Effect of surroundings on recorded or reproduced sound.

AGC Automatic gain control (of an amplifier).

Afocal lens A lens having no image-forming power of its own, but modifying the acceptance angle of other lenses when placed in front of them. It is used in wide-angle and tele attachments and also as the variable element of a zoom lens.

ALC Automatic level control (in a sound recording amplifier).

Ampere Unit of electric current flow, usually abbreviated to A in relation to film.

Amplifier Electronic apparatus to boost the strength of sound, radio or television signals nowadays usually using transistors or integrated circuits. Formerly valves (vacuum tubes) were used.

Anamorphic lens (A-lens) Lens or lens attachment having different magnifications horizontally or vertically, used in the taking and projection of wide-screen films such as CinemaScope.

Animated viewer Accessory used for film editing, producing an enlarged, moving image when a length of film is pulled through it. The viewer is usually operated by hand, but some are motorized.

Animation Filming inanimate objects or drawings in such a way that they appear to move when the film is projected.

Animation bench Device for holding camera, artwork and suitable lights for animation and cartoon work, usually fitted with register pegs so that the artwork can be positively located in position.

Aperture The hole inside a photographic lens that limits the amount of light passing through it. Aperture is normally adjustable in camera lenses. The maximum aperture (e.g. f/1.2) is a measure of the light-gathering power of a lens; it is one of the two common characteristics by which a given lens is described, the other being focal length.

Aperture scale A series of marked numbers used for adjusting the amount of light transmitted by a camera lens (see F/STOP). Many amateur cine cameras have this scale visible in the viewfinder, allowing the user to check the exposure while filming.

ASA The abbreviated title of the American Standards Association, a body issuing various commonly-used national standards. In photography and film-making, ASA is especially associated with a numerical method of measuring and quoting the sensitivity of film stocks.

Aspect ratio Shape of a projected image, given as a ratio of width to height, as in 1.33:1 (Academy), 2.33:1 (Scope) and so on.

Asynchronous motor Type of motor commonly found in film projectors, whose speed is mainly dependent on the frequency of the mains supply.

Attenuator Resistive network for reducing levels of signals.

Auto-exposure metering An automatic system which adjusts the camera lens aperture to the brightness of the image being filmed, taking into account the film sensitivity and usually the exposure time. This produces correctly exposed results without the intervention of the operator.

Auto-focus Complex electronic and mechanical servo-system that focuses the camera lens automatically on the nearest main subject near the centre of the area at which the camera is pointed.

Auto threading Device fitted to most modern 8mm projectors to guide the film along the correct path through the mechanism and usually to the take-up spool once the end of the film is fed into a slot and the motor started.

B

Back-light Light coming from behind the main subject being filmed. It can be used to separate a subject from its background.

Back-light compensation A control on auto-exposure cameras that opens the lens aperture by around one f/stop to give acceptable over-all exposure with back-lit subjects. These would otherwise come out as silhouettes.

Back projection Picture projection onto a translucent screen from the side opposite to that seen by the audience.

Backwind Mechanism for moving or running back a length of film in the camera to allow effects, such as superimpositions and dissolves, to be made.

Balance stripe A narrow magnetic stripe applied on the opposite edge of the film to the MAIN STRIPE. Originally its purpose was to ensure even winding of the film on the spool, but it is now also used for recording a second or stereo sound track on Super 8 film.

Barn doors Adjustable flaps fitted to the front of a spot- and some flood-lights, allowing the spread of light to be restricted when desired.

Battery A set of electrical CELLS connected in series. Batteries are used to power most modern movie cameras, especially in the Super 8 and Single 8 gauges; most of these run off two, four or six cells of the small 'penlight' type.

BCU (Big Close Up) Very tight shot of a face, usually excluding the hairline and point of chin.

Beaded screen Projection screen covered with myriads of tiny glass beads partly embedded in the surface, which reflects most of the light back in the direction of the source.

Beam splitter Partially-reflecting prism or mirror, mainly used in reflex viewfinding systems to divert some of the image-forming light from the lens to the finder optics instead of the film, and also in some cases to the cell of the auto-metering system.

Bias Firstly, a steady high-frequency (40-100kHz) signal mixed with the audio current in the record head of tape recorders and stripe projectors to reduce distortion and permit high quality recordings to be made. Secondly, unwanted color cast in a photographed scene, usually due to processing errors or a mis-match between the type of film sensitisation and the colour of the light illuminating the scene.

Blimp Sound-absorbing housing for movie cameras to prevent running noise — from mechanism and film — being picked up by microphones during sound shooting.

Blooping Blacking out a short length of an optical soundtrack at splices to eliminate 'plops' during replay.

Blow-up Enlargement of film images, normally onto a wider gauge of film — 8mm to 16mm, for instance. The process is carried out by

specialised film laboratories using optical printers.

Boom Pole-like device for positioning microphones in the set — usually just above the camera's field of view. Many Super 8 cameras have a fitting allowing a short telescopic boom carrying a small directional mike to be mounted to the camera.

Breakdown script Document, prepared from the shooting script, listing common locations, sets, artists, props etc in a scripted film to help determine the most rational shooting order of various scenes.

Breathing Rapid movement of film towards and away from the lens, causing unwanted changes of focus and magnification. It is usually caused by insufficient gate pressure on the film.

Butt-join Film or tape splice where the cut ends lie next to each other and do not overlap at the join. It is a commonly-used adhesive-tape splicing method.

Cable release Mechanical device that allows the motor to be started and stopped without disturbing the camera.

Cable release socket Threaded hole in the camera into which a cable release can be screwed for remote starting and stopping.

Capacitor mike A

microphone generating a signal from changes in capacity between two closely-spaced plates. It produces high quality results and can be easily made directional.

Capstan Rotating circular shaft used in tape recorders, sound cameras and projectors to obtain smooth motion of the tape or film over the record and/or play heads.

Cardioid A common type of directional microphone. Its name comes from the fact that its pick-up pattern is heart-shaped.

Cartooning Animations produced from sets of drawings, each differing slightly from one another to produce movement of various objects within the frame.

Cartridge Light-tight housing, usually of plastic, containing a fixed length of factory loaded film-stock, with light-trapped openings allowing the film to emerge to pass the gate — and, if appropriate, a sound-head — on suitable cameras.

Cartridge notches Cut-outs at specified locations of Super 8 and Single 8 cartridges used to set the meter's light-metering circuit — and, on many models, the position of the conversion filter — to suit the type of film contained in the cartridge.

Cassette Firstly, sealed container for audio or video tape permitting fast, foolproof drop-in loading of a recorder without the need for lacing the tape over guide rollers. Secondly, a metal or plastic light-tight housing for a length of film, similar to a cartridge, though sometimes reloadable by the user. Also used in

some specialized 8mm projectors, often with the film joined up in an endless loop.

Cel Thin, transparent plastic sheet used in cartooning to carry those parts of the image which have to be changed from frame to frame to provide motion.

Cell Electro-chemical device for generating or storing electric power. It can be either a primary (use and throw away) or a secondary (re-chargeable) type. Several cells joined together form a BATTERY.

Change-over Starting a second projector at the end of the previous reel shown on another machine to allow unbroken projection of a film that is too long to be accomodated on a single projector.

Change-over cues Black circular marks printed, or sometimes crudely scratched, in the upper right-hand corner of the picture on multi-reel releases. The first eight seconds from the end of the reel, warns the operator to start the motor of the incoming machine, allowing it to get up to speed for the actual sound and picture change over. This is made at the second mark, one second before the end of the reel.

Chamfered splice A film join in which the two ends are scraped or ground to a wedge shape before cementing, so that the overlap is hardly thicker than the film itself.

Changing bag Light-tight cloth or plastic bag, allowing loading and unloading of film at any location without recourse to a darkroom.

Charger Electrical device for passing a controlled flow of current, usually from the mains supply, through a re-chargeable battery to restore its capacity to deliver electric power.

Ciné camera Camera that allows the recording of a series of images on a length of perforated photographic film in rapid sequence, usually at speeds of 18 or 24 frames per second.

Ciné film Photographic film of a specified width carrying perforations at regular intervals by which it is transported through the camera.

CinemaScope First professional wide-screen system using a namorphic lenses on the camera to compress a wide (2.55:1) aspect ratio onto a normal 4:3 film frame. A similar lens on the projector restores correct appearance for presentation in the cinema.

Circle of confusion The amount of unsharpness permissible in a photographic image so that it will still appear tolerably sharp when viewed at a 'normal' magnification. Used in calculating DEPTH OF FIELD.

Clapper board Two hinged pieces of wood that can be brought together sharply in front of the camera at the start of a take. It is used in double-system sound shooting to make audible and visible marks on sound-track and picture that can later be used for synchronization.

Claw Metal 'tooth' in a camera or projector gate, driven up and down as well as in and out to pull the film down to the next frame.

C-mount One of the most common interchangeable lens-mounts used on many 16mm and a few Super 8 cameras.

Coating
Applying a very thin transparent layer of magnesium fluoride or similar substance to the air-to-glass surfaces of a photographic lens to reduce reflection and light scatter. Light transmission and particularly contrast of the image is thus improved. Also known as Blooming and Anti-reflection Coating.

Color temperature Spectral distribution or color quality of a continuous light source, expressed on the Kelvin Scale (°C + 273). It is of importance in matching the color sensitivity of color films to the type of light illuminating the scene being filmed.

Commag Combined magnetic - sound on stripe on the same length of film as the picture.

Comopt Combined optical - photographic soundtrack on the same length of film as the picture - the normal projection release print.

Continuity Ensuring that the position and action of people and props in scenes that follow one another are consistent, even if filmed out of order. Also smooth transition from one scene to the next.

Conversion filter Colored filter designed to considerably modify the quality of existing illumination to match the color sensitivity of the film stock being used. A Wratten 85 for instance, is used to film with Type A tungsten-balanced materials in daylight.

Cross-cutting Editing together shots of two or more events, so they appear to be taking place simultaneously.

CU (Close up) Shot in which the camera appears to be close to the subject; with people, the term applies only to head and shoulders shots.

Cue Audible or visible signal to make some action or movement, normally pre-arranged, and so expected.

Cue-light Small red L ED on the front of many Super 8 sound cameras to warn the people being filmed when the camera is running.

Cue marks Another term for same as CHANGE-OVER MARKS (q.v.).

Cut The normal, sudden transition from one shot to the next and the action of separating scenes and joining them up in the required order and duration. Also, the command given by the director to stop the camera.

Cut-away A shot that appears to be related to, but not a part of, the main action in a sequence.

Cut-out animation Animated film largely made up from cut-out figures and other shapes that are moved frame by frame to give the appearance of being in motion.

Cutting copy Rough positive print made from a camera original that can be used for editing and track-laying without danger of damaging the original material.

DC A direct electric current flowing continuously in one direction.

DC motor Particular type of permanent-magnet motor. It is used in many modern film projectors because of its high torque and because it is easy to regulate its speed electronically.

Decibel Unit expressing the ratio of two electrical quantities such as power, voltage or current on a logarithmic scale, often with respect to a standard reference. The abbreviated form is dB.

Depth of field Range of subject distances that will appear to be reasonably sharp in the final viewed image at any given camera lens settings of focal length, aperture, and focus-scale.

Depth of focus Total amount that the film can move from its designated plane behind the lens in a camera or projector and still produce an acceptably sharp image at a given distance. Again this depends on focal length, aperture and working distance.

Developer Chemical solution capable of reducing exposed silver halide grains to metallic silver. Color developers form suitable dyes in the film layers of color materials from the development by-products.

Delayed-action release Timing mechanism, nowadays usually electronic, that starts the camera motor a short time after the release is pressed. In some cases, it also stops it after a predetermined amount of film has been shot, so allowing the user to appear in his own shots without wasting film footage.

Diaphragm Adjustable 'hole' or aperture inside a camera lens that governs the amount of light passed on to the film.

Dichroic Multiple ultra-thin layers of transparent material that reflect one part of the spectrum and transmit another, by optical interference. The reflectors of projector lamps are usually treated with such material to concentrate the light from the filament on the film but the long-wave infra-red (heat) radiation passes straight through to be absorbed in the lamp house.

Diffusion Scatter of transmitted or reflected light by a substance placed in its path.

DIN Deutsche Industrie Norm The German industrial standards organisation, whose DIN rating is the European equivalent of ASA.

DIN plugs and sockets Standardised connectors with two to seven pins, widely used for interconnecting audio equipment, projectors and recorders.

Diopter The 'power' of a lens, expressed as a reciprocal of its focal length in metres. The diopter figure is prefaced by + if convergent and − if divergent.

Diopter lens A positive supplementary lens mounted in front of the camera lens to permit it to focus on closer distances than its normal focus-mount allows.

Directional microphone A microphone that is more sensitive to sounds coming from some directions than others.

Direct sound camera Movie camera in which sound is recorded on stripe at the edge of the picture at the time of shooting. Also called a live-sound camera.

Dissolve The gradual merging of one image or sound into another. The effect is produced by fading out the first image

and superimposing this on a fade-in of the second.

Distortion Reproduction of an audio signal, or an image, that is not a true copy of the original.

Documentary film A film recording or re-creating a true happening or event.

Double-8 (Double-run 8) Length of film 16mm wide, but with twice the usual number of perforations along each edge. The film is run through the camera twice, images being recorded on half the width on the original run-through and on the opposite half during the return passage. After processing, the film is slit down the middle and the two halves joined end to end, giving an 8mm wide Standard 8 film of twice the original length.

Double-Super 8 Super 8 perforated film in double 16mm width, wound on spools. It is used in a few 'professional' cameras in a similar manner to Double-8.

Double-system sound Method of sound recording, editing and sometimes projection, in which the sound is on a different strip tape or film stripe to the picture. Its use involves special synchronization procedures.

Dual gauge Equipment capable of handling two gauges of film, particularly projectors that can run both Standard 8 and Super/Single 8 films.

Dubbing Transferring sound from one medium to another — from tape to stripe, for example — or mixing of several constituent parts of a soundtrack into a composite track.

Duo-play Simultaneous mixed replay of two

separate soundtracks recorded on the same tape or main plus balance stripe.

Dupe In film language, a commonly used abbreviation for duplicate.

Dupe neg Duplicate picture negative made from a positive original, used for the production of release prints.

Dynamic range The ratio between the loudest and quietest sounds that can be handled by a sound system, measured in decibels.

E

Editing Arranging position and length of various shots to compile a film in the most logical and artistically suitable order.

Effects filter Specialized filter or attachment placed in front of the camera lens to modify or distort the colors, shapes or contrast of the scene being filmed for artistic purposes.

Emulsion Mixture of light-sensitive silver salts (halides) suspended in gelatine and coated on a base of film or paper.

Erase head Magnetic head fed with high frequency current that removes any previously recorded signals on tape or stripe passing over it.

Establishing shot General view filmed as a scene-setter for subsequent action at that location.

Exciter lamp Auxiliary lamp in an optical sound projector, illuminating the sound-scanning slit

and soundtrack.

Exposure Quantity of light reaching the film in a camera. The figure is a product of the intensity of the light and the time it has to act on each frame.

Exposure meter Electrical instrument used to measure scene brightness or illumination as an aid to adjusting the camera controls — lens aperture and sometimes exposure time — to expose the film correctly. An exposure meter is a built-in feature of most Super 8 and Single 8 cameras.

Exposure override Manual control for modifying the working aperture selected by an auto-exposure mechanism.

F

f/number The relative aperture of a lens — a measurement of its light-gathering power — equal to the focal length divided by the effective diameter of the entering light-beam, and expressed as a ratio. Written as f/8, say, in most parts of the world and 1:8 in Continental Europe. Except for the largest aperture, marked f/numbers run in a standardised series — 1.0, 1.4, 2, 2.8, 4, 5.6, 8, 11, 16, 22.

Fade in The gradual lightening of a scene from black to its normal brightness on the screen. Also the increase of a sound signal from zero to its normal level.

Fade out Darkening of

the end of a scene to black, or reduction of a sound signal gradually to zero. The opposite of a FADE IN.

Feedback In amplifiers, the return of some of the output signal to the input, which modifies the amplifier's performance. Feedback can be negative (or antiphase), which reduces distortion with some loss of gain, or positive (in phase), which causes oscillation. Acoustic feedback, or howl-round, occurs when a microphone picks up the output signal of a loudspeaker it is feeding.

Feed spool The spool in a camera or projector on which film to be exposed or projected is wound.

Field of view Limits of the area being filmed at a given camera set-up. These are determined by the focal length of the lens and the dimensions of the gate mask.

Fill light Light used to soften shadows cast by the main illumination source.

Film cement Liquid applied to the film during splicing. It partially dissolves the base and causes the ends of the film to weld together under pressure.

Film speed (film sensitivity) Measure of the amount of light needed to correctly expose a given film material. The figure is usually expressed in ASA. The term should not be confused with running speed.

Filter Firstly, a transparent material that absorbs some parts of the spectrum and transmits others, modifying the colour of light passing through it. Secondly, an electrical network that passes some frequencies but stops others.

Filter Factor The

exposure increase needed to compensate for the light loss in a filter due to the holding back of some colours. It is expressed either in f/stops or 'times' — two stops or 4X, for instance.

Fixed Focus A lens whose position relative to the film, and hence the distance it is focused on, cannot be varied. Such lenses are common in simple movie cameras; they are generally set so that all objects from infinity down to a few metres are covered by the depth of field at or near the maximum aperture.

Fixer A chemical, such as hypo, or ammonium thiosulphate, used to convert any silver halide remaining in the emulsion after development into soluble silver salts that can be removed by washing.

Flare Unwanted light arriving at the film due to internal reflections or scatter in the lens. It produces a reduction in image contrast, or bright spots in parts of the frame.

Flashback Interruption of narrative development in a story film by scenes taking place at an earlier time. The device is frequently used to explain motivation or reaction to a situation.

Flash frame Over-exposure of the first frame or so of a shot. It can be caused either by a delay before the camera comes up to full speed or by light leaking past the shutter while the camera is stopped between shots. The second failing is common with some electrical remote releases that do not stop the camera mechanically in the shutter closed position.

Flash socket A 3.5mm co-

axial socket on cameras, connected to contacts that close momentarily while the shutter is open. It is used for triggering electronic flash units for time-lapse and single frame filming and also for generation of sync signals in double-system sound shooting.

Flicker Rapid fluctuation in the brightness of a projected image at a rate too slow to be overcome by the PERSISTENCE OF VISION of an observer's eye.

Floodlight A lamp providing general illumination of a scene, with gradual fall-off at the sides. Floodlights are used mainly as fill lighting and to illuminate backgrounds.

Fluid head Pan and tilt head whose motions are damped with viscous fluid.

Flutter Either a warble in reproduced sound, caused by rapid cyclic speed variations of the film or tape at the recording or replay point. Alternatively, the rapid and repetitive changes of position, focus or density of a projected image.

Focal length The distance at which a lens focuses an infinitely distant image sharply, measured from its rear nodal point. For a given image area, the longer the focal length, the smaller the field of view and the larger the scale of reproduction.

Focus Point of convergence of light rays from an optical system.

Focus aid A microprism, rangefinder or ground glass screen in a viewfinder system that indicates to the user when the taking lens is correctly focused on the desired subject.

Focus puller A member of the camera crew,

whose main job is to adjust the focus of the taking lens to bring the parts of the scene being filmed into sharp focus.

Fog An unwanted change in photographic density unrelated to the image. It is usually caused by light-leaks, exposure to X-rays, or faulty processing.

Footage counter — Firstly, a moving pointer or dial on a movie camera, showing the amount of film that has been (or remains to be) exposed from a given loading. Secondly, a digital counter coupled to a sprocket that measures lengths of film during editing, track-laying and so on.

Four-track recorder A tape recorder allowing one or two tracks to be recorded with the tape passing in one direction, and two further tracks to be interleaved when the tape is turned over and run through in the opposite direction. Each recorded track is called a QUARTER-TRACK.

Fps The taking and projection rate of film, expressed in frames per second.

Frame Either an individual picture on a length of film or a rectangular mask that limits the FIELD OF VIEW of the viewfinder system and thus indicates the area being filmed.

Frame counter Dial showing the individual number of frames exposed. It is useful in trick work, animation, and especially in back-winding for superimpositions, dissolves and so on.

Frame line Unexposed bar separating adjacent frames. The line is black in a positive image.

Framing Firstly, the

adjustment of the position of the film in a projector relative to the gate mask so as to eliminate the frame line being projected on to the screen. Secondly, adjusting the camera to include just the required part of a scene.

Frequency Repetition rate of a cyclically varying quantity (such as voltage) in a given time, now measured in Hertz (Hz) but formerly in cycles per second (c/s).

Frequency response The relative response of an electronic circuit or system at various frequencies. It is expressed in graphical form, or as figures denoting the maximum departure (in decibels) form, or as figures denoting the maximum departure (in decibels) from reference level over a specified frequency range (e.g. ± 2dB, 60-10,000Hz).

Front projection The usual form of projection on to a screen, from the same side as the audience. Alternatively, the special process of combining a projected background with foreground action being filmed. This is done by using a highly directional screen behind the actors and projecting on it via a beam-splitting mirror that places the projector in effectively the same position as the camera.

Fullcoat Perforated film, coated over its full width with magnetic oxide (similar to that used on tape). Fullcoat is used in some types of double-system sound recording and editing.

Gain control The knob on a recorder or sound projector that alters the level of signal being recorded or replayed. The latter is also called a volume control.

Ganging Coupling together of film transport sprockets, used for synchronising picture with one or more sound tracks during the editing (e.g. two-gang, three-gang etc).

Gate The part of a camera and projector that holds the film flat and steady at the correct distance from the lens. It consists of one fixed and one sprung plate, but, in Super 8 cameras, the latter is part of the film cartridge.

Gate mask A rectangular aperture cut out of the front plate of the camera gate, and both plates of a projector gate. It limits the area of film being exposed or projected.

Gauge The overall width of movie film stock.

Ghost Semi-transparent figure, produced by double-exposing figure and background on separate passes of the film through the camera.

Ghosting White vertical streaks, visible particularly from the highlights during projection. These are caused by the camera or projector shutters not cutting off all the light during film pull-down. Alternatively, a faint secondary image obtained when filming or

projecting via a normal, rear-silvered mirror. This is caused by partial reflection at the front glass surface.

Governor Electro-mechanical or electronic speed control device for a camera or projector motor.

Grading Assessing the variations of exposure and color correction needed to be made from scene to scene when printing a film in order to iron out exposure and color-balance errors that have arisen during shooting and processing.

Graduated filter Filter whose color or density varies from top to bottom. When correctly orientated in front of a lens, it allows differential filtration of various parts of the scene, such as reducing exposure in the sky area without affecting the foreground.

Grain Uneven distribution of silver or dye particles in a developed film, appearing as a sort of moving mottle pattern during projection. In general, faster films have more grain than slower ones of similar type.

Ground glass Glass with a finely ground or matted surface on which a real image can be formed in a viewfinder system.

Guide-track A temporary, rough sync or commentary track on tape or fullcoat which acts as a guide to the recording of the final track with correct relationship to the edited picture film.

Gun mike A highly directional type of microphone. It can be aimed at the sound-source and so partly eliminates sounds coming from other directions.

Halation Scatter from the rear of the film base, or a bright camera pressure plate. This results in unwanted exposure in the vicinity of very bright objects in the scene. The effect is minimized in modern film stocks by a black anti-halation coating on the rear of the film.

Half-track Firstly, recording on tape occupying half the total width; two stereophonic half-tracks may be recorded simultaneously in the same direction, but it is more common for a mono track to be recorded on one pass of the tape, which is then turned over for a second track to be recorded in the opposite direction. Secondly, half-width recording on 16mm film stripe, allowing two separate tracks to be carried by one film, or mixing of two separately-recorded tracks, such as music and commentary, played on a full-track head. Thirdly, a half-width stripe applied on top of an optical track on 16mm film, allowing either the optical or the magnetic track to be reproduced.

Halogens A group of elements including iodine, bromine, chlorine and fluorine, used as an additive to the filling of high efficiency tungsten halogen lamps to prevent blackening of the bulb-wall with age. They are also used to form light-sensitive silver halides in film emulsions.

Howl-round A whistle arising when a microphone connected to an amplifier receives sound from a· loudspeaker connected to its output.

Hertz Unit of frequency, abbreviated to 1Hz. 1Hz = cycle per second (c/s).

Hum Unwanted pick-up of mains frequency, or one of its low multiples, in an amplifier. Howl is often caused by induction, due to lack of screening.

Hum-bucking coil Small auxiliary coil connected in the replay head circuit of tape recorders and stripe projectors. Its position can be adjusted to largely cancel out induced hum.

Hypo Common name for sodium thiosulphate (or hyposulphite) crystals or solution, which acts as a FIXER.

I

Image Two dimensional representation of objects or scenes formed by a lens or mirror system on a plane surface (real image) or in space (virtual image).

Impedance The complex resistance of a circuit to the flow of alternating current, measured in ohms.

Inching Moving a film forwards or backwards by small amounts in a projector (or camera) to check proper lacing or positioning a given frame in the gate to set up correct synchronism.

Incident light measurement A special form of exposure measurement in which the light falling on a scene, rather than the light reflected from it, is measured. The meter used has its cell covered by a diffusing dome or plate.

Induction motor Simple form of AC motor, whose speed is largely determined by mains frequency but varies slightly with load and temperature. It is commonly used for tape recorders and film projectors.

Infra-red Radiation beyond the red, long, wavelength end of the visible spectrum perceptible by humans only as radiated heat.

Inserts Shots of static subjects, such as letters, books and clocks, which can be filmed at any convenient time or place.

Integral screen projector Film projector with a back-projection screen built into its cabinet. It is thus instantly ready for projection without the need to set up a screen or black out the room.

Integral tripack Most common form of modern color film, with three dye-forming emulsions coated one on top of another on a common base. It is used for producing subtractive color negatives or positives.

Intercutting Editing together shots from two or more events so that they appear to be related or take place simultaneously.

Interlock Mechanical or electrical coupling together of several machines, such as a projector and tape recorder, so that they all run at the same rate, or 'in sync'.

Intermittent Stop-go transport for film. The transport moves the film through the camera or projector gate frame by frame, with a regular period of rest to allow exposure or projection.

Intermittent mechanism Claw (or sometimes sprocket) and its drive train that produces intermittent pull-down of the film.

Intervalometer Electronic or electric device that exposes single frames of movie film at pre-determined intervals. It is used for time-lapse work and is a built-in feature of a number of modern Super 8 cameras. On others, it is available as an accessory.

Iris diaphragm One form of adjustable lens stop, made up of a number of thin, overlapping leaves forming a near-circular aperture.

J

Jack plug and socket A long, thin electrical connector with two (sometimes three) poles, of which the tip is normally 'live' (signal carrying) and the sleeve part earthed. Two-pole types are available with various standardised diameters — 2.5mm, 3.5mm and 6.35mm (¼in); the latter is also on the market in a three-pole type, with a ring between the tip and sleeve.

Jump cut Interruption of the smooth flow or continuity of a shot, caused by stopping and re-starting the camera or cutting out a few frames of film, while there are moving subjects in shot. This makes them appear to suddenly jump from one place to another.

K

Kelvin scale Scale of temperature measured from absolute zero (—273°C) with the same intervals as degrees Centigrade. It is used for measuring and quoting COLOUR TEMPERATURE. The abbreviated form is K (previously °K).

Key light Source of the main light illuminating the chief subjects in a scene.

Keystoning The distortion of a projected image into a trapezoid instead of a rectangle. It occurs when the optical axis of a projector is not at right angles to the projection screen.

Kodachrome The first popular color film material, originally introduced in 1935, and, in an improved version, still the most widely used amateur movie film to date. Since it does not contain the color-forming chemicals in the emulsion (they are in the developers), it has higher resolution (sharpness) and finer grain than other materials with the same sensitivity.

L

Lacing Threading the film through the various parts of a projector or camera mechanism by hand.

Laminated stripe Magnetic stripe made from tape slit to the appropriate width and cemented with a special solvent to the base of the film in the sound-track area.

Larsen effect Another name for HOWL-ROUND.

Latent image Invisible record of light distribution in a scene existing in an emulsion after exposure and capable of development to a visible form.

Latitude Ability of film emulsion to render an acceptable image despite incorrect (or non-optimal) exposure, usually measured in stops or fractional stops.

Leader Length of film or tape at the beginning of the spool used for lacing through the camera, projector or recorder and not intended to be used for picture or sound recording. It also serves as protection for the useful parts of film underneath it.ç

LED (Light emitting diode) A solid state device that emits light of a specific color (red, yellow, green) when a small voltage is applied to it. The device is long lasting and consumes little power, so it is widely used as signal lights on movie cameras

and projectors. Another use is to form numbers in digital displays such as some frame- or pulse-counters.

Lens Curved, optically worked glass — sometimes a special plastic — capable of forming an image of a subject by the bending of light-rays emanating from it. Practical movie lenses are made up of a combination of many elements, which are designed to overcome faults in image formation (see ABBERRATION).

Lens cap An opaque plastic, rubber or metal cover that can be attached over the front of the camera lens in order to protect it from dust and dirt.

Lens hood Circular or rectangular shade attached to the front of a camera lens to keep out stray light from outside the image field.

Lens mount Standardized fittings by which interchangeable lenses can be mounted on a camera. These are usually either of the screw-in or bayonet type.

Lenticular screen A screen surface embossed with a large number of ribs or pits that modify the scatter angle to prevent light being wasted outside the audience area.

Level sync In double-system editing, the alignment of picture and sound films on sprockets so that each picture is next to its corresponding sound. In single-system-sound editing, using special re-recording equipment to similarly align picture and sound on the film, reversing the procedure after editing to restore projection sync.

Light That part of the electromagnetic spectrum visible by the

human eye, having wavelengths in the range 400 to 700 nanometres.

Light-balancing filters Pale filters used for making slight corrections to raise or lower the effective color temperature of the exposing light.

Line input High level input to a projector or recorder amplifier, between about one-tenth and one volt magnitude, used for feeding in a signal from other equipment incorporating an amplifier, such as cassette, tape recorder or gramophone.

Lip-sync Originally the exact matching of a speaker's filmed lip movements with the corresponding speech sounds; nowadays the term is used as a generic for accurate synchronization between picture and sound-track, and the practice of recording sound synchronously while filming.

Live action Filming real movements of people or things, as opposed to creating movement by animation techniques.

Location Natural surroundings, outside the studio, where a film is being shot.

Loop The slack length of film intended to cushion the transition between the intermittent movement through the gate and continuous movement elsewhere in a camera or projector. In dubbing a continuous sound effect, played off a tape or fullcoat joined up in a loop. It allows infinite repetition and so increases the running time available.

LS (Long Shot) A set-up where the camera appears to be far away from the subject and taking in a

correspondingly large area, with any people appearing quite small in the frame.

Loudspeaker Transducer for converting audio signals to sound waves, normally connected to the output of a recorder or projector amplifier.

M

Macro focusing The ability of many modern zoom lenses to focus on very close distances, often right down to the front glass, achieved by shifting a group of internal lens elements.

Magazine Light-tight reloadable container for rolls of film stock, designed for quick attachment to and removal from professional cine cameras. It is designed to feed the film via light-traps to the camera gate and to wind it up in another roll after exposure. Also a small, light-tight metal housing, incorporating the whole film path (including the gate), fitted to a few double-8 and 16mm amateur cameras. This enables speedy film changes to be made, even under adverse conditions, without danger of fogging.

Mag/Opt A projector capable of replaying both optical and magnetic sound-tracks. Alternatively a film print carrying both optical and magnetic sound tracks.

Mag-stripe (Magnetic

stripe) A narrow ribbon or track of magnetic material applied near one (or both) edges of a film. This can have sound signals recorded on it in the form of variation of magnetisation of the particles in the coating.

Main Stripe In films carrying more than one, the stripe in the normal sound track position (usually the widest).

Married print Print of a film carrying both picture and sound (usually optical track).

Matte Opaque mask limiting the area of frame being exposed. It is placed either in front of the camera lens or in some specialized cameras, just before the film. In professional filming, the matte can be an opaque area on another length of film run in contact with the stock being exposed.

Matte box A box or bellows containing a frame to take mattes. It can be positioned in front of a camera lens to produce special photographic effects.

Mega- Prefix meaning one million times, used mainly for values of resistance. It is usually to abbreviated to M, as in (two megohms or 2,000,000 ohms).

Microphone Transducer for turning sound waves into audio signals.

Microprism Tiny pyramid-shaped indentations in the focusing screen of a reflex viewfinder system. When a lens is not correctly focused, they break up the image but almost disappear when the focus is set correctly.

Mirror shutter A camera shutter with a 45° mirror attached to its front to deflect light to the viewfinder — or sometimes only a light

measuring system — during the time interval that the film is being pulled down to the next frame and thus not being exposed.

Mix In filming, the same as a DISSOLVE, but in sound recording, combining several sound sources onto one track or recording.

Mixer Electric circuit for combining several sound sources into a single signal, with individual gain controls for each channel. The operator performing the mixing operation is also known as a mixer.

Monitoring Listening to the sound signal being recorded to check the quality, level of various signals and for correct cueing.

Monitor head A third head fitted to some tape recorders and projectors to allow monitoring of the actual recorded signal. It does this by replaying the signal off the tape or stripe a fraction of a second after it has been recorded.

Montage Semi-abstract, representational assembly of short scenes used to create a specific mood. Superimpositions and dissolves are frequently used in this technique.

Movielight High intensity light source using a tungsten-halogen bulb in a compact reflector. Movielights are specifically intended to be fitted to amateur movie cameras.

Movielight socket Screw socket or slot designed to mount a movielight on the camera. Fitting the lamp in place means that the Type A conversion filter inside the camera lens to match the color sensitivity of the film to the 'tungsten' light from the movielight usually

has to be removed.

MS (Medium shot or Mid-shot) A camera set-up in which the principal figures appear around full length in the frame.

Narrow gauge Film and equipment for film of a smaller gauge than standard 35mm, such as 16mm, 9.5mm and the various 8mm gauges.

ND filter (Neutral density filter) A grey filter for reducing the amount of light passing through the lens (or a window) without altering its colour.

Negative Image on film in which the tones (and, where appropriate, colors) are reversed — light parts of the object photograph black and dark parts as almost clear film. Used for making copies on positive film, which reverses the tones back to normal.

Noise Unwanted sounds or electrical signals which tend to spoil the quality of the wanted sounds or signals, and reduce the available DYNAMIC RANGE.

Non-substantive Integral tripack color film in which the color couplers that produce the dyes when silver is being developed up are not contained within the emulsions, but in the color developers. Three separate color developing stages are necessary, making this material suitable for processing only by the manufacturer or his

agents. The best known film of this type is Kodachrome.

Ohm Unit of resistance and impedance to current flow, abbreviated to Ω.

Omnidirectional A term meaning equally sensitive in all directions. It is applied mainly to microphones that do not discriminate in their sound pick-up.

Optical effects Special effects, such as dissolves, wipes, fades, and superimpositions, produced by a laboratory using an optical printer. Some of these can also be produced in the camera.

Optical framing Method of centering the film in the gate mask by a projector to remove the frame-line by moving the pivot-point of the claw and thus not moving the boundaries of the image on the screen.

Optical printer Machine for producing prints using projection rather than contact printing. This allows prints to be made with the emulsion on the same side as the original and various effects to be incorporated if desired.

Optical sound Audio signals recorded as changes of transparent area (or sometimes density) of the sound-track. They are placed near one edge of 16mm or Super 8 film prints.

Optical viewfinder Description of a simple direct vision camera viewfinder, separated from the taking lens.

Overlap splice Cement-type splice in which the two ends of the film to be joined are overlapped, and welded together with cement. It is the opposite of a BUTTSPLICE.

Overload Driving an amplifier, transducer or recording medium to a higher level than its designed capacity resulting in distortion.

Override Manual control over an automatic system, such as in the control of exposure or sound level.

P

Pan To move the camera horizontally to scan a scene, or follow moving objects.

Pan and tilt head Device placed between the camera platform and legs of a tripod to allow the camera to be moved side to side (pan) and up and down (tilt).

Parallax The difference between the view seen through a viewfinder and the area being filmed if the finder axis is displaced from the lens, as in most OPTICAL FINDERS. It is only serious when filming small areas especially close to the camera.

Parallax compensation Method for tilting the axis of a finder system via a cam, calibrated in distances so that it 'sees' the same area as the taking lens at the specified distance.

Paste stripe Magnetic stripe coated on to the film in a paste form, containing oxide, binder and solvent. It is either extruded from a nozzle or 'printed on' by a transfer wheel.

Pause control A key or lever that allows tape and cassette recorders to be started and stopped instantaneously without producing unwanted clicks or noises. This works by lifting off the PINCH ROLLER at the capstan; the tape may be held paused and ready for instant starting on cue.

Perforations Regularly-spaced holes of standard dimensions punched near one or both edges of film and used for transporting it through cameras, projectors and printers. Perforated ¼ in tape has similar holes for synchronization.

Persistence of vision The inability of the human eye to distinguish rapidly presented images or flashes of light. If these are repeated quickly enough, they appear to be fused into a continuous image. In this way, movement is created from a series of stills, making movies and television possible.

Perspective The apparent variation in the size of objects with their distance from the camera or viewer's eyes, used to give depth to scenes imaged in a plane, such as a projected picture.

Phono-socket (RCA jack) U.S.-originated small diameter co-axial audio plus and socket, commonly used for line-level inputs and outputs on tape recorders, and all the inputs on amplifiers. The plug consists of a central pin carrying the signal, with a cup at the rear connected to the cable screen and earth.

Photo cell (Photo-electric cell) A device capable of converting variations of light intensity into related variations of electric current or voltage. It is used in exposure measuring systems and for the replaying of optical sound-tracks.

Photo-conductive cell A special type of photocell whose resistance varies inversely with the strength of light falling on it. It needs to have a small current passed through it to produce any output; because of its high sensitivity, it is used in virtually all current auto-exposure metering systems.

Photoflood A highly overrun tungsten filament lamp giving a great deal of light for the power consumed, but with a correspondingly short life (burning two to six hours, depending on the type). Its color temperature matches that of Type A balanced films (3,400K).

Pick-up A transducer used to convert small movements into electrical signals, used to convert small movements into electrical signals, used mainly for replaying gramophone records. Alternatively the unwanted induction of hum or noise into an amplifier, replay-head and connecting lead.

Pilot tone A signal related to camera running speed recorded on tape alongside the audio information, in double-system sound filming. It is later used for the synchronization of sound to picture.

Pinch roller Elastic roller used to press film or tape against a CAPSTAN to minimise slippage between the driving and driven parts.

Pistol grip The handle at the bottom front of movie cameras, usually incorporating the start/stop button. It allows cameras to be supported and released with one hand, freeing the other to operate various controls.

Pitch The distance between successive perforations in film and tape, or the subjective impression of the position of sounds in the musical scale. It is related to frequency, but not always identical with it.

Polarising filter A special filter that restricts the vibrations of light-waves to a single direction. It is used in front of a camera lens to reduce glare and unwanted reflections and to darken a blue sky with color film under certain conditions. Two filters used together can be used to produce fades by rotating one of them 90°.

Polavision A near-instant home-movie system developed by Corporation, using special color film in a cassette. After exposure in the Polavision camera, this only needs to be inserted in a slot in the 'player' (rear-screen projector), where it is automatically developed and then projected some 90 seconds later.

Positive Film or image in which the tones (and colors, if appropriate) are the same way round as in the original scene; in film, positives are normally produced by printing from a NEGATIVE

Post- sync (Post-synchronization) The recording of sound to a previously photographed film, in which the sounds should relate closely to the images.

Power Zoom The ability to alter the focal length of a camera lens smoothly via a motor drive. The facility is usually built into Super 8 cameras, though it sometimes operates only when the motor is running.

Pressure plate The sprung half of a gate in a camera or projector that presses against the film in order to keep it stable and flat and to place the emulsion in the focal plane of the lens.

Print Copy of a film, produced either from a negative or positive original. A print can be produced by contact, in which case the emulsion in the copy is on the opposite surface to the original, or by optical projection, in which case the emulsion is the same way round and the print may therefore be intercut with original material.

Processing The act of using chemicals to make an exposed image visible on photographic film.

Projection Sync The synchronization of picture and accompanying sound track for projection or printing. The method takes into account the displacement between the picture gate and sound head in the projector, amounting to 18 frames (sound ahead) for Super 8 magnetic, 22 frames for Super 8 optical, 26 frames for 16mm optical, 28 frames for 16mm magnetic, and 56 frames for standard 8 magnetic.

Projector Apparatus for enlarging the image from .the film and throwing in onto a screen for viewing. A movie projector has to advance the film intermittently at the correct rate of either 18 or 24 fps.

Prop (property) Any movable inanimate object appearing in the scene, particularly if especially placed there, as in a studio.

Pull-down The act of moving the film in camera or projector intermittently from one frame to the next. The light is normally cut off by a shutter while the film is moving, so the film is exposed or projected only while it is stationary.

Pulse track In double-system shooting a series of plops or beeps, each corresponding to one frame exposed by a camera and generated by sync-contacts in it, recorded on the sync track of the tape (alongside the audio). The track is used later for synchronization during transfer and (occasionally) projection.

Quad-8 Special method of producing mass Super 8 copies for sale by printing on to specially perforated 35mm wide film, which is later slit into four 8mm wide strands.

Quarter-track Width of one track in a four-track tape recorder. Also used to describe the matching record/play head.

Quartz Mineral from which crystals can be manufactured to control an electronic oscillator frequency to a very high degree of precision.

Quartz-sync Method of double-system sound shooting without interconnection between camera and recorder. In this, the camera speed is controlled by one crystal oscillator, while a matching one lays down a pilot tone on the tape recording.

Racking Another name for framing, removing the frame-line from the screen.

Rangefinder Method for measuring the distance of a subject optically, often built into a camera viewfinder. Two separate images are seen, or a straight line appears split, when the image is not in focus.

Rear Projection Alternative term for BACK-PROJECTION.

Recording Capturing of sounds (and images) in permanent form. The most common forms of sound recording are magnetic, optical and disc.

Record Head. Electro-magnetic head that records the signal on to tape or stripe. It often also doubles for replaying the signal and is therefore called record/play head when this occurs.

Record level The strength of the signal being fed to the record head. This has to be within fairly narrow limits to produce optimum results.

Record Level Indicator A meter or led-chain fed from the recording amplifier allowing the user to check for correct recording level (and, on some machines, to make adjustments to set the level correctly). It is especially useful in preventing overloading.

Reel Spooled film as used in projectors. One reel lasts some 11 minutes at sound speed, 16 minutes at silent speed, these times corresponding roughly to 200ft of 8mm, 400ft of 16mm and 1000ft of 35mm film. Also used to describe the spool on which film or tape is wound.

Reflex finder Viewfinder system operating through the taking lens of a camera, thereby eliminating PARALLAX and also permitting visual focusing if a FOCUS-AID is fitted.

Remote control Provision for electrically releasing a movie camera from a distance, via a switch and a pair of wires plugged into a socket on a camera. However, flash frames will be produced between shots unless the camera incorporates a solenoid operated pin that stops the mechanism with the shutter closed.

Replay head Electro-magnetic head for converting variations of magnetization on a tape or stripe to electrical signals. The head is usually combined with the record head in sound projectors and many tape recorders; some of the latter, however, use a separate head so that recording can be monitored, and to give higher quality replay.

Resistance The opposition of an electric circuit to the flow of current.

Resolution The ability of a lens, or lens plus film, to resolve fine detail. Resolution is usually measured in lines per millimeter (1/mm).

Retake Repetition of a shot or recording that has for some reason proved unsatisfactory.

Reversal film Film intended to be processed directly to a positive image, thus making the camera film suitable for projection. All amateur cine films are reversal types, since the process greatly reduces cost as only one positive is needed.

Reversal process Chemical treatment used for forming a positive image from reversal film.

Reverse action Projecting a scene in reverse time order, either by running the film backwards in the camera or projector, by using a special optical printing process, or by filming with the camera upside down and then turning the strip of film end-for-end for projection.

Reverse Shot (reverse angle) A set-up in which the camera's point of view is almost exactly the opposite to the preceding one — when shooting close-up dialogue, for instance.

Rewind Geared winding device for returning projected film to its original spool, head out. The device is built into many projectors; hand-operated rewinds are used for editing.

Rim Light Light shining from behind the subject, outlining it with a sort of halo.

RMS (Root-mean-square) Used mainly to measure the true continuous power output of an amplifier with a continuous sine-wave applied.

Rostrum A table for holding titles and animation drawings, with the means of mounting a camera and lights above it. The camera distance is usually adjustable. Alternatively, a collapsible platform used

to position the camera at levels higher than can be reached by a tripod alone.

Rough cut Intermediate stage in film editing where the various shots are assembled in something like their final order, but not yet finally trimmed to length.

Running speed The rate, in frames per second (fps) at which film runs through cameras and projectors. Normally, this is 24fps for sound and 18fps for silent (and many amateur-made sound) films.

Rushes First print from the lab, viewed to check the previous day's shooting. In the USA they are also called dailies.

Safelight Light filtered to pass only those colors to which a photographic emulsion is not sensitive. Modern movie films are sensitive to all colors and must be handled in darkness.

Safety film Film on a slow-burning base, such as acetate or polyester.

Scene Term relating to the filming of seemingly continuous action in a single location, which may be covered in one or more shots or set-ups.

Scope Popular abbreviation for CinemaScope, and similar anamorphic images with a squeeze ratio of 2:1.

Scraper The part of a splicer that removes the emulsion from one end of the film (and often

roughens the other end) to allow film cement to be applied to the film base so that the two ends can be welded together.

Screen Flat surface specially prepared for the projection of images on it, often having directional characteristics to limit the spread of light to the likely audience area.

Screened lead Signal-carrying cable surrounded by a braided or twisted wire sheath connected to earth, used to prevent pick-up of unwanted signals such as hum. In the USA, the cable is known as shielded lead.

Script Document from which a director or film-maker works, detailing the manner in which the story is to be filmed, and describing the settings, action and dialogue (if any) as well as camera set-ups. It is also known as a scenario.

Semi-automatic exposure A form of exposure metering, where the user has to manually move the iris control ring in order to centre a needle visible in the viewfinder.

Sensitivity Measure of the amount of light needed to correctly expose a given film material.

Sepmag (Separate magnetic) Sound and picture on different films, as in double-system sound filming.

Sequence Group of related shots covering a continuous event or action that is more or less complete in itself.

Set Surroundings in which a scene is filmed, usually specially built.

Set-up The positioning of the camera relative to the action being filmed at the start of each shot.

Servofocus Trade name for a variant of a FIXED-

FOCUS zoom lens, in which the distance on which the lens focuses varies with the focal length in such a manner that the maximum depth of field is achieved at all settings.

Servo-motor A motor used for moving or positioning a component in response to a control signal. A servo-motor is used in some auto-exposure metering systems to set the lens iris to the desired value.

Shooting script Final version of a SCRIPT, ready for filming.

Shot The basic element from which a film is made, consisting of action recorded from one run of the camera or from a single set-up. The term is also used to describe the apparent distance between subject and camera when combined with adjectives, such as long, medium, close and so on.

Shot-gun mike An extremely directional microphone. It has to be pointed at the source of sound and is largely insensitive to sounds arriving from other directions.

Shutter Opaque blade that interrupts the light from or to the lens in cameras and projectors respectively so as to obscure the film while it is moving during pull-down. Projector shutters normally interrupt the light beam two or three times per frame in order that the projected picture should be free from visible flicker.

Shutter angle Measurement of the open sector or sectors of a shutter. The result is a measure of its efficiency and thus also indicates the amount of light allowed to reach the film or screen.

Shuttle bar A dark or light near-horizontal stripe produced when filming images from a television screen. It is caused because the exposure time for each frame differs from the repetition period of the television signal. A number of the TV lines are therefore not recorded on each film frame.

Silver halide Light-sensitive salts of silver — such as silver chloride, bromide and iodide — contained in photographic emulsions. These, after exposure to light, are capable of being reduced to metallic silver by the action of a developing solution to form a visible image.

Single-8 One of the current film gauges, originating in Japan. The film has identical dimensions (except thickness) to SUPER 8, but the cartridges and cameras are quite different, with the feed and take-up rolls placed one above the other and a rear pressure plate that is part of the camera.

Single-frame release A device that allows film frames to be exposed one at a time in a camera. Its chief use is for titling and animation.

Single-system sound A method of sound recording in which the sound (usually on magnetic stripe) is carried on the same support as the picture. It is used in Single-8 and Super 8 direct sound cameras and for projection.

Skylight filter An extremely pale, straw ultra-violet absorbing filter, used to prevent excess blue in the rendering of distant scenes, specially in the mountains or near the

sea. It also 'warms up' scenes shot on an overcast day.

Slow motion Technique for slowing down the movement of objects on the screen by running the camera at a faster speed than normal.

S/N ratio (Signal-to-noise ratio) The relationship between the greatest undistorted signal that can be obtained from an electronic system and the residual background noise, which limits the achievable dynamic range.

Soft-light A large light-source that casts no appreciable shadows. It is used for filling in shadows from the main light.

Solenoid An electromagnet which moves a nearby lever when it is energized. It is used for starting and stopping camera mechanisms with minimal pressure on the release button, for remote control and to apply pressure in sound-heads.

Sound editor Equipment allowing a moving picture to be seen and the associated sound to be heard during editing. It is often made up of an animated viewer with a clip-on sound head, and rewind arms.

Sound head The part of the camera or projector concerned with the recording and reproduction of sound on film, including the magnetic, optical and mechanical transport components.

Soundtrack The area on the film used for sound recording and reproduction, either optical or magnetic and the contents of the final sound signals recorded on the film.

Special effects Various

illusions that can be achieved with the camera on the set, or in the laboratory by special 'trick' techniques to achieve results otherwise impossible or too expensive to film in the normal way.

Spectrum Band of electromagnetic radiation expanded to show the various wavelengths or frequencies of which it is composed. The classic example is passing white light through a dispersing prism.

Splice Join between two pieces of film or magnetic tape.

Splicer Equipment for making joins in film (or tapes). It can be wet (cement) or dry (adhesive tape).

Splicing tape Thin, clear, tough tape coated with a non-oozing adhesive, used in dry splicers. It can be pre-perforated or plain.

Split-field lens A close-up lens with part of its diameter cut away. It can be positioned in front of the camera lens so that both nearby objects and the distant view beyond them are sharply focused on the film.

Spool Narrow core with circular side-plates on which film (or tape) can be wound. Spools are used in projectors, recorders, and some cameras.

Spot effects Sound effects needing to be in sync with action in the picture.

Spotlight Lighting unit that concentrates light in a relatively narrow beam, usually fitted with a stepped Fresnel lens at the front. Changing the lamp-to-lens distance varies the width and intensity of the beam. It produces a hard shadow.

Sprocket A drum carrying regularly

spaced teeth of the same pitch as film perforations. It is used to transport film at a constant speed through projectors, printers and some cameras.

Sprocket holes Stamped-out holes near one or both edges of cine film, used for transporting it through equipment.

Sprocket-hole Modulation Warble in the reproduced sound from stripe tracks placed very close to the sprocket holes. It is sometimes caused by distortion of the film base near the sprocket holes.

Squeeze-lens Popular name for an anamorphic lens, which compresses the picture horizontally during filming and expands it again during projection to give an oblong, wide-screen picture.

Squeeze Ratio The compression/expansion power (in one plane) of an anamorphic lens. The professional standard is 2:1 (giving a 2.3 to 2.6:1 aspect ratio); many amateurs however use a ratio of 1.5:1, which produces a screen image twice as wide as its height.

Standard-eight The original 8mm film gauge, resulting from splitting a 16mm film with twice its usual number of perforations down the middle. It is now obsolescent.

Standard gauge Ciné film 35mm wide.

Start marks Identifying marks punched or drawn on the leaders of several strips of film, sound-track, or tape to allow them to be repeatedly run or printed in the correct relationship to one another.

Still Photograph of a scene from a film, or showing the filming of a scene (production still), used mainly for publicity purposes.

Stock Unexposed ciné film.

Stop The APERTURE that stops or limits the passage of light through an optical system.

Stop-action A trick photography technique which makes it possible for objects to appear, disappear or move from place to place instantaneously. It is produced by temporarily stopping a firmly mounted camera and moving the object concerned; if there are any live actors involved, they must freeze in their places during the interruption.

Stop motion A method for animating titles, models and cut-outs by exposing single frames in a rigidly mounted film camera, moving the object slightly, exposing another frame, and so on. Either one or two frames can be exposed at a time.

Story board Sketches to show how shot set-ups will finally appear in scripted order. They are drawn as an aid to visualisation of the final film and for reference during shooting.

Sub-standard Term used to describe film narrower than standard gauge. Also referred to as NARROW-GAUGE

Substantive Term referring to color film that has color couplers incorporated in the emulsion during manufacture, which form dyes of the desired color when activated by silver-oxidation products in the color developer.

Subtractive color film: The most common type of color film, in which the image colors are produced by three transparent dyes that

each filter out (or subtract) one third of the spectrum. The dyes are yellow (= minus-blue), magenta (= minus-green) and cyan (= minus-red).

Super 8 Improved 8mm gauge, introduced by Kodak in 1965, with very small perforations that allow a 40% larger image area. The film is enclosed in a light-tight cartridge for fast and foolproof camera loading, with co-axial feed and take-up rolls. The gate pressure-plate is a part of each cartridge.

Superimposing Combining two images one on top of another on one length of film — such as titles on a moving background — either by running the film twice through the camera, or using a special partially-reflecting mirror, such as a beam-splitter, to combine images in one exposure. Alternatively, in a magnetic stripe projector or some tape recorders, recording an audio signal on top of a previous one with only partial erasure, so that the first will be heard as a background under the second.

Supplementary lens A weak positive lens placed in front of the camera lens to enable it to focus on closer distances than its normal focus-mount allows. With the camera lens focused at infinity, sharp focus will be achieved at a distance from the supplementary equal to its focal length.

Sync The exact correspondence of picture and the accompanying sound. This has to be exact to the frame for critical scenes, such as spoken dialogue.

Synchronizer An electrical or electronic

device for keeping picture film in step with the matching sound, usually on tape, for editing, projection or transfer to stripe. Alternatively two or more sprockets ganged on a common shaft and used in editing to keep picture and sound films — or two picture films — locked together in sync. The sprockets are usually geared to a footage and frame counter.

Sync-lead The connection between camera and tape recorder carrying the synchronizing signals to be used later to keep picture and sound in step.

Sync-mark Firstly visible marks, usually made with wax pencil by film editors on picture and sound films. They enable sync to be restored easily even when removed from the synchronizer. Secondly marks scratched and punched into picture and sound-film leaders to enable the laboratory to make a combined print with the correct synchonization.

Synchronous Motor An electric motor, used in some tape recorders, whose speed is only dependent on the frequency of the supply feeding it. The motor cannot run at any other speed, so it remains unaffected by changes of load or temperature.

Take Film resulting from one run of the camera.

One shot may be taken several times until the director or film maker is satisfied, and the best take selected in editing.

Take-up Drive provided to wind up film or tape on a core or spool after passage through the camera, projector or recorder mechanism.

Tank A light-tight container into which film is loaded for processing. The film is usually wound on special reels carrying spiral grooves.

Tape Plastic ribbon coated with magnetic oxide, capable of storing a pattern of magnetisation, representing the audio signal from a record head over which the tape has passed. The tape is capable of later replaying the pattern repeatedly through the use of a similar head into which it induces a minute signal voltage.

Telecine Equipment for scanning film for television, converting the images into a TV signal.

Telephoto A special type of lens design in which the overall length is shorter than the focal length. The term is generally applied to all camera lenses with a focal length considerably longer than a normal one for a given image size.

Tempo In film language, the pace of a piece of film, created by choice of shot length and speed of movement in frame.

Threading Inserting film in the projector, or some camera, mechanisms by hand and leading it through its correct path over sprockets, through the gate and to the take-up.

Throw The distance between the projector and the screen. This, together with the focal length of the lens, determines the image size.

Tilt Up and down movement of a camera during filming.

Tilt adjustment A device for raising the front of a projector in order to align the projected picture with the screen.

Time lapse The filming of single frames at carefully spaced intervals to greatly speed up any movement when the film is projected. The technique can be used for purposes as diverse as comic effects and the study of very slow movements such as cloud patterns and plant growth.

Titler Accessory for holding title cards, the camera and lights in order to allow titles to be filmed easily. Some titles make provision for the taking distance to be adjusted so that different sizes of card may be covered; more elaborate models allow the lettering to be placed on a drum or blind to produce what are known as crawling titles.

Track To move the camera bodily backwards, forwards or sideways smoothly to follow a moving subject or alter the appearance of a shot.

Track laying An advanced editing technique, in which various sounds, such as spot sound effects, are recorded on a separate length of perforated film and then cut into sync with the picture on a multiway synchronizer by spacing them out from the start-mark with leader. The technique can only be used when equipment capable of running several tracks in sync with each other is used for the final mix.

Trailer The protective length of blank film or tape placed at the end of reels to prevent damage to the actual film. Alternatively, a short collection of scenes from a film edited together with titles, used to advertize forthcoming releases.

Transducer Electro-mechanical or optical device capable of changing one form of energy to another. Examples include microphones (sound to electric voltage), loudspeakers (electric power to sound), gramophone pick-ups (velocity of movement to voltage) magnetic heads (current to magnetisation or vice versa) and photocells (changes in light intensity to voltage).

Transfer Re-recording from one medium to another — particularly from tape to stripe — in which sync is maintained.

Treatment The preliminary stages of a script, showing broadly how the story line develops.

Tripod Common support for a camera, having three adjustable legs. Movie tripods should be fitted with PAN-AND-TILT HEADS.

T-stop An aperture calibration system that takes into account light-losses. It therefore represents the true light transmission at any set aperture.

TTA (Through the aperture) A type of automatic exposure metering with the photocell placed after the lens iris, which allows the system itself to check that it is functioning correctly.

TTL (Through the lens) An exposure metering system that receives its light through the taking lens, usually via a beam-splitter in the viewfinding system.

Tungsten halogen A tungsten filament lamp enclosed in a small quartz or hard-glass tube having a filling containing one of the halides — iodine or bromine. These prevent the bulb-wall blackening and greatly extend bulb's life. The lamps are used for projector, movielight and floodlamps, with color temperatures between 3000K and 3400K according to application.

Tungsten lamp A common type of lamp in which light is produced by passing current through a coiled tungsten-wire filament, which heats up due to its resistance. Such lamps, if intended for photography, have a color temperature of around 3200K; household lamps are appreciably redder at 2800K.

Turrets Sliding or rotating mounts for several camera lenses, allowing rapid change of focal length. They have now been largely superseded by ZOOMS, though 16mm cameras still have them.

TV-style projector Sound or silent film projector with built-in back projection screen, looking rather like a television set and ready for projection at any time.

Twin-track The recording of two magnetic tracks on one support. Some sound projectors and tape recorders allow each track to be recorded separately but replayed together with automatic mixing of the two signals.

Type A film Amateur color film intended to be exposed with 3400K illumination (from photofloods or movielights). It can be used in daylight with the Wratten 85 filter. Virtually all Super 8 films are of this type.

Type B film Professional color film, balanced for 3,200K tungsten lamps. It can be used in daylight with the Wratten 85B filter.

Type D film Daylight-balanced color film. It can be used with tungsten 3200K lights with Wratten 80A filter, or 3400K lamps with 80B; the filters, however, absorb an appreciable amount of light.

Type G film General-purpose Super 8 color film that can be exposed under any illumination (including fluorescent light) without a filter and still produce acceptable results.

U

Universal motor Series wound electric motor that can be run off A.C. or D.C. supplies. Its speed can be easily varied over a wide range by a simple series resistor. It can also be fitted with an electro-mechanical governor when used on sound projectors, but this system is now obsolescent.

UV (Ultra-violet) Invisible electromagnetic radiation of wavelengths shorter than violet, to which films tend to be very sensitive.

Fortunately most U.V. is filtered out by glass, while all of it is stopped by the 85 conversion filter used in daylight on Super 8. Daylight color pictures would come out far too blue, if this was not the case.

UV Filter Clear or pinkish filter that stops the passage of U.V.

V

Variable shutter A camera shutter whose open angle can be reduced from normal 170° to zero to create fades. Most variable shutters can be locked in intermediate positions to reduce exposure and produce sharper individual images.

Viewer An editing tool, showing film images magnified in motion when film is pulled through it.

Viewfinder An optical system delineating the area included by the camera's taking lens. Various direct vision, zoom or reflex arrangements are available, but the latter is by far the most common and satisfactory.

Viewpoint The positioning of the camera relative to the scene being filmed.

Vignetting The darkening of the corners of an image produced by a lens. The fault is either due to poor design, in which case it will be most visible at full aperture, or due to lenshood or filterring too small for the camera being fitted.

These then showing up more at smaller lens apertures.

Volt Unit of electrical pressure or potential, abbreviated to V.

VU meter Strictly speaking, a level indicating meter calibrated in Volume Units as standardized for broadcast use in the USA; generally any level-indicating meter on a sound projector or recorder, even if it does not have the correct dynamic characteristics.

W

Watt Unit of electrical power, abbreviated to W.

Wide angle lens A lens having a considerably shorter focal length than is considered normal for a given image area and so including a wide angle of view.

Wide screen Projection of films with an aspect ratio greater than the 1.33:1 'Academy'. The effect can be produced by masking the top and bottom of the gate in the projector or printer (giving aspect ratios of around 1.85:1), or by using ANAMORPHIC LENSES, with aspect ratios of 2.35:1 or more.

Wild track Sounds of a general nature recorded at or around the time of filming, without any special sychronization between camera and recorder. The effect can be used later to dub an underlay of sound for a series of shots or, even for a whole sequence.

Wipe A transition effect,

in which one picture appears to push another off the screen, or a moving line apparently uncovers a new picture while covering up the existing one. It can be hard or soft-edged. The effect is normally produced in an optical printer, but it can be created in the camera with the aid of a MATTE-BOX.

Work print Rough ungraded copy used for editing and sound-track compilation. Saving the original from excessive handling. When editing is complete, the original is cut to match the copy (in professional practice, this is done by the laboratory, who then make a splice-free print from it).

Wow Slow cyclical variation of pitch, caused by small changes of film or tape speed past the record or replay points. The effect usually due to some unevenness in the drive mechanism is very unpleasant to the ear and cannot be corrected.

X

Xenon lamp High-efficiency discharge lamp used in a few high-priced Super 8 and 16mm projectors when showing films to very large audiences. Light is produced by an arc in a tube containing Xenon gas, fed via a special rectifier and control unit from the mains. The term is also used colloquially to cover other, metallic

arc discharge lamps used in projectors, such as the Marc series from General Electric. All give near daylight-quality light, bluer and brighter-looking than that produced by tungsten lamps.

XL (existing light) A form of camera design that maximises the amount of light reaching the film by fitting very fast lenses (f/1.1-1.3), large-sector shutters (up to 235°) to the camera and minimising the amount of light taken from the film by viewfinding and exposure metering. In extreme cases, these two systems do not depend on the taking lens at all, but have separate entrance 'windows'. Combined with the ability to take a fast film-stock (typically ASA160), these cameras can produce well-exposed results at extremely low light levels.

Z

Zoom The variation of focal length of the taking lens while filming.

Zoom lens A lens made up of many elements, of which some can be shifted along the optical axis to vary the focal length and so the taking angle. The relative aperture normally remains constant.

Zoom range Ratio of maximum to minium focal length of a zoom lens; in practice, this ranges from 2:1 up to 15:1 and even greater figures.

Leading Manufacturers

Aäton (France) 16mm cameras. Agfa (Germany) Super 8 cameras, projectors, accessories. Arri (Arnold & Richter) (Germany) 16mm cameras. Bauer (Germany) Super 8 cameras, projectors and accessories; 16mm projectors. Beaulieu (France) Super 8 cameras, projector; 16mm cameras. Bell & Howell (USA) Super 8 cameras, projectors; 16mm cameras, projectors. Bencini (Italy) Super 8 cameras, projectors, Bolex (Switzerland, Austria) Super 8 cameras, projectors, accessories; 16mm cameras, projectors. Braun-Nizo (Germany) Super 8 cameras, projectors, accessories. Canon (Japan) Super 8 cameras, projectors; 16mm cameras, lenses. Capro (Japan) Super 8 cameras. Carena (Liechtenstein) Super 8 cameras, projectors. Chinon (Japan) Super 8 cameras, projectors. Cinema Products (USA) 16mm cameras. Cinerex (Japan) Super 8 cameras, projector. Cine Sales (india) 16mm projectors. Copal (Japan) Super 8 cameras, projectors. Cosina (Japan) Super 8 cameras. De Brie (France) 16mm projectors. Eclair (France) 16mm cameras. Eiki/Elf (Japan) 16mm projectors. Elmo (Japan) Super 8 cameras, projectors accessories; 16mm projectors. Eucelec (France) Super 8 projectors. Eumig (Austria) Super 8 cameras, projectors, accessories. Fairchild (USA) Super 8 projectors (back-projection sales type). Frezzolini (USA) 16mm cameras. Fujica (Japan) Single 8 cameras, accessories, projectors (also run Super 8). Fumeo (Italy) Super 8 projectors; 16mm projectors. Gioca (Italy) Super 8 projectors. Graflex/Singer (USA) 16mm projectors. Halina (Hong Kong) Super 8 cameras. Hanimex (Australia) Super 8 cameras, projectors, accessories. Heurtier (France) Super 8 projectors. Hokushin (Japan) 16mm projectors. Horison (France) 16mm projectors. Imac (Italy) Super 8 projectors. Kalart-Victor (USA) 16mm projectors. Keystone (USA) Super 8 cameras. Kodak (USA) Super 8 cameras, projectors; 16mm projectors. Krasnogorsk (Russia) 16mm cameras. Leitz (Germany) Super 8 cameras. Lentar (Japan) Super 8 cameras. Lomo (Russia) Super 8 cameras. Magnon (Japan) Super 8 cameras, projectors. Meopta (Czechoslovakia) Super 8 cameras, projectors; 16mm projectors.

Microtecnica (Italy) Super 8 projectors; 16mm projectors. Minolta (Japan) Super 8 cameras, projectors. Mitchell (USA) 16mm cameras. Mupi (Italy) Super 8 cameras, projectors. Nalcom (Japan) Super 8 cameras. Nikon (Japan) Super 8 cameras. Noris (Germany) Super 8 cameras, projectors. Pathé (France) Super 8 cameras, projectors; 16mm cameras, projectors. Photophone (India) 16mm projector. Plus (UK) Super 8 cameras, projectors, accessories. Polaroid (USA) Polavision (Super 8 format) camera, projector. Quarz (Russia) Super 8 cameras. Raynox (Japan) Super 8 cameras, projectors. RCA (Jersey) 16mm projectors. Ricoh (Japan) Super 8 cameras, projectors. Sanyo (Japan) projector (back projection sales type). Sankyo (Japan) Super 8 cameras, projectors. Silma (Italy) Super 8 cameras, projectors. Tacita/Tacnon (Japan) Super 8 projectors. Videotronic (UK) Super 8 projector (back projection sales type). Viewlex (USA) 16mm projectors. yashica (Japan) Super 8 cameras, projectors. Yelco (Japan) Super 8 projectors.

Index

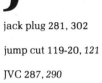

10/07 new front hinge LG